READING BUCHI EMECHETA

Recent Titles in
Contributions to the Study of World Literature

Shakespeare's Proverbial Themes: A Rhetorical Context for the Sententia as *Res*
Marjorie Donker

Promptings of Desire: Creativity and the Religious Impulse in the Works of D. H. Lawrence
Paul Poplawski

The Second Best Bed: Shakespeare's Will in a New Light
Joyce E. Rogers

Literary Selves: Autobiography and Contemporary American Nonfiction
James N. Stull

Storied Cities: Literary Imagining of Florence, Venice and Rome
Michael L. Ross

Women Writers in Russian Literature
Toby W. Clyman and Diana Greene, editors

Writing the Good Fight: Political Commitment in the International Literature of the Spanish Civil War
Peter Monteath

Money: Lure, Lore, and Literature
John Louis DiGaetani, editor

Smollett's Women: A Study in an Eighteenth-Century Masculine Sensibility
Robert D. Spector

English Country Life in the Barsetshire Novels of Angela Thirkell
Laura Roberts Collins

Bakhtin, Stalin, and Modern Russian Fiction: Carnival, Dialogism, and History
M. Keith Booker and Dubravka Juraga

Aspects and Issues in the History of Children's Literature
Maria Nikolajeva, editor

READING BUCHI EMECHETA

Cross-Cultural Conversations

Katherine Fishburn

Contributions to the Study of World Literature,
Number 61

GREENWOOD PRESS
Westport, Connecticut • London

Library of Congress Cataloging-in-Publication Data

Fishburn, Katherine
    Reading Buchi Emecheta : cross-cultural conversations / Katherine Fishburn.
        p. cm.—(Contributions to the study of world literature, ISSN 0738-9345 ; no. 61)
    Includes bibliographical references and index.
    ISBN 0-313-29589-1 (alk. paper)
    1. Emecheta, Buchi—Criticism and interpretation. 2. Africa—In literature. I. Title. II. Series.
PR9387.9.E36Z67 1995
823—dc20   94-39245

British Library Cataloguing in Publication Data is available.

Copyright © 1995 by Katherine Fishburn

All rights reserved. No portion of this book may be reproduced, by any process or technique, without the express written consent of the publisher.

Library of Congress Catalog Card Number: 94-39245
ISBN: 0-313-29589-1
ISSN: 0738-9345

First published in 1995

Greenwood Press, 88 Post Road West, Westport, CT 06881
An imprint of Greenwood Publishing Group, Inc.

Printed in the United States of America

The paper used in this book complies with the Permanent Paper Standard issued by the National Information Standards Organization (Z39.48–1984).

10 9 8 7 6 5 4 3 2

. . . we should let everything human be spoken to us.
Hans-Georg Gadamer (1976c)

. . . the discovery of the plurality of cultures is never a harmless experience.
Paul Ricoeur (1965)

I dedicate this book to my students
and to my beloved husband, Tom,
whose understanding always helps to shape my own

Contents

Preface: A Hybrid Text — ix
Acknowledgments — xv
Introduction: A Question of Power — 1
    Interactive Readings
    Hidden Prejudices
    The Self-Contextualized Critic: Foregrounding Our
        Prejudices and Traditions
    The Language of Perspicuous Contrast

1. The Author—and Reader—as Other: A Postmodern Approach to African Fiction — 17
    Hermeneutic Charity
    Questioning Liberalism and Liberal Feminism
    A Postmodern Approach
    Reconfiguring Authors and Readers

2. Aesthetics, Language, and Politics — 33
    Definitions of Individuality and Aesthetic Consequences
    Art for Art's Sake?
    Artistic Commitment—To Whom and to What?
    Dialogic Heteroglossia: Whose English Is It?
    Epistemology and Narrative Form

3. Life as an Emigré — 51
    A Double Marginality
    Intelligibility and the (Social) Construction of Rationality
    A Difference in Values: The Individual and the Community
    Retaining and Translating a Cultural Heritage
    Love, Marriage, and Narrative Consequences
    A Defense of African Culture and Corruption in the West
    A Matter of Signifying and Dialogic Heteroglossia

4. The Sense of an Ending — 77
    A Matter of Genres
    Narrative Intentions
    Epic or Novel?
    Heteroglossia and Textual Plurality
    Competing Discourses and the Construction of Reality
    Narrative Telos
    A Mélange of Customs and Hybrid Constructions
    Questions of Enslavement, Prologues, and Endings
    Human Constants and Dialogic Heteroglossia
    Christianity and the Role of Nigerian Women
    The Competing Voices of Tradition and Modernization
    Signifying and the Question of Endings
    Inscribing the Feminine

5. The Difference of View — 127
    Traversing (Traditional) Boundaries
    From a Woman's Perspective
    Sexual/Textual Politics
    Double-Voiced Discourse and Interpretive Dilemmas
    Didacticism and Heteroglossia
    That Which Divides Us
    Limitations of Cultural Relativism
    Enlarging Our Horizons
    The Agonistics of Language Games
    Textual Ambiguity: Moments of Misunderstanding
    A New Community of Interpreters

Bibliography — 169
Index — 185

Preface: A Hybrid Text

> A person skilled in the "art" of questioning is a person who can prevent questions from being suppressed by the dominant opinion.
>
> *Hans-Georg Gadamer*
> Truth and Method (1989, 367)

This book is, broadly speaking, an attempt to theorize how Westerners might—more responsibly—read African literature. More specifically, it is my rebuttal to much of the (white) Western feminist criticism that has been generated on Buchi Emecheta and her fiction. As such, it also presumes to enter the current conversation that is focused more generally on issues of cross-cultural understanding.

Even so, my project does not pretend to participate in the related, but ultimately different, ongoing intellectual project of theorizing an African approach to African literature (see, for example, Chinweizu et al. 1983, Bjornson 1990, and A. Williams 1991). Nor does it participate in the related intellectual project of theorizing and documenting the cultural/linguistic continuities between Africans and African Americans (see, for example, Herskovits 1990, Mintz and Price 1992, Levine 1977, Asante 1987, J. Holloway 1990, Mudimbe 1990, K. Holloway 1992). I would hope, however, that participants in these two sister projects would find my ideas not entirely incompatible with, or always irrelevant to, their own—especially as I am trying to theorize my own cultural and intellectual relationship to Africa and, in the process, more than once have found myself raising objections to Western thought and criticism that will be familiar to readers of Molefi Kete Asante.

By entering the conversation as I do here, I hope to raise questions about the nature of understanding across cultures, questions that feminist scholars of

Emecheta all too often have failed to ask, let alone address.[1] Part philosophy, part anthropology, part literary theory and criticism, this project, then, speaks to the problems inherent to reading across cultures. I take as my working premises that (1) texts are not the privileged aesthetic objects so dear to the hearts of New Critics,[2] (2) readers do indeed help to produce meaning in texts, (3) readers themselves are constructed in language,[3] and (4) readers have a cultural history and material existence that affect their understanding and help to determine the meaning they produce.[4] What I have attempted to set out here is a contextualized postmodern approach to African literature—an approach that allows for some measure of understanding, but nonetheless (and just as important) gives full voice to the differences that separate the Western critic from the African text. (That there is a crying need for such an approach—most especially among white Western feminists—I consider to be self-evident.) Mine is also a theory of reading that openly acknowledges the function of my Western "prejudices" or fore-meanings (their being the precondition of my ability to understand any text) even as it calls these prejudices and their usefulness into question. In formulating such a theory, I have found the philosophical hermeneutics of Hans-Georg Gadamer to be particularly helpful. Although I most assuredly do not embrace his project—and its reliance on Truth—in its entirety, his work has provided me with a point of happy departure.[5]

Before getting on with the work before us, however, I need to situate my project in relation to one final project: the current attempt, found on most campuses today, to devise a multicultural curriculum. Lest I be accused of preaching to the choir, let me say that it has been my experience that far too many otherwise well-meaning people have treated lightly the task of teaching outside their area of expertise. Those trained as New Critics have been particularly tempted to teach African (African American, Native American, and so on) texts absent of the material circumstances surrounding their production (and reception). It is, thus, a major aim of this book to demonstrate just exactly how difficult cross-cultural understanding is. Such understanding, achieved as best it can be (though, I would argue, never entirely), at the very least demands of us all (need I say it?) that we familiarize ourselves with the culture that has produced the text in question; it further demands that we recognize the limitations in ourselves that hinder full understanding. Finally, it demands that we recognize the fact that the text itself is not necessarily trying to make itself clear to us (on this, see Dasenbrock 1987)—or even necessarily addressing us at all.

I would argue finally that reading across cultures also demands that we read ourselves. I mean this quite literally. When I call for a cross-cultural conversation with a novel, I mean a give-and-take, where I question it, and it questions me. In this post-New Critical era, when the text as aesthetic object is in decline and the reader still in ascension, we cross-cultural readers must do double duty by reading ourselves even as we read the text. On my view, interrogating ourselves in this way offers us the most promising means of achieving an equitable dialogue with an alien text. This, perhaps, is the closest I can come to what I mean by attempting multiculturalism: accepting the responsibility of scrutinizing myself and the cultural texts that constitute my intellectual, emotional, and psychological baggage—in other words, taking nothing for granted, not even myself.

This is really what my project is about: the joys and dangers, the rewards and difficulties that await the cross-cultural reader. My example is chosen narrowly: a single-author study intended to illustrate the depth of the problem. In its composition as well as its contents, this book, then, is a hybrid. It is, in part, a close reading of Emecheta's novels. But it is also a close reading of the Western thought and theories that have gone into the making of many Western literary critics, including this one. As I read Emecheta's novels and allow them to "inhabit" and interrogate me,[6] I find myself attempting to negotiate a new kind of relationship—within the expanding confines of my own cultural heritage—between the needs of communities and the rights of individuals. As I do this, I also attempt to negotiate a new kind of interpretive relationship—a more symmetrical one—between African texts and Western theories, traditions, and epistemology. I am trying, in other words, to critique my own cultural inheritance even as I encounter an alien text. I thus try to counter my anthropologizing of Emecheta with a similar anthropologizing of the West. In Gadamer's terms, I am trying to expand my horizon without foolishly thinking I can escape it altogether.

In the introduction, I lay out my argument for the need to read interactively (where I read the text and allow it to read me); as part of this argument I stress the further need to focus on what I call moments of misunderstanding, those passages in Emecheta's texts where her African experience and my (white, middle-class feminist) Western experience seem most significantly to diverge. In chapter 1 I explain why both liberalism and feminism actually interfere with our ability to read African literature and then argue for a contextualized postmodern approach. As part of this argument I reject the death of the author, calling instead for a recognition of the author—and reader—as Other. In chapter 2 I explore the aesthetic differences between African and Western literature, using the ideas of Chinua Achebe and Mikhail Bakhtin to argue that the English Emecheta writes in is not the English we read in, making a case for the interrelationship between epistemology and narrative form. The rest of the book is devoted to discussion of Emecheta's novels.

Because I have set out quite self-consciously to describe how a Western reader experiences an African text, my book is necessarily interdisciplinary. Because I am interested in the literary version of what happens when cultures intersect, I have borrowed heavily from recent debates in anthropology and the philosophy of the social sciences, citing, for example, the work of Thomas McCarthy, Richard Bernstein, Clifford Geertz, Alasdair MacIntyre, Charles Taylor, and Peter Winch. Much of what I have to say here is intended to contribute to these debates. But even as I draw on the social sciences to frame some of my questions, my purview remains literature. I have tried, therefore, to explain how both literary criticism and theory can be enriched by an infusion of ideas from anthropology and the philosophy of the social sciences, especially when two cultures as distinct as Emecheta's and mine come into contact.

Though I do not think that I have burdened my study unnecessarily with any technical terms, I do feel a note on terminology is in order. First, perhaps, is the term "postmodern." In my usage, postmodern theory works from the premise that the world is our text and all the people in it are texts, too—unstable, contested selves that have been, and are continually being, constructed in discourse.[7] This theory rejects, as a consequence, foundational thinking, exemplified by notions of Truth, Beauty, and Justice (thus my difficulties with Gadamer), embraces as its operating principle the ungrounded philosophizing (or conversation) of Richard Rorty, recognizes with Foucault the conjunction of power, truth, and knowledge—and works to unjoin them. Postmodernism is, in short, a theory with an attitude.

Second is the notion of "alien." Though Buchi Emecheta's and my culture have much in common, what concerns me are the values and traditions that separate us, that make it difficult (sometimes impossible) for us to understand one another. I have, therefore, quite intentionally chosen a strong anthropological term in order to characterize what I feel are, indeed, fundamental differences between her culture and mine. In choosing "alien," I have assumed the Gadamerian (and perhaps Herculean) task of trying to rehabilitate a term that, I think it is fair to say, has fallen of late into disfavor, not to mention disrepute. But just as "prejudices" are central (necessary) to Gadamer's theory of understanding, "alien" is central to mine. Many of the differences I describe later are relatively minor and thus what the social scientists would call incompatible but commensurable. Some, however, are extreme and may even be incommensurable. All, however, can be, and should be, discussed. It has been so tempting for many of us Westerners to try to evade opposition altogether by flattening out differences so they seem not to exist. This temptation leads some of us who read African fiction to imagine that we have understood it when we have not.[8] Those who fall into this category seem either to feel, innocently enough, that they have found truly culture-free universals from which to evaluate Emecheta's fiction or, less innocently, to think that they can utilize Western ideas as universal tools of understanding. Thus I make it a point to insist on differences.

Third is the notion of "Africa" itself. I have taken the liberty of occasionally invoking a larger sense of Africa here, raising the question of what Africa has meant to me—what received ideas of Africa mark me as a Western scholar. I do this not to blur the many distinctions among African cultures but to insist on the differences between Emecheta's texts and my own Western experiences. My goal is similar to that of Maria Torgovnick in *Gone Primitive* (1990), where she retains the term "primitive" in order to interrogate what this concept has

Preface: A Hybrid Text   xiii

meant to the West and how we Westerners have been ethically implicated in its use. A similar interrogative impulse lies behind my project, which has also been inspired by Edward Said's work on Orientalism (1979b), as I, too, employ a trope ("Africa") in order to deconstruct it. Any cultural generalizations I employ are therefore those provided by African scholars and writers themselves. Other cultural explanations I provide to help explain Emecheta's novels refer specifically to her Igbo heritage. It is not my intention to perform a kind of Orientalism on Africa. It is my intention to call upon what we in the West think we know of this vast and complex continent and compare it with what Africans say of themselves.

Finally, it is possible to question whether Emecheta herself should even be called an African writer since she writes in English and has lived in London since 1960. To this objection I would respond that, from my perspective as a Western critic, Emecheta's fiction has been deeply enough informed by her African heritage to make understanding her novels an extremely challenging cross-cultural reading experience.

NOTES

1. For an exception, see K. Holloway 1992; see also Alcoff 1991-92, Kaplan 1987, Mohanty 1984, and Lugones and Spelman 1983.

2. This claim is particularly pertinent to African texts; see the discussion on art for art's sake in chapter 2. Compare also to Asante's claim that "African art is never l'art pour l'art; it is always functional" (1987, 63).

3. This assertion seems to echo the African concept of *Nommo* (see Jahn 1990 and Asante 1987)—though my sources are Western poststructuralism and reader-response criticism.

4. Compare this with Asante when he condemns "the inability of European thinkers, particularly of the neo-positivist or empiricist traditions, to see that human actions cannot be understood apart from the emotions, attitudes, and cultural definitions of a given context" (1987, 164). As Diana Fuss (1989) would argue, these "premises" constitute the essentialism at the heart of my own postmodern/poststructuralist project.

5. Asante faults Heidegger's hermeneutics, for example, for being "inextricably absorbed in European culture" (1987, 161). This is the same kind of cultural narrowness I critique in Gadamer by showing how hard it is to transport some of his key ideas into a cross-cultural hermeneutical situation.

6. Though they will never, à la Asante, possess me entirely (1987, 189-90). On my view, they cannot.

7. Again, I think of Nommo.

8. I am not engaging Afrocentric readings here.

Acknowledgments

Thanks go to many people: Nellie McKay, for her friendship and for introducing me to Emecheta's fiction during her own postdoctoral fellowship at Michigan State University in 1981; Henry Louis Gates, Jr., for encouraging me to pursue this project; Aldon Nielsen, for his enthusiastic and helpful response to an earlier version of this manuscript; Douglas Peterson and Kevin McCarron, for taking the time to read a much earlier version; Nancy Eckelbarger and her staff, for the work they do that helps to make my own work possible.

In addition, I am deeply grateful to the Department of English, Michigan State University, for giving me release time to begin this project.

I wish also to acknowledge the contributions of my students—all of whom, over the years, have helped me think through my ideas. I wish to give particular recognition to Kevin Asman, Delecia Seay Carey, Amy Elizabeth Markley, Wayne Smith, and Sherry Wynn.

Finally, I wish to thank Tom for his loving support (without him, nothing) and all the doggie-persons who help make life worth living: Cindy Lou Fishburn Beagle; Charlie Boy Fishburn Lab; and Chloe Gene Fishburn Beagle (the Beagle Queen).

READING
BUCHI EMECHETA

Introduction: A Question of Power

What we see in a text is what our ideology has equipped us to see.
Lewis Nkosi
Tasks and Masks (1981, np)

Sometimes what is required to communicate—to establish a reciprocal "we"—is rupture and break—a refusal to accept the common ground laid down by the "other."
Richard J. Bernstein
"The Rage Against Reason" (1986, 206)

INTERACTIVE READINGS

My purpose in this introduction is to argue for a model of reading that will permit us Westerners to engage African texts on a more equal and, thus, more ethical interpretive footing. In short, I am arguing for a model of reading that will help critics overcome the lingering habit of cultural domination and dogmatism that historically has marked most of the West's encounters with Africa. In this introduction and throughout the rest of this study, I have contextualized my arguments in the philosophical hermeneutics of the contemporary German theorist Hans-Georg Gadamer. I do so for many reasons, not the least of which is Gadamer's standing as one of the preeminent philosophers of the art of conversation.[1] I include him also because his attempts to explain how (textual) understanding occurs have deeply influenced my own attempts to explain how misunderstandings arise—even among Western readers who approach African texts with the best intentions. Less respectfully, I also include his ideas because I think, at times, they represent what is wrong with a great many theories of reading that fail to address the serious interpretive problems that result when reader and text come from two different cultural traditions; this oversight is especially troubling, I would argue, in those interpretive situations that are marked by an imbalance of power between reader and text. Gadamer's own dialogic model of understanding, while informing the interactive model I propose here, seems to be, for example, overly idealistic, depending as it does not only on the good intentions of readers but also on their willingness to submit to the authority (or truth claims) of a relatively stable and unified tradition. Based as it is on the Heideggerian concept of the hermeneutic circle and a fundamental reliance on the role of tradition in determining meaning, his theory also seems to be unavoidably culture-bound. But, unexpectedly enough, Gadamer's argument that tradition helps to govern our understanding is precisely what permits me to theorize how misunderstandings almost inevitably occur when we attempt to read outside our own literary/cultural traditions.[2]

In both his magnum opus *Truth and Method* (originally published in 1960) and his essay "The Problem of Historical Consciousness" (originally published in 1963), Gadamer endorses Heidegger's position that the hermeneutic circle is not vicious but rather productive of all meaning. As Heidegger himself argues in *Being and Time,* in the hermeneutic circle is "hidden a positive possibility of the most primordial kind of knowing"—in short, it enjoys an ontological status—and we "grasp" or "take hold" of this possibility only when we ensure that our various kinds of foreknowledge are not corrupted by "fancies and popular conceptions" but informed by "the things themselves" (1927, 153).[3] As Gadamer remarks, Heidegger is not recommending a method of reading here but is describing how understanding is achieved (1989, 266; see also 293). Following Heidegger, Gadamer also argues that understanding involves "a pre-understanding," which itself is shaped "by the determinate tradition in which the interpreter lives" (a claim that helps to formulate my own theories of misunderstanding) (1987, 87). That is, understanding can occur at all only because of the foreknowledge that the reader brings to a text from his or her own tradition. What we bring to a text Gadamer calls our "prejudices," the foremeanings that make understanding possible. Of these prejudices, some are legitimate or enabling and permit understanding, while others are disenabling and actually obstruct understanding (1989, 277). On Gadamer's view, in order to achieve understanding, whenever we encounter others—in person or in art or in texts—we should be willing to suspend our prejudices and open ourselves to them.[4] That is, we must be prepared to accept the fact that others are "potentially right" and allow them to "prevail against" us (a claim that I find congruent with my own project) (1987, 87).[5] In so doing, ideally we will set aside those prejudices that block understanding and invoke those that facilitate it. But, as persuasive as Gadamer is in describing what makes understanding possible, I am not convinced of the applicability of all his arguments to my own project. In response to his idealized scenario of how understanding is achieved, for example, I would ask, are the "authentic" intentions (1987, 132) we Western critics bring to the act of reading enough? Or is it not more likely that, because of deeply entrenched political and cultural differences separating the West and Africa, the ontological status of the hermeneutic circle also involves spinning in the ugly rut of monologic ethnocentricity? Necessary as prejudices are to our understanding (and I agree they are), are not our (unspoken, unrealized, unacknowledged) prejudices enough to undermine even the best intentions of the best of us? Making ourselves receptive to the newness of African texts may be a necessary gesture if we hope to understand them in their alienness, but I wonder if it is sufficient. Perhaps only African readers of Western criticism can help answer this question for us.[6]

Conversely, I would also ask of Gadamer's apparently culture-bound theories, how many of our Western prejudices are, indeed, legitimate ones that lead to cross-cultural understanding? How in the world can we tell them from the false ones? Gadamer offers us some help when he challenges what he calls the naive claim of historicism that somehow we can learn to think the way our (literary) ancestors did and therefore achieve a kind of "historical objectivity" that will allow us to understand the text the way it was written. Arguing that it is impossible to overcome this temporal gap, which necessarily separates us from traditionary texts (and which has helped produce us as beings-in-the-world), Gadamer urges us, instead, to think of the gap as productive of understanding (1989, 297). Because Gadamer is respectful of the authority (or truth claims) of traditionary/historical texts, he is able to argue that the very act of reading such a text necessarily forces our false prejudices into perspective, where they can be isolated and subdued, an act that permits us, in turn, to submit ourselves to the higher truth(s) of the text in question (299). He thus describes "the hermeneutically trained mind" as one incorporating "historical consciousness" (299). Theoretically, at least, I think for Western readers an encounter with an African text could probably serve the same purpose of highlighting our (ethnocentric/critical) prejudices. Rather than trying to overcome this cultural gap and pretending to read like Africans, we might instead think in terms of utilizing this gap in order to learn more about ourselves and our prejudices. What we might want to add to Gadamer, then, is the claim that the hermeneutically trained mind will also include transcultural consciousness.

But, as I have suggested, Gadamer's argument is based on the authority of tradition (1989, 279-85)—which complicates its applicability to our cross-cultural reading situation. He rejects, as too narrow, the Enlightenment prejudice that authority only unseats our judgment (or reason) and argues instead that authority is also potentially "a source of truth" that is actually "productive of knowledge." On Gadamer's view, those in authority, then, have earned the right to the respect they command; that is, we are willing to acknowledge someone else's authority if we perceive that he or she is "superior [to us] in judgment and insight" (1989, 279). Gadamer finds this same authority in tradition (and traditionary texts). But we must then ask, whose authority—and which tradition—is invoked when Westerners encounter African texts? Whose "truth"? Do African texts have sufficient authority to convince us of the validity of their truth claims? Equally to the point, what does it mean for us to invoke tradition as a source of authority? The possibility that Gadamer's own use of tradition is nothing more than camouflaged essentialism is addressed by John D. Caputo, who reads Gadamer (accurately, I think) as arguing that it is "the task of hermeneutics . . . to learn how to mine [the] wealth [of meaning in tradition] and to pass it along to the current generation." In his own Derridean reading of Gadamer, Caputo finds this view nothing more than "transcendental naïveté" (1989, 262).[7] In our current context, I would ask, is such a view naive or is it disingenuous? On Caputo's view, "tradition is largely the story of the winners while the dissenters have been excommunicated, torched, castrated, exiled, or imprisoned" (264). We might add that dissenters have been those who are (or have been) colonized (see Fanon 1968).

What, then, is to take the place of a tradition we do not share? What happens when the tradition we are situated in is alien (or hostile) to the tradition the texts were written in? What happens when the tradition we encounter is one that has been deeply marked by Western colonization? Under these circumstances do we not have an ethical obligation to find a methodology[8] that permits us to question our own tradition even as we read the texts of an alien tradition?[9]

At various points in his writing, Gadamer reminds us that conducting a conversation or dialogue involves helping the other person make his or her argument—and not, as so often occurs, seeing the exchange as a competition that must be won at any cost (see, for example, 1989, 292, 367). For Gadamer, then, the act of interpretation should be construed as a conversation between an I and a Thou. He has, thus, insisted on the "reciprocity" of understanding that necessarily occurs between the two when a text has been successfully interpreted (Gadamer 1989, 358-60 and 1987, 127). Inspired by this conversational or collaborative model of reading, I call my own approach an interactive reading strategy. By this I mean that, in reading Emecheta, I am not just reading her and her African heritage—I am also reading myself and my Western heritage. I am allowing the Thou (her text) to interrogate me, even as I interrogate it. As with other forms of perception, the act of reading moves from the reading agent to the object being read; as readers, then, our attention is necessarily focussed not on ourselves but on the text in question. As a result, we reading agents, in effect, seem to disappear in the act of reading, with our training and our prejudices providing a kind of (omnipresent but unacknowledged) frame or background against which we perceive (or read) the text. (A disappearance of which far too many Western readers have tried to take advantage.) With few exceptions, previous theories of reading, therefore, have given little attention to the actual person doing the reading. Even reader-response critics have tended to theorize only general differences between readers, such as those Patrocinio

Schweickart finds characterize men and women readers (1986). In the interactive reading model I propose here, I argue that we need to turn attention back to the reader, to ask ourselves what Gadamerian prejudices inform and motivate us as we read African texts. What I am asking in the pages that follow, therefore, is that we attend not only to the *text* but also to *ourselves* as readers. Theoretically speaking, which we decide to focus on (the African text or ourselves) at any given moment is arbitrary (to us, if not the Africans). But we must never lose sight of the fact that at least two systems of thought (two traditions) have been brought together in this reading experience—and while these traditions are necessarily related to one another, their relationship is not completely *harmonious* (read: congruent and friendly).

I take it as a given, therefore, that when we are faced with the problem of reading an African or any other text alien to our own Western experience, we must recognize that our ability to understand will be impeded (to one degree or another) by fundamental differences that separate the two cultures.[10] Because of these differences, I want to suggest that, as we read, we concentrate on what I have called moments of misunderstanding, wherein we isolate the passages that puzzle, irritate, or alienate us. The point is not to bracket these problematic passages. The point is to make good use of them. For these are the moments true learning can occur: when we admit to the authentic strangeness of alien customs and, in Paul Rabinow's words, recognize how truly "exotic" and historically constituted our *own* sense of reality has been (1986, 241). Though it is possible that we may never fully understand these alien practices, we may learn more of ourselves from our very inability to understand. There will also be moments when, for one reason or another, we will as Westerners wish we had not understood, when what we learn so deeply violates our philosophy, values, or worldview that we must overturn our very selves (or a good portion of them) in order to embrace or even tolerate these alien concepts—as occurs for me, for example, during a discussion of clitoridectomies in Emecheta's 1983 novel *Double Yoke*. But even a moment like this—when we refuse to accept another culture's values—can provide us with an important opportunity to learn more about ourselves as we investigate the cultural biases that lead to our refusal.[11] At the very least, therefore, it is incumbent upon us Western readers of African texts to acknowledge our Gadamerian prejudices—the fore-meanings that we bring to the reading of any text and that are basic to how we understand it.[12] At the same time that we look for the problem passages in African novels, there will, of course, always be passages we feel confident we do understand, passages with which we can make connections. In order to avoid a too facile understanding of the text, however, I would urge that even these passages be problematized.[13]

HIDDEN PREJUDICES

In *Truth and Method*, Gadamer suggests that it is not uncommon for readers to overlook or disregard their prejudices—to act as though they can come to a text unencumbered by fore-meanings or tradition.[14] This conviction, of course, itself reflects an idea central to modern Western thought: the possibility and necessity of intellectual neutrality—the corollaries to which are the further convictions that European reason is the only reason, scientific rationality the only rationality, and the largely unstated but always assumed conviction that European man is the measure of all things, the neutral baseline against which all other peoples and their cultures are to be measured (and found wanting).[15] In short, Western readers are encouraged by their own intellectual traditions to believe that they can come to a text (African or other) unburdened by tradition. In the past, having been schooled in the principles of intellectual neutrality, universal values, and universal reason, Western readers have found it all too easy to misread African texts by presupposing that these texts speak to them in the language (forms) they share.

But how can we discover, in Gadamer's terms, that the language the text is using is different from the usage we are accustomed to? How can we discover that the so-called universal meaning we expect to find in African texts is not there? Gadamer would respond by arguing that normally we make this discovery when the text takes us by surprise. That is, we get no meaning from the text, or the meaning is not what we had anticipated. But ordinarily we will have little difficulty in understanding texts that have been written in our own language; whenever we do have trouble, it is primarily because the text is using words in ways that are unfamiliar to us (Gadamer 1989, 268). Since his focus is primarily on the process of (historical) understanding, Gadamer does not seem to be terribly interested in these isolated incidents when the text fails to make itself clear to us. But in my cross-cultural reading project, I focus specifically on misunderstanding—on why and how understanding is not achieved. In fact, I intend to argue more fully later that the failure to understand (the language and, thus, the text) that occurs only infrequently when we read *within* our tradition almost always occurs when we read *across* traditions—that is, when English-speaking Westerners read texts written by Anglophone African novelists. I argue, in other words, that the English Africans employ in their fiction, appearances to the contrary, is not the same English we in the West are familiar with (see my discussion of Bakhtin and Achebe in chapter 2).[16] But because critics have assumed it is the same, we have failed to have the experience that Gadamer describes of being caught off guard. Far from having a harmless effect, this assumption has interfered with our ability to understand these African texts. For, rather than reading an African novel in the proper context of a specific African literary tradition and worldview, we (white feminists especially) have read as though it were part of our own Western tradition; in other words, we have imposed on African texts the meanings we expect them to have.

But, Gadamer asks, what happens if we are not "pulled up short" (1989, 268)? What happens if we think we understand, when, in fact, we do not? Though it is not a complete answer, he suggests, much as I do, that we must always be conscious of our biases so the text is free to appear in its full difference and thus affirm its truth in the face of our prejudices (269).[17] Then he really seems to address my project, by claiming that it "is the tyranny of hidden prejudices" that prevents us from heeding "what speaks to us in tradition"—or, to apply his ideas more precisely to mine, what speaks to us in an-Other's tradition (270). For the idea is not protecting ourselves from the tradition expressed in the text but instead eliminating anything that interferes with our ability to understand tradition (269-70).[18] To Gadamer's optimistic advice about excluding that which would obstruct understanding, which in the main I find useful, I feel compelled to add the more sobering reminder that our hidden prejudices have the capacity to deafen us even more profoundly when the tradition involved is that of a historically despised continent such as Africa. Christopher L. Miller, for example, describes these hidden prejudices at work in the ethnocentric thinking of the Marxist literary critic Georg M. Gugelberger, whom he accuses of knowing "in advance what the nature of African literature should be." But unlike those literary critics who have found much to disparage in African literature, Gugelberger is faulted by Miller for making the opposite but equally offensive mistake—for seeing African literature as an "antidote to Western lassitude and stagnancy" (1988, 79).[19] Nor are Western feminists immune to similar charges of ethnocentricity. Though Katherine Frank, for example, self-consciously attempts to overcome her Western ethnocentrism, she nonetheless has argued that the African woman in "order to be free and fulfilled as a woman . . . must renounce her African identity because of the inherent sexism of traditional African culture" (1982, 478). As the following pages show, much in Emecheta's fiction seems to invite Western readers to draw Frank's conclusion. At one time I would have drawn it myself. I am more inclined now, however, to argue that conclusions like Frank's are less inspired by the texts themselves than by the hidden biases of the critics.[20]

THE SELF-CONTEXTUALIZED CRITIC: FOREGROUNDING OUR PREJUDICES AND TRADITIONS

This tendency of the West to impose meaning on others is certainly not limited in any way to literary criticism. Charles Taylor, for example, faults "transcultural and comparative social science" for perpetuating ethnocentrism by giving more credence to Western "scientific" accounts of a culture than those provided by the indigenes themselves (1985, 124; see also Asante 1987).

That we have been able as Africanists to exercise what Taylor calls this "ethnocentric prejudice" (124) is a reflection of the power we in the West have historically enjoyed over African peoples and their cultures. For Richard Bernstein, the exercise of this prejudice among anthropologists results in a "commonality [that] is not really shared, it is *violently* imposed" (1986, 205). Or, as I have been arguing, when unselfconscious Western readers (Marxist, feminist, or other) approach African texts, a "false 'we' is projected" that elides meaningful differences between subject and object (205).[21] The elision is the same whether it is between scientist and culture or critic and text. Sometimes it is not commonality that is sought, however, but pure power. Both physical and cultural anthropology, for example, originated in a colonizing desire to focus the Western scientific principles of measurement and observation on the so-called primitive peoples of the world.[22] What these "objective" studies of Africans (on the Continent and off) reported as factual information is too well known to need repeating here.[23] But even though few people now place credence in craniology or in the Great Chain of Being, these outmoded belief systems and their ilk seem to have had lingering effects on the intellectual commerce between African and the West. Abiola Irele, for example, argues that even today, with few exceptions, scholarship done by Africans "is at best marginal, and at worst nonexistent, in the total economy of intellectual and scientific endeavor in the world today." Irele finds, moreover, that African scholarship is "characterized by a state of dependence in relation to the Western frame of reference" (1991, 63).[24] Clearly, what Irele describes is an example of the Western "regime of truth" in action (see also Mudimbe 1988).

In order to begin to dismantle this regime, Mark Poster urges all theorists to "acknowledge the will to power behind and within the truth claims of [their] discourse" (1989, 8). Poster argues that only by contextualizing their ideas, can theorists help to make sure that their "discourse does not emanate from a transcendental ego, a subject sharply opposed to the realm of objects" (7-8). For me, Poster's timely advice involves the necessity of maintaining a thoroughly self-conscious reading stance, where I continually ground my ideas in my Western heritage. This is yet another reason for me to read the West even as I read Emecheta. Given my own desire to dismantle the Western regime of truth, I often position myself in opposition to its teachings. At the same time, by contextualizing my readings in this way, I acknowledge (and yet hope to undermine) the will to power behind what I claim ("my reading is better than yours"). In doing so, I am not unaware of the fact that I have placed myself in the awkward and paradoxical position of claiming the superior virtue of my own humility. I also am not unmindful of the possibility that contextualizing may not be enough and stand willing to be corrected by the force of a better argument. Finally, I recognize (with Alcoff 1991-92) that my attempts to represent others, however self-consciously they are undertaken, must entail certain ethical responsibilities.

Introduction: A Question of Power

In this introduction I have so far stressed my conviction that the relationship between Western readers and African texts has historically been one of power, suggesting that "prejudice" is all too appropriate a term to describe the fore-meanings we bring to these texts. Now I want to return to Gadamer's attempts to rehabilitate this concept. Working from the premise that human beings are historically defined and placed, Gadamer argues that it is crucial to acknowledge not only the hidden (or disenabling) prejudices we have already discussed but also more legitimate prejudices, those that make understanding possible. The fundamental question of a historically defined hermeneutics then becomes one of distinguishing the two prejudices so the disenabling ones may be overcome (Gadamer 1989, 277). The same question might be formulated of a cross-cultural hermeneutics where the problem of prejudice(s) seems equally organic. Echoing Gadamer, Miller argues, for example, that a Western critic must be able to acknowledge his or her "own biases and prejudices; failing some measure of self-reflexivity, chances of fairness are slim" (C. Miller 1988, 75). I would go farther and proclaim that more than simple fairness is at stake: if we fail to foreground our prejudices, the chances of achieving more than the most minimal understanding are slim.

In describing the relationship of the present to the past, Gadamer gives me reason to hope that cross-cultural conversations that lead to understanding are theoretically possible when he introduces the metaphor of horizons into his discussion of the relationship of readers to traditionary texts. Gadamer refers to the epistemological limitations of both text and reader as horizons, arguing that the perspective of text and reader alike is limited by our respective points in time. The horizon of both text and reader has both scope and borders, but the borders of our vision, like those of a real horizon, are capable of infinite expansion. The secret, then, is recognizing our limits as readers and learning to see past them (Gadamer 1989, 302). I think it can be argued that Gadamer's metaphor is transferable to our purposes; rather than defining a horizon in time, we can define it in culture (assuming that there is enough familiarity in these texts to make understanding possible—and enough strangeness to make it difficult). Ideally, what should occur as we encounter the horizon of an alien text, then, is what can occur as we encounter the horizon of a traditionary text—that is, we can experience (or achieve) the genuine understanding that Gadamer calls a fusion of horizons (306). When critics fail to acknowledge their horizon, they run the risk of thinking it encompasses the world. In this case, rather than a fusion of two dissimilar horizons occurring, we have one horizon (that of the West) engulfing the other. Paradoxically, then, only by acknowledging that the world beyond our horizon is genuinely different from (though necessarily related to) our own do we make the connections we (feminists and Marxists) long for.

Gadamer defines the "*true locus of hermeneutics*" as that which falls between what we find strange and what we find familiar in the traditionary text

(1989, 295). As we in the West approach an African text, however, I would ask, what constitutes the true (in contrast to the falsely presupposed or imposed) familiarity of the African text in question? The strangeness Gadamer describes is here in abundance, but where is the familiarity we need for understanding?[25] I have already suggested that the notion of a common language is more fantasy than reality (an idea I shall return to in the chapters that follow). What, then, is there in an African text that Western readers share? Although there is much of Africa in our own culture and much in Africa of our culture (we have, after all, had commerce of one sort or another for nearly 400 years),[26] the fact remains that our informal knowledge of Africa is often just plain wrong and inflected by our Western prejudices toward rationality, legitimation, and individualism (on this, see Asante 1987 and Torgovnick 1990). Even some of our most obvious points of historical convergence, such as the slave trade and colonialism, are events that would have been experienced far differently by the Africans and the Western slavers and colonizers—and thus left different marks on the respective traditions involved (see Visel 1988). Nor do we really share a literary tradition, if by sharing we mean a reciprocal relationship. Though most African novelists have, indeed, been educated in, and influenced by, Western literature, many Western readers (especially white ones) have had little or no experience with African oral and literary traditions.[27] Moreover, some African writers, like the South African novelist Lewis Nkosi, argue that the novel itself may inherently contain "a view of life that is essentially hostile to African traditional society" (1981, 5). Whether or not they are willing to go as far as Nkosi, most African novelists nonetheless are working fundamental changes on the form as they adapt it for their own purposes and traditions.[28] Thus, it would appear that we, whose critical faculties have been shaped to a greater or lesser degree by the European novel, are generally ill-prepared to understand—or even to recognize—the true context of African fiction.

By insisting on these differences, I obviously do not mean to suggest that Africa has been isolated in the world; I do mean that Africans know more of us than we do of them. Given the preponderance of the strange over the familiar in our relationship with African texts (even allowing for the necessary continuities and a certain degree of intertextuality that make understanding possible), then, how can we possibly negotiate between them in order to achieve a fusion of horizons? To put it in Bernstein's terms, what are our qualifications for participating in these cross-cultural "dialogic communities" (1989, 231)? In short, what competencies can we bring to a cross-cultural interpretive community? Perhaps the most important quality we can bring is a willingness to self-consciously interrogate our own tradition(s) and foreground our prejudices (whatever our background).

THE LANGUAGE OF PERSPICUOUS CONTRAST

To the question, Is it theoretically possible for Westerners to understand African texts on their own terms as African texts?, I would respond, obviously we cannot. But I do insist that we can understand them as something *other than Western texts*. In this endeavor the ideas of Charles Taylor can be useful. Taylor has formulated an "interpretive" approach or "*verstehen* view" that is designed to avoid two common anthropological errors: assuming that we in the West can approach an alien culture from a purely objective standpoint; or, conversely, accepting the self-description of an alien culture with such credulity that we treat their accounts as "incorrigible" (1985, 124). Since we can never learn to see another culture as a native would, is not ethnocentricity our only option? Taylor thinks not. In fact, Taylor rejects this Hobson's choice, arguing, instead, that it is more likely that as we challenge "their language of self-understanding, we may also be challenging [our own]" (125). This is the very idea that I have been arguing in my interactive theory of reading: while we read Emecheta (or any African or non-Western novelist), we perforce are reading (or questioning) ourselves.[29] In order to manage this coeval interrogation of two alien self-understandings, Taylor suggests working in a "language of perspicuous contrast," a solution that has been influenced both by Gadamer's horizons and by Peter Winch's concept of limiting notions. Winch has suggested that three "fundamental notions" have helped to organize all human society: "birth, death, [and] sexual relations." Because they are, indeed, basic to human life, they provide guidance when "we are puzzled about the point of an alien system of institutions" (1964, 322).[30] Quite similarly, Taylor's language of perspicuous contrast is an attempt to describe two ways of life "in relation to some human constants at work in both. It would be a language in which the possible human variations would be so formulated that both our form of life and theirs could be perspicuously described as alternative such variations" (1985, 125).

Applying Taylor's principle of perspicuous contrast to a consideration of alien literary texts, we would find a similar process occurring, where we would learn to see our own cultural texts differently. In my postmodern adaptation of Taylor's approach, the human constants at work in these two sets of cultural artifacts (Western and African texts) become (in part) narrative poetics: narrators, narrative audiences, narrative voices, narrative structures, and so on. By treating these African texts as cultural artifacts (and artifacts as texts), I intend to show how their various narrative poetics reflect a culture alien and occasionally incommensurable—but also comprehensible—to our own.[31] Still borrowing from Taylor, I want to suggest, then, three possible basic readings of alien texts: an ethnocentric one we impose on them from the outside that has its basis in the so-called neutral language of New Criticism[32]; an indigenous one that arises naturally from within the alien culture itself (and in which we cannot participate); and—the one I am advocating—a cross-cultural or hybrid reading that speaks a language of perspicuous contrast.

Reading interactively in the language of perspicuous contrast is not a particularly pleasant activity, as it has the side effect of never letting us forget that we are reading (and thus interferes with our being "possessed" by the literature). It is, in fact, a kind of metareading wherein all texts become metafictional—that is, reminders that the reality we inhabit is a text and the "we" that inhabits this text is itself textual (a product of discourse, both socially and individually constructed). Besides finding this reading unpleasant, some may feel that this interactive reading strategy necessarily (if inadvertently) marginalizes Emecheta. To this potential criticism I would reply that, as a Western reader, I do not see how I could possibly leave out my own tradition. For, as Gadamer himself would argue, we are always already placed in traditions—there is just no getting away from them (1989, 282). They help determine who we are even before we are aware of their existence. Rather than pretending my Western tradition has had no effect on me, I feel it is absolutely essential to bring my intellectual background into the foreground, where it can be scrutinized even as I use it to try to understand Emecheta (as I have been doing with Gadamer throughout this introduction). This is the most ethical reading strategy I, as a non-African, have been able to devise for myself. I am trying to see where Emecheta's and my cultures intersect and where (and, if possible, why) they diverge and what consequences these intersections and divergences have for reading. What follows in this book, therefore, is a theoretically framed but ultimately practical model for how Western readers can relinquish sufficient institutional power to *begin* to understand African texts—or, at the very least, begin to see what it is we cannot understand. In Gadamer's terms, it is an attempt to delineate the boundaries and conditions of our own Western horizon while at the same time opening it up to the influence of an African horizon. In Taylor's terms, it is an attempt to introduce a language of perspicuous contrast.

As I anticipate what is to come (which I have, of course, already completed), I find myself torn between hope and despair. On one hand, I do think we can read and even understand African texts with a modicum of success—all the arguments I muster against this position to the contrary. Thus, I find myself caught somewhere between believing in meaningful differences and believing in correspondence.[33] I muster the arguments against the hope of perfect understanding because I think that, historically, we have been far too sure of our success, far too convinced that we as Westerners know what an African text means. To correct for this hubris, I want to stress, on the other hand, the *difficulty* of reaching such an understanding—thus, my epigraph from Bernstein: "Sometimes what is required to communicate—to establish a reciprocal 'we'—is rupture and break—a *refusal* to accept the common ground laid down by the 'other'" (1986, 206; see also Gadamer 1989, 334). Similarly, I also feel the need to insist that there are times when *I know I do not understand* an African text—when, for whatever reason (and there are many), it simply makes no sense to me. At other times, having understood (or at least having thought I understood) an African text, *I refuse to allow* its meaning to fuse with (enter) my own horizon.

Though I am utterly convinced we never can understand African texts on their own terms, at the same time, as I have suggested, I am equally convinced that we can see them with fewer Western presuppositions and prejudices. I am also convinced that we must learn to do this—that we no longer really have a choice in the matter.[34] The world has grown suddenly so small that we are deluded if we think we can ignore other peoples, other cultures or smugly imagine them inferior copies of ourselves. But, as Bernstein soberly reminds us, we are also deluded if we "think that the 'other' can always be heard in a friendly dialogue" (1986, 206). From my own experience with Emecheta's fiction—and Gadamer's urgings aside—I have to say that Bernstein is absolutely correct. Thus, I feel compelled to warn readers that some of what follows will be friendly, and some (alas) will not. But just because we have no choice in the matter is no reason, finally, to despair. Reading interactively through a language of perspicuous contrast, then, is not, as some might imagine, a reinstatement of the Western regime of truth. Instead, it is a realignment of the balance of power where (African) text and (Western) reader are equal partners in a cross-cultural conversation.

NOTES

1. See Dallmayr 1984, 195. See also Gadamer's influence on Richard Rorty's theories of conversation (Rorty 1982 and 1985).

2. Gadamer argues that "[t]he anticipation of meaning that governs our understanding . . . proceeds from the commonality that binds us to the tradition." But he also argues that we ourselves help to produce tradition "inasmuch as we understand" (1989, 293). This argument would, of course, supplement Asante's counter-arguments (1987). But see Butler 1985 and Gilroy 1993. My system, too, requires some commonality for understanding to occur; I just do not find evidence of as much as others have found.

3. "The 'circle' in understanding belongs to the structure of meaning, and the latter phenomenon is rooted in the existential constitution of Dasein—that is, in the understanding which interprets. An entity for which, as Being-in-the-world, its Being is itself an issue, has, ontologically, a circular structure" (Heidegger 1927, 153). Following the practice of others, I cite the original pages numbers to *Being and Time*.

4. For a second reading of these ideas, see also Bernstein 1989.

5. Later he cautions us that he has not been arguing that we should "forget our own opinions or shield ourselves against" formulating an idea about what is come. Openness means, instead, that the opinions of others "are *situated* in my system of opinions, or better, that I situate myself in relation to them" (1987, 132; see also 1989, 268).

6. See Mudimbe's use of Gadamer (1990) to critique Herskovits.

7. "It is true that Gadamer has made much of the need for hermeneutic openness to the other," concedes Caputo, "and that is his most profound moment—but he allowed this radical theme to be undermined by a metaphysics of the tradition inspired by Hegel and German Romanticism and by a metaphysics of the dialogical soul inspired by Plato" (1989, 264).

8. Because I do not intend to propose or endorse a specific methodology per se, this term should be read as written under erasure. Perhaps "approach" or "attitude" would be better.

9. See also Mitchell 1992.

10. I remind readers that I do not intend here to engage the Afrocentric debate. Compare my work on literary differences to K. Holloway 1992 and Okhamafe 1989.

11. Gadamer and I are not quite of the same mind when it comes to understanding and its consequences. He does acknowledge that there are circumstances wherein we, indeed, do understand and yet choose to disobey an order, for example (1989, 334). He and I both endorse the negativity of experience (353). But Gadamer, who is more convinced than I am that tradition is the repository of truth, argues that allowing ourselves to remain open to others means that we must "accept some things" that are "against" us (361). Though I agree that acquiring new knowledge does involve changing our minds, I am not sure how much of his argument is applicable to a cross-cultural reading situation since it would appear that his view of understanding entails application. He argues, for example, that we need to regard "not only understanding and interpretation, but also application as comprising one unified process" (1989, 308). In the philological and historical realm, moreover, hermeneutics, on his view, does not involve "'knowledge as domination'—i.e., an appropriation as taking possession; rather, it consists in subordinating ourselves to the text's [superior] claim to dominate our minds" (311; see also 1987, 131, 138). On my view, African texts historically have had neither the power to dominate the Western mind nor the authority to induce our subordination.

12. Gadamer's own intention is to rehabilitate the concept of prejudice from the disgrace it has known since the Enlightenment. In this context, Bernstein reminds us that the German word Gadamer uses is *Vorurteil*, which "can be translated as 'prejudgment,' in order to avoid the exclusively pejorative meaning that 'prejudice' conveys in English" (1989, 249, n. 19). (See also Gadamer 1989, 270.) Though there might be good cause to use this less inflammatory alternative, I personally am unwilling to defang the conventional English translation, regarding "prejudices" as all too appropriate a term to discuss the hermeneutical issues facing Western readers of African texts.

13. Whether we ever do understand one of these texts can never be proved, of course; our understanding in this case, as with any interpretation, can best be measured by how it is received by what Stanley Fish calls our interpretive community. I would ask whether the "acceptable" readings of Emecheta (and other African writers) have historically been a function of informed scholarship or political power—the discursive power wielded, for example, by American (and European) newspapers, magazines, learned journals, and publishing houses (see Fish 1980 and Foucault 1971).

14. This, of course, is a conviction codified by the principles of American New Criticism. See also Gadamer 1989, 268.

15. See Hawkesworth 1989 and Young 1990a and 1990b.

16. Again, I do not mean by this to engage the various Afrocentric debates. For a range of arguments see Herskovits 1990, Mintz and Price 1992, Levine 1977, Smither-

Introduction: A Question of Power   15

man 1988, Mudimbe 1990, and J. Holloway 1990. For discussion of literary connections, see K. Holloway 1992.

17. As a poststructuralist, I would amend Gadamer's notion of Truth here—and elsewhere—to one of provisionality.

18. He takes this unsettling view because he is convinced that a culture's tradition is the repository of truth. But his ideas are applicable here, in that I am arguing for the need for Westerners to see a kind of truth (though not the Truth) in African texts.

19. See also C. Miller 1990.

20. Elsewhere Frank acknowledges the "fundamental opposition between western [sic] and African values that permeates African literature" and its criticism. She asks, for example, "whether European-style literary criticism can or should be used on African texts" (1984, 47). Florence Stratton explores the "possibility" that there might be a "female literary tradition that transcends all cultural boundaries," but she reminds us that critics must "be neither indifferent to the . . . cultural elements that a writer has incorporated into her text, nor ignorant of their form and function in the cultural milieu outside the text" (1988, 144).

21. Compare my approach to that of K. Holloway 1992.

22. See, for example, Uzo Esonwanne's 1990-91 critique of current anthropological approaches to Africa (including Miller's "Theories of Africans"). For a discussion of the hostility scientific discourse harbors toward narrative discourse, see my application of Lyotard to Emecheta's *The Rape of Shavi* in chapter 5. For an account of scientific racism, see Gould 1981.

23. See, for example, Goldberg 1990.

24. Ngugi claims that the "most important area of domination was the mental universe of the colonised, the control, through culture, of how people perceived themselves and their relationship to the world" (1989, 16).

25. I do not intend by this claim to engage the Afrocentric debate here; see also K. Holloway 1992.

26. Many of these connections are evident in African American culture and traditions (see, for example, Herskovits 1990, Levine 1977, and J. Holloway 1990).

27. I am not concerned here with Afrocentric arguments but with how readily white Western readers have claimed Buchi Emecheta and other African women writers for their own projects.

28. Ngugi asks, "Why should not the African peasantry and working class appropriate the novel?" (1989, 68). He also argues for a connection between the African novel and orature, finding that the central ingredient "in the oral tale as in that of the novel is still the story" (69).

29. My use of "reading ourselves" to mean critiquing and challenging our way of seeing things is analogous to its use in the black vernacular.

30. S. P. Mohanty feels Winch's "cross-cultural comparison of 'forms of life' is pitched at such a high level of generality that his versions of human culture and rationality cannot register and include significant moral and imaginative practices and choices" (1989, 18). Mohanty, therefore, proposes a "more specific commonality" that is based on the view that human beings are "seen as individual and collective *agents* in their world," a conception wherein "their practices can be specified for analysis without a necessary reduction to their subjective beliefs" (19).

31. Clearly, this is where my project and Afrocentrism part company—but politely, I

hope, as we are both in search of a better understanding of our connections to Africa.

32. Or what Asante (1987), with good cause, would call a Eurocentric reading; see 6-7, 160-67.

33. See Geertz's essay on anti-anti-relativism (1984), which describes the kind of intellectual dilemma I face.

34. See also Geertz 1983, 234 and C. Miller 1988, 102.

1

The Author—and Reader—as Other: A Postmodern Approach to African Fiction

> ... the trouble with these so-called experts is that they are not sufficiently humble about their knowledge of Africa.
>
> *Anonymous source quoted in Joseph Okpaku*
> New African Literature and the Arts (1970a, 7)

HERMENEUTIC CHARITY

In this chapter, having argued in the introduction for the necessity of an interactive reading model, I begin to answer the more practical question of what we must do if we hope to understand African fiction in general—and Buchi Emecheta's fiction in particular. By understanding, I mean participating in a transcultural conversation in which my own cultural discourse has been enriched and even modified, in Peter Winch's terms, by my encounter with the "internal relations" of an alien discourse—which permits me to grasp "the *point* or *meaning*" of what has been written (1990, 115). As I argue more fully in chapter 2, what occurs when we in the West read African fiction is really a matter of language differences—but not because this fiction is written in foreign languages. To the contrary. Because it is written in "our" language(s), we must protect ourselves from the comforting, but ultimately false, idea that the discourse (and thus the culture) is already familiar to us.[1] Although distinguishing between Western discourses (of scientific instrumentality and individualism) and African discourses (of wholeness and interrelatedness) is particularly crucial for a discussion of rationality (since the world we experience is largely defined by the language we inhabit), it is also crucial, as I discuss in the next chapter, to the language forms we call novels. But let me for the moment focus on what literary critics can learn from certain philosophical issues facing the social sciences.

A key text in this debate is Winch's "Understanding a Primitive Society," an essay in which he lays out what has become known as his principle of hermeneutic charity. Although this principle has fallen on hard times of late,[2] I think it can be a helpful guide for those of us who desire to understand African fiction as something other than an exotic variant of Western literature. Winch takes it as a given that "standards of rationality and intelligibility" vary from culture to culture. He then argues that these variations can make it quite difficult for Western scientists to understand another culture—especially a "primitive"[3] one, whose standards can differ fundamentally from our own (1964, 315). In order to resolve the interpretive problems posed by these differences, Winch urges Western scientists to accept the responsibility for changing their way of thinking. The example he uses to illustrate his argument is the institution of magic in the African Azande culture. Because we are the ones who wish to understand this magic, Winch argues that the burden is "on us to extend our understanding so as to make room for the Zande category, rather than to insist on seeing it in terms of our own ready-made distinction between science and non-science" (319). In other words, he wants to find a method by which we in the West can incorporate the perspectives of an alien society into our own way of looking at the world (317-18). Exercising this hermeneutic charity would serve not only to promote our understanding of an alien culture but also to change ourselves and our view of the world. In short, Winch is calling upon Western social scientists to engage in the philosophical activity of extending our own categories of thought in order to understand the (thought) behavior of other cultures.

If we are sincere in wishing to understand the texts and beliefs of an alien culture, we literary critics also ought to follow Winch's lead and extend our categories of thought. For how else are we to understand those novelistic expressions of traditional African beliefs that involve such things as magic, ancestor worship, and the spirit world? Surely, then, this extension must also include the modification or even outright rejection of old models of interpretation when they reveal themselves to be too culture-laden to be useful. The difficulty of trying to extend ourselves in this way may discourage us, but it should not stop us if, indeed, we wish to understand what these other cultures are about. If we are uncomfortable (as perhaps we should be) with the idea of invoking the principle of hermeneutic charity, perhaps we should invoke the virtue of cultural and intellectual humility. Doing so should allow us to learn how other cultures organize and explain the world and to achieve a better understanding of our own epistemology—seeing it as one of many systems of knowledge.

QUESTIONING LIBERALISM AND LIBERAL FEMINISM

As I argue in the introduction, when we engage a text outside of our national culture, a primary interpretive principle should be that of contextualizing ourselves as readers by interrogating our cultural prejudices and our theoretical and critical assumptions—and modifying them when they can be seen to interfere with our understanding.[4] As a general rule, then, I think it is imperative for all Western readers (most particularly, feminist readers) to ask ourselves whether we are really being open to the newness in these texts, or whether we are so beholden to our liberal humanist (or liberal feminist) tradition that we close ourselves off from their newness and strangeness. It is my argument that our heritage of liberal humanism has heretofore interfered with our ability to understand other cultures in their full difference from ourselves—an argument also put forward by the eminent ethnographers George Marcus and Michael M. J. Fischer, who claim in *Anthropology as Cultural Critique* that the Western intellectual tradition is "biased toward attenuating the importance of alien cultural differences" (1986, 38). It is biased in this direction precisely because we in the West conceive of the self as atomistic, autonomous, and originating outside or prior to society, a conception based on what Iris Marion Young calls the "illusory . . . metaphysic of a unified self-making subjectivity" (1990b, 45). Differences among peoples, thus, are seen as being nothing more than "relatively superficial" variations played out upon "a certain fixed human nature which is modified but not fundamentally created by social circumstances" (Jaggar 1988, 125).[5] If human beings are all the same (as liberals hold), it is a small step to imagine that all women, for example, share a common experience irrespective of their cultural or material differences—an assumption that has marked much of the Western feminist approaches to African women's writing (but see Okhamafe 1989, 33). In hopes of affirming an international sisterhood and eradicating sexism, white liberal feminists in particular, like their liberal humanist counterparts, have claimed to find similarity and sameness where none exist (see also C. Mohanty 1984). But it is not only a matter of longing for connections that can lead us astray; it is also our determination to find a standpoint theory that would provide universal explanations for why women have historically been oppressed by men.

Contrary to this liberal humanist view of subjectivity, I want to argue here for the (advantages of the) poststructuralist position that subjectivity is a constantly shifting construction of social—and personal—discourse. Such a view of subjectivity reminds us that, although we are, indeed, products of our socialization, we can use language itself to redefine or "rewrite" ourselves (see Weedon 1987, 29-30). This view also holds that people, having no subjective existence which precedes socialization, really are markedly different from one another and that their literatures reflect these differences. This, of course, is where anthropology can be helpful to literary critics, as it helps us recognize cultural differences. That these differences historically have been used to support the so-called superiority of the West is no reason not to use the evidence today to undermine the false universalism inherent to a liberal point of view. As part of our strategy for contextualizing ourselves, therefore, it can also be quite helpful to hear how African critics represent us—to learn, in short, how culture-specific many of our own ideas really are.

An example of what the African Left finds wrong with the tenets of liberal humanism can be found in Ngugi's position paper, "Literature and Society," where he insists that liberalism tries to encourage "the illusion in the exploited of the possibilities of peaceful settlement and painless escape from imperialist violence"—even as it has functioned as the handmaiden of Western imperialism (1981, 20).[6] Ngugi is particularly bothered by the fact that the liberal (bourgeois) agenda fails to endorse violent change and also deeply troubled by the fact that liberalism manages to disguise so well the "antagonistic" tensions between classes. He finds the clearest expression of liberal thought not so much in openly political writings but in "imaginative literature" (20).[7] Though Western liberalism may, indeed, obscure antagonistic *class* contradictions, it does, as Ellis reminds us, insist on the "opposition between the individual and all those institutions that would impose limits upon him or her—feudalism, monarchy, big government, 'experts'—in a word, 'society'" (1989, 42). This opposition between the individual and society is certainly more Western in its origins than African. In fact, as I am at pains to point out frequently in the pages that follow, the Western concept of individualism serves us poorly as we try to understand Emecheta's African fiction. This, then, is just one of many cultural differences that interfere with our understanding of African literature. Western feminists are faced with others.

Rhonda Cobham, for example, faults those feminists who invoke the rallying cry of "universal sisterhood as a means of achieving goals in their societies that are irrelevant to—not to say exploitative of—women in other countries" (1988, 138). Carole Boyce Davies, though she finds points of congruence between Western and African feminism, describes the "failure of Western feminists to deal with issues that directly affect Black women and their tendency to sensationalize others." Davies also reminds us that white women have themselves been the oppressors "of both African women and men" (1986a, 10).[8] In her introduction to *The Black Woman Cross-Culturally*, Philomina Chioma Steady challenges the feminist scholarship that has less to do with African realities than the "male/female antagonisms that derive from Western middle-class experiences." She also argues that many Western scholars, motivated by their own feminist agenda, have been unwilling to address the economic oppression of African men (1981, 28). Cynthia Ward argues similarly that a (Western) feminist approach "frequently reinscribes the image of Africa as the dark continent where 'primitive' cultural practices must be guided into productive paths by enlightened Europeans" (1990, 85). Barbara Christian reminds us that African novelists like Nwapa, Head, and Emecheta reject "the narrowness of the western [sic] version [of feminism], which does not see sexism as related to class exploitation and racism in an established hierarchy of dominance" (1985a, 147). Perhaps because of these serious challenges to feminism, the Nigerian critic Chikwenye Okonjo Ogunyemi has forgone the concept altogether, preferring instead, like Alice Walker (1983b), to use "womanism," though she apparently came to this decision independently of Walker's essays on the subject. Ogunyemi defines black womanism as binding together African and African American women writers, as "a philosophy that celebrates black roots, the ideals of black life, while giving a balanced presentation of black womanhood" (1985, 72).

In part, because of criticisms like these, I suggest we learn to utilize moments of misunderstanding to help us see (and critique) Western theory itself. For, clearly, it is a reconceptualized feminist theory that Western readers must take to African fiction.[9] For my part, then, rather than adopting the term "womanism," I prefer to redefine my Western feminism by working in the language of perspicuous contrast. This means walking that fine line between ethnocentric positivism and what Taylor calls the incorrigibility thesis. We must neither assume that our way (our feminism) is the only way of doing things and seeing the world nor assume that there are no flaws in the African way(s). In short, we should not identify ourselves so completely with African heroines that we assume their experiences are our experiences. If we Western feminists look only for connections with African women, it is far too easy (as others have found) to regard their various cultures as narrowly chauvinistic.[10] To give their *cultures* a fair reading, we must, on principle, also look for difference. As we do this, however, we must not ignore or try to explain away the very real and deeply serious complaints that African women have articulated. These, too, we need to bring to bear on our understanding of African fiction.

Several scholars have written eloquently about the kinds and scope of the problems faced by African women today. In 1972, for example, Audrey Wipper described the social disapprobation facing urban African women, who were "seen as a major force undermining traditional values" (346). In 1987, Biola Babatope described the hardships she has faced as a member of the Nigerian House of Representatives. In this sometimes bitter essay she writes that even elected women "are still being used as cannon fodders [sic] by political parties. Though a handful of our kind are in exalted positions as ministers and commissioners, we are still made to eat off the crumbs from the men's table." She continues with her bleak assessment of conditions by reminding her readers that "the fact of our subjugation is evident" if it is only remembered that most of the power, "including the coercive force of the police, is entirely in male hands" (21). In the same issue of *Présence Africaine*, Flora Nwapa suggests that because Nigerian women are less vocal than Western women, they are often "taken for granted, not only by politicians and political aspirants but by almost everybody" (1987b, 120). According to Christian, African women novelists have responded to this situation by condemning the "debasement of the African woman and man wreaked by colonialism, but they also protest the mores of the traditional society that condemn women to a prescribed fate of subsistence, subservience, and silence in the political world" (1985a, 147). Irene Assiba d'Almeida goes so far as to suggest that the writing of contemporary African women can be "characterized by a certain malaise. This malaise emerges from the dilemma women face in wanting to keep traditions while, at the same time, wanting to reject what, in society, ties women down" (1986, 167). Davies echoes this thought, reminding us that life for many women in Africa "is fraught with contradictions, tensions and oppositions, most arising out of the colonial domination of Africa, others intrinsic to the organizational structures of particular societies" (1986b, 241).

As these accounts indicate, African women do have much to complain about, and there is legitimate, impassioned political protest in their fiction. But this protest must be seen in a larger perspective than the one provided by (white Western) feminism or (white Western) socialism. Without this wider perspective, it is just too easy to represent the lives of African women as so similar to ours that they can be judged on our terms. All too often this has meant, as Chandra Mohanty (1984) demonstrates, that Third World women's lives and cultures have been found to be inferior to ours. To avoid this false universalism, what is needed is a politically grounded interpretive approach that challenges, rather than reinscribes, the discourses of Western critical "truth."

A POSTMODERN APPROACH

In *Critical Practice*, Catherine Belsey rebukes Stanley Fish for failing "to recognize that a plurality of readers must necessarily produce a plurality of readings" (1980, 33). Belsey goes on to suggest that because Fish "makes no attempt to account in theoretical terms for the relationship between experience and language, ideology and history," he can be cited for practicing nothing more than "a sophisticated form of New Criticism" (34). In short, Fish, like most (male) reader-response critics, fails to theorize how differences in readers themselves can lead to differences in interpretation.[11] Thus, for Belsey, Fish's version of reader-response criticism "becomes the literary equivalent of populism, challenging the privilege of the author but offering instead the reader's intuition as a new source of authority" (34).[12] This populist stance, I would argue, is especially tempting to those Western readers of African fiction who are not, in the words of one of the epigraphs to this chapter, "sufficiently humble about their knowledge of Africa." Not only do such critics insist on a Western reading of African fiction, but they defend their right to do so by insisting on the "universality" of aesthetic values. In other words, either by argument or implication, they make the imperialist claim for the universality of their own values—their own ideology. As Chinweizu et al. argue, such readings work to judge "African literature as an appendage of European literature, and to deny its separateness and autonomy" (Chinweizu 1983, 10). The ultimate effect of applying these so-called universal values is to distort African literature. By forcing alien texts into the Procrustean beds of known aesthetic systems, Western critics impoverish the rich, unplumbed plurality of African fiction.

I certainly do not mean to suggest by this phrasing that there exists today a "dark continent" of African literature ripe for colonization by Western critics. What I do mean is that African fiction contains complexities and subtleties that are sometimes literally unimaginable to Western minds. The best we Western critics can hope to do, therefore, is, wherever possible, fuse our own (defamiliarized) Western horizon with an (alien) African horizon and thus enlarge our perspective. Though a complete fusion is probably out of the question, we can do better than we have in the past in interpreting these texts. At minimum, in my own efforts to achieve fusion, I hope to avoid the flagrant imperialism so roundly condemned by Ngugi, who complains that African writers like himself are "encouraged [by Western critics] to produce and are applauded for producing the kind of literature that perpetuates decadent western [sic] bourgeois values and class world outlook." As evidence of the West's attempts to control African literature, he points to "the mad rush of European critics who only a few years ago . . . were so disparaging about African literature and African writers. Now they are the new interpreters, interpreting African literature for the African" (1981, 24-25). In postmodern terms, Ngugi's complaints remind us that a plurality of readings is only as productive as the critical systems on which these readings are based. For if all (Western) readers take the same (unexamined Western) prejudices and preconceptions to the African fiction they read, their interpretations will all sound pretty much the same. None will do justice to the novels they purport to explain, for a Western reading will produce nothing more than a Western(ized) text. As Chinweizu et al. put it, "Eurocentric criticism of African fiction stems from colonialist attitudes whereby these critics see the African as an apprentice European whose literary production has no other canons to adhere to but those of [the critic]" (1983, 8).[13] Under these critical conditions, African novelists cannot win. When held to Western standards, their fiction either lacks unity (is too undisciplined, too journalistic, without a strong plot line) or contains too much (is too tight, too short, too simple).

If the universalist/European aesthetic principles of New Criticism cannot help us understand an African text, perhaps we should look to a new kind of reader-response criticism—one that has been informed by the principles of poststructuralism. What I want to do in the remainder of this chapter, therefore, is play with the possibilities and pitfalls inherent to a postmodern approach to African fiction.

Certainly, there is much to be said in favor of postmodern thought, most especially in its challenge to the *grands récits* of liberal humanism and its interrogation of Western epistemology. At the heart of my own contextualized approach to African fiction, for example, is the postmodern challenge to the Western concept of universal reason, a concept premised on the notion of a transcendent, rational self, which under scrutiny reveals itself to be nothing more than a privileged white Western male, middle-class rational self. As a Western reader of African texts, I have therefore found quite useful those postmodern strategies that would engender a proliferation of meaning in Buchi Emecheta's novels—strategies that would prevent Western parasitism by insisting on textual differences, strategies born of postmodern theories that are themselves based on what Linda Hutcheon identifies as "multiplicity, heterogeneity, plurality" (1988, 61). If we are to have any chance at all of submitting ourselves to the sociocultural truths (or local narratives) of an African novel, surely we ought to be cognizant of what Foucault calls the "circular relation" of truth "with systems of power which produce and sustain it" (1984, 133). Since the West controls (or has until recently) the publishing houses and educational systems, it has determined what can even count as African literature. Or, as Irele puts it, the West "has exerted such pressure upon our experience and our awareness that it is no exaggeration to say that all forms of modern African expression have been massively conditioned by it" (1991, 58).[14]

Closely related to these issues of truth and power is the question of authorship itself. By now everyone has noticed how ironic it is that Barthes and Foucault (surely two of the best-known "names" in current intellectual circles) have argued for the "death of the author"—Barthes claiming that assigning a text an "Author" means, in effect, limiting its meaning (1986, 147); Foucault arguing that authors function to prevent "the free composition, decomposition, and recomposition of fiction" (1979, 159). Perhaps, if the author does, indeed, impose limits on texts, we would be well advised as Western readers of African texts to accept this death and read without the father's signature.[15] Perhaps, if the "author principle" is, indeed, tied to a Western concept of "*identity* whose form is that of *individuality* and the *I*," we have further reason to invoke *his* death (Foucault 1971, 222). But are these arguments about the author really all that liberating in the context of a cross-cultural reading experience? Or do these intellectual positions, in fact, have the opposite effect of reinstating the regime of Western truth? Do they not permit Western readers to engage in the "control and delimitation of discourse" so anathema to Foucault and other postmodernists (1971, 220)? Do they not permit, even encourage, the kind of commentary that limits "the hazards of discourse through the action of an *identity* taking the form of *repetition* and *sameness*" (222)?

Let me begin with the admission that I am intrigued by the "death of the author" and find it *theoretically* quite appealing as a disruptive strategy. But for all its apparent revolutionary promise, I must confess (with others)[16] that I have found it disrupts nothing at all. Though on the surface the death of the author seems to free us from patriarchal authority, it has the unwanted effect of ungendering our fiction—or at least making the female signature (and the text's ideology) more difficult to detect. I do not want to slip into the kind of sexual essentialism that Toril Moi finds so naively characteristic of American feminism (1985). Nor do I want to suggest that all individuals in a particular gender category are alike. But the existence of an author has allowed feminist critics to problematize their relationship to novels that have been authored by men.[17] It has also allowed feminist critics the added (and perhaps unexpected) advantage of problematizing their relationship to novels that have been authored by women.[18] It has certainly allowed me to problematize my relationship as a (white) Western feminist to a (black) African woman writer's fiction. For me, then, the subject who is doing the reading is just as important as the subject who has written the text. In short, as a Western critic facing the task of reading African fiction, I have found myself unwilling to embrace the death of the author. In the contextualized postmodernism I am proposing here, I must have an author. I am convinced that I have needed to have the author in this project as a constant reminder not to impose my own Anglo-American centrism on what, after all, are alien texts. I take my inspiration in part from Edward Said, who sees a text's situatedness as the foundation of an ethical criticism, arguing that there is "an ambition on the part of a writer to deliver his text as an object whose interpretation—by virtue of the exactness of its situation in the world—has already commenced and is therefore already constrained in, and constraining, its interpretation" (1979a, 171).

RECONFIGURING AUTHORS AND READERS

I contend, therefore, that the birth of a decentered Western reader, contrary to Barthes, must be accompanied by the birth of the author as Other—or in this particular case, the birth of the author as African. Without the ever-present author as Other, it is just too easy to be reassured by what we think is discursive familiarity[19]—when what these texts, instead, are asking us to do is defamiliarize (and even anthropologize) the dominant Western narratives to which we are heir.[20] It is too easy, in other words, to end up talking to ourselves, to think we have engaged a stranger in a friendly dialogue when, in fact, we have only met ourselves in the mirror.

Drawing on the work of Albert Memmi, Nancy Hartsock argues that the subject envisioned by Enlightenment philosophy (and virtually naturalized today in the West) depended on "the philosophical and historical creation of a *devalued Other* [as] the necessary precondition for the creation of the transcendental rational subject outside of time and space" (1987, 191; emphasis added). Speaking herself as an-Other, Hartsock argues that one of the first tasks (facing her and all those who have been marginalized as Others) is to *construct* "the subjectivities of the Other, subjectivities which will be both multiple and specific" (195). On her view, "we need to engage in the historical and political and theoretical process of constituting ourselves as subjects as well as objects of history" (204). I, however, do not see it as my task to *create* the Other. I see it as my task to *recognize* the (preexisting but also always provisional) subjectivity of the Other. But, as Alcoff reminds us, in representing other persons, we do inevitably help to construct their "subject-positions" (1991-92, 9). We thus need to take particular care, even as literary critics, to let the Other speak to and through us—and to let ourselves be changed by the conversation. My purpose in acknowledging the presence of the Other, therefore, is not to shore up the Enlightenment notion of a transcendent rational self, outside space and time. It is precisely to challenge this self—and the Western epistemology that gives it voice. In short, if we are hoping to practice an ethical criticism in a cross-cultural reading situation, we must have an author—an author who is Other.

At the same time, we must have a reader—a reader who is Other. With Gadamer, I would argue that readers are situated (within their own cultural horizons) as well as texts. If, indeed, we wish to understand the African text as a new experience (in Gadamer's terms, a negative one), as readers, then, we must at the very least be willing to reconfigure our role as that of a conversationalist rather than combatant or, as Hutcheon puts it, that of "collaborator" rather than a "consumer" (Hutcheon 1988, 80). This notion of a situated collaboration returns me to the interactive reading strategy I am proposing, where the Western reader, on behalf of the African author, reads (or questions) herself and her Western intellectual tradition even as she reads (and questions) the African text. Though we may not, as Westerners, ever be able to read ourselves as an African would, we can, I think, use the strangeness in the African text to interrogate our (familiar but perhaps unacknowledged) Western prejudices—and so reverse what we find familiar and what we find strange. Drawing on the insights of Hegel and others, Iris Marion Young reminds us that "persons necessarily transcend one another because subjectivity is negativity. The regard of the other is always objectifying" (1990b, 231). To apply this, then, to my own project: because the text and its author do not reflect my experiences or perspectives, as I permit them to read me, I am, then, in Young's terms, "always faced with an experience of myself different from the one I have"—which, in Gadamer's terms, allows me to argue that I have acquired knowledge (Young, 231; Gadamer 1989, 353-55).[21]

But what view of language and subjectivity does my position entail? In short, who are the parties engaged in the cross-cultural conversation I have undertaken here? These questions return us once more to Gadamer, who argues that the "*hermeneutical conversation*" occurs in the "common language" that the *text* and reader mutually discover during the course of interpretation (1989, 388). The text is able to bring "a *subject matter* into language" largely because of the cooperation of the reader (388; emphasis added).[22] As a result of its being written down, the text has, in effect, "detached itself" from being dependent on its origins (395) and is thus free to circulate in conversation with readers. Because the text is detached from its author, the validity of its "truth" claims (quotation marks added) is decided by "the understanding reader" (394). For Gadamer, then, the major effort involved in understanding is not that of recovering the author but of finding the common language that text and reader can share. In sum, an author's subjectivity is neither recoverable nor necessary to understanding (395). Because Gadamer has constructed his hermeneutical conversation on the "logic of the question," however, he does invite us to consider an author's sociocultural subjectivity, if not an individual subjectivity (370). For Gadamer, what is said—or written—is, in effect, one of many possible answers to a question. Moreover, once "we go back *behind* what is said, then we inevitably ask questions *beyond* what is said." That is, once we achieve or enter into the "horizon of the question," we will realize that it is capable of generating an abundance of (different) answers—thus expanding the meaning of what has been said (or written down) (370). This returns us to the arguments I make in the introduction. Putting it in terms of the logic of the question, I would formulate my own question thus: without foreknowledge of African cultures, how can we Western readers begin to "question what lies behind" the text (370)? Without this knowledge, how can we formulate the question the text replies to—and thus begin to "answer the question the text asks us" (374)?

In arguing for the author as Other, then, I am not claiming the other as Author. I am trying to find a tolerable middle ground that would permit us to read the subject behind the *subject matter* without insisting on the existence of some sort of rational transcendental self—or relying on the metaphysics of presence. It may very well be that African readers (or Nigerian readers of Emecheta—or similarly exiled Nigerian readers of Emecheta) will not need to conceptualize the subject behind the subject matter. But as a Western reader of an African text, I feel it is (absolutely) necessary for me to do so. I would thus offer the postmodern paradox of absent presence. I want to suggest that Emecheta's novels contain the presence of an author who is absent. I have no particular interest in trying to recover the author behind the text. I do believe, however, that these novels have been authored by a (black) African woman whose subjectivity is fundamentally different from (alien to) my own (white) Western subjectivity. But because there is enough "discursive familiarity" in these texts to keep me reading (and to permit my understanding), I need the presence of an alien subjectivity to prevent me from being too reassured by what I read. I need it, in other words, to remind me that subjects cannot be transparent to one another (see Young 1990b, 230-31).

In response to my own hermeneutical situation, like any good conversationalist, I am seeking a compromise, where, in an effort to understand the African text in question, I never forget its particular African origins. Thus, the interpretive model I propose acknowledges the mutual interdependence of understanding and misunderstanding, and that of community and rupture. At the same time, our encounter with the discourse of Others necessarily changes us, by calling into question how we perceive the world and ourselves in it. As Taylor, Gadamer, and others have argued, the negative experience of freely opening ourselves to the alien horizon of the Other necessarily clarifies and modifies our own horizon. It is precisely because an alien text has this extraordinary capacity to change our own subject-position that, in the pages that follow, I occasionally find myself refusing to assume the (unfamiliar) role the text would assign me as reader. But, if, in the poststructuralist model I am proposing here, we are truly to know (rewrite/revise) ourselves rather than just retranscribe ourselves, we must make sure we encounter (and, yes, submit to) an alien horizon: an-Other who is truly different from us.[23]

In describing the conversational experience, Gadamer suggests in *Truth and Method* that we "fall into" it, giving ourselves completely over to the joy of conversation (1989, 383). In a later essay, he characterizes the dialogic game of giving and taking as marked by "accident, favor, and surprise—and in the end, of buoyancy, indeed, of elevation." For him, then, reading and understanding a text are analogous to entering into a friendly conversation, a dialogue with someone whose language we share (1976b, 57). But here I feel I simply must strike yet another cautionary note. As we read an African text, we must not be too quick to assume we have found a common language. We must not get so caught up in the hermeneutical game, in the delightful buoyancy of (a false) understanding, that we silence the Other with whom we would speak. After all, both as teachers and critics we are (quite literally) in the business of representing others to students and colleagues alike. There are material consequences to those we represent as well as to those to whom we make our representations. Even if we see ourselves as *only* literary critics, the question of power still obtains if it is *our* interpretation, *our* representation that is circulated. How can our cross-cultural conversation with a text be a conversation between equals if power is distributed unequally outside the text?[24] Perhaps we should, ideally, in a Barthean moment (be able to) dispense with the particularities of author and reader. Perhaps we should comply with Hillis Miller's suggestion that we (simply) submit ourselves to the words of the text. Perhaps that is the route to an ethical and just criticism.[25] But as a feminist, I am profoundly skeptical of Barthes's poststructuralist argument and Miller's American deconstructionist ethics—as is Alcoff, who insists that "political theory must base itself on the initial premise that all persons, including the [literary] theorist, have a fleshy, material identity" (1988, 433).[26] If I were to try, therefore, to assume a Rawlsian veil of ignorance and "forget" that these novels have an African author and that I am a Western reader (harboring both enabling and disenabling prejudices), I am utterly convinced I would do nothing more than impose a Western meaning on them. This, I contend, would be an injustice.

I want at this point, therefore, to endorse Hutcheon's definition of a contextualized postmodernism, a definition that relies on the paradoxical relationship between postmodernism and its predecessor. For Hutcheon, postmodernism is a "questioning of commonly accepted values of our culture (closure, teleology, and subjectivity), a questioning that is totally dependent upon that which it interrogates" (1988, 42). Though I am not comfortable in arguing that an African text is *totally dependent* upon that which it interrogates, the idea has its uses—especially for its Western readers. It seems especially pertinent to the arguments I have been making here, and it does coincide with the Gadamerian approach I am taking: since *we as readers* cannot escape or otherwise circumvent our own cultural context (our horizon), perhaps we should approach African texts in the knowledge that they will invoke what we already know (the familiar: West) only to interrogate it through the unknown (the unfamiliar: Africa).[27] Perhaps for us, if not for African readers, an African text is indeed dependent on that which it interrogates. I would like to propose, then, that for Westerners the very act of reading an African text constitutes the postmodern condition—and engages us in an archetypal hermeneutic dialogue where we are poised between the foreign and familiar and called upon to contextualize (and even anthropologize) ourselves.[28] Such a model of reading has the decided advantage of helping to explain how it is that Westerners can understand African texts at all, since it presupposes an overlapping of Western and African tradition(s). The difference in (and benefits of) the negative experience of reading across cultures rather than within our own is that the "truth" claims of these African texts will often involve challenging the very "truth" claims that constitute our own tradition and its texts.

NOTES

1. I remind readers that my quarrel is not with Afrocentric readings but white feminist ones.

2. See, for example, Matustik 1989, where he reads Winch's principle of hermeneutic charity as "an appeal to the critical modernist type of rationality. Winch's reflective, essentially modern use of rationality is not available in primitive cultures. Thus such a 'charity' is also ethnocentric [in that it] condescends to those who [apparently] cannot make a rational case for themselves" (161). Matustik's criticism may be valid, but it does not entirely obtain to the act of literary interpretation. To be sure, African novelists have no need of Western critics, so we are not charitably making a case for those who cannot speak for themselves. But Western readers of African novelists do have need of us—or at least access to an approach that would aid their understanding.

3. I certainly do not mean to endorse the notion that African cultures are somehow primitive. Nor have I been able to find a term to use myself that is not somehow value-laden. Even the apparently innocuous "non-Western" suggests that the West is the standard by which all else is to be judged.

4. For me personally, this means interrogating my particular version of feminism and finding a balance between it and the principles of poststructuralism.

5. Chris Weedon describes this view of human nature, in which crucial cultural differences are overlooked or discounted, as "presuppos[ing] an essence at the heart of the individual which is unique, fixed and coherent and which makes her what she *is*" (1987, 32). See also Asante 1987.

6. See also Mazrui 1983, 66-67.

7. Perhaps Ngugi should have qualified the last statement to read that nowhere is liberalism so clearly seen as in imaginative *Western* literature, for it does not seem particularly prevalent in my experience with African fiction.

8. For Davies, African feminism (1) "recognizes a common struggle with African men" against the forces of colonialism and neocolonialism; (2) "recognizes that certain inequities and limitations existed/exist in traditional societies," inequities that were strengthened by colonialism; (3) "recognizes that African societies . . . [historically] addressed the problems [of women]"; (4) "examines African societies for institutions which are of value to women and rejects those [which are not]"; (5) "respects African woman's self-reliance and the penchant to cooperative work"; (6) scrutinizes objectively the status of women in countries that have experienced wars of "national liberation and socialist reconstruction"; and (7) recognizes the true power of women in African society (1986a, 8-10).

9. Examples of the new sensitivity to otherness are suddenly abundant; especially recommended are Fuss 1989, Lugones and Spelman 1983, Meese 1990, Rosaldo 1980, Spelman 1988, Young 1990b. At this point let me also note for the record that I am not trying to discredit either the political Left or feminism. I am trying to correct our political position from within by illustrating how our longing for connections can lead us astray.

10. But see K. Holloway 1992 for a positive reading of cultural connections.

11. Patrocinio Schweickart begins to undertake this project in her work (1986), though she fails to distinguish among women readers. See also the collection by Jardine and Smith (1987).

12. Fish responds to some of these charges in a 1987 essay by arguing that the community does "the work of transforming the landscape into material for its own project; but that project is then itself transformed by the very work it does" (433).

13. Compare this with Said's contention that Western methodology and discourse have been employed in order to make non-European cultures appear inferior, with the result that they have been relegated "to a position of subordination" (1979a, 180).

14. Noting the recent discrediting of scientific positivism even among scientists, Irele describes the analogous relationship between "the new scientific spirit . . . and the profound intuition of the fundamentally unsettling nature of the world within those non-Western modes of apprehension that have been qualified as 'mythical' and have thus tended to be dismissed out of hand" (1991, 67).

15. For Said, the "inherent authoritarianism of the authorial authority" gains much of its power from "the patrimony of texts," which is founded on the "displacing power of the Bible, whose centrality, potency, and dominating anteriority inform all Western literature" (1979a, 179). How much the (displaced) biblical authority that Said attributes to Western texts is evident in African literature is another issue. It is present, to a degree, in Emecheta. But even when it appears, I do not think it carries the same weight

that it does in Western fiction. When the author of a text is an African, therefore, it seems likely that it will be (or at least it has been) the *Western critic* who is regarded as the "father" and owner of the work.

16. Nancy Hartsock finds it "highly suspicious that it is at this moment in history, when so many groups are engaged in 'nationalisms' which involve redefinitions of the marginalized Others, that doubt arises in the academy about the nature of the 'subject'" (1987, 196). See also Huyssen 1986, N. K. Miller 1986, and Mascia-Lees et al. 1989.

17. See, for example, Fetterley 1978, Kolodny 1985, Baym 1985, and Schweickart 1986.

18. See, for example, Coward 1985, Jacobus 1986, Spelman 1988, and Meese 1990.

19. I take this phrasing from Belsey 1980; this notion of discursive familiarity is one I discuss in detail in chapter 2.

20. On the relationship of African American readers to African literature, see K. Holloway 1992 and Gourdine 1994.

21. See also Bhabha 1990.

22. For commentary on this, see Dallmayr 1984.

23. For a discussion of subject-positions in reading, see Fuss 1989, 32-34.

24. See, for example, Thompson 1982.

25. Miller contends that the "ethics of reading is the power of the words of the text over the mind and words of the reader" (J. H. Miller 1981, 41). Miller's model of reading (like Habermas's model of speech) seems to be built on a necessary (and necessarily idealized) combination of good intentions and a balance of power. Tobin Siebers, for example, summarizes Miller's ethics of reading as requiring readers to deny their urge to choose a particular interpretation while they "allow the paradoxical and undecidable character of textuality to shape and coerce them" (1988, 38). Siebers counters that "the creation of an isolated linguistic morality robs ethical theory of its social context and renders ethics ineffectual" (39).

26. I would argue further that we experience our material identities through the mediating effects of language—though to what degree our bodies are mediated remains in some dispute. See, for example, Martin 1987 and Jaggar and Bordo 1989. Alcoff conceives of the subject as "positionality," which permits her to argue that even though "gender is not natural, biological, universal, ahistorical, or essential," it is still useful "as a position from which to act politically" (1988, 433).

27. As I have said throughout this project, I am not engaging Afrocentrism here. No doubt, the balance between familiarity and strangeness will vary from reader to reader. See K. Holloway 1992.

28. See Bialostosky 1986, in which he proposes that readers "self-consciously represent the voice-ideas of others and involve others in dialogues they had not anticipated, but . . . also self-consciously expect unexpected replies and foresee unforeseen uses of our own words and ourselves by others" (791).

2

Aesthetics, Language, and Politics

A nation's literature . . . is not only a reflection of that people's collective reality, collective experience, but also embodies that community's way of looking at the world and its place in the making of that world.

Ngugi wa Thiong'o
"Literature and Society" (1981, 7)

Art for art's sake is just another piece of deodorised dog-shit.

Chinua Achebe
"Africa and Her Writers" (1975c, 19)

DEFINITIONS OF INDIVIDUALITY AND AESTHETIC CONSEQUENCES

I have already suggested that many of the differences that distinguish the many dozens of African cultures from Western culture can be traced to the fact that the presence of European thought is a relatively recent phenomenon on the continent of Africa. In this section I want to suggest some aesthetic consequences of this late arrival. The first deals with the relationship between artist and society, a topic I explore at some length, concluding with a discussion of some of the problems facing contemporary African writers. As part of this discussion, I use the ideas of Mikhail Bakhtin to argue that even though Buchi Emecheta has written her novels in English, it is not the English with which we in the West are familiar. Then I return to the question of Western philosophy by raising some questions about the relationship between epistemology and narrative form. Following that, I compare how Marxists and poststructuralists regard realism, suggesting that it is a mistake (though extremely tempting and even reasonable) for Westerners to try to read Emecheta's fiction as though it were European realism.

Because it is so central to the differences I find between the tradition of Western fiction and Buchi Emecheta's African novels, however, I want to begin this chapter by reiterating the history of the term "individual" that Raymond Williams traces.

Williams reminds us that in medieval times the term "individual" was used primarily in theological debates "about the nature of the Holy Trinity." As such, it originally meant "inseparable" and referred to "a member of some group, kind, or species." Over time, however, the concept lost the idea of affiliation, a loss that now allows those of us in the West to conceive of an individual "as a kind of absolute" (1961, 73). Accompanying these changes—which Williams traces to the social and philosophical changes brought by the Renaissance, the Reformation, and the start of capitalism—was a process that increasingly abstracted "'society'" to a "thing in itself" (76). The initial move to separate these newly conceived "individuals" from the repressive authority of church and state was all to the good. But over time the two terms took on opposite valences, "individual" coming to represent wholly positive values and "society," mainly negative ones (109). What began, then, as the beneficent and laudable process of freeing individuals from institutional authority has become the more harmful exercise of separating individuals from each other, contributing in no small measure to what Williams describes as an endemic Western alienation (95-96). Robert Bellah et al. trace a similar pattern of alienation, describing American society as one where individuals only occasionally see their lives "as interrelated in morally meaningful ways with those of other, different Americans" (1985, 50). Bellah attributes this concept of what he calls "an unencumbered self" to the heritage of Western philosophy found in Descartes, Locke, and Hume (80) and argues that American literature is organized around the dominant theme of a "hero who must leave society" (144). In 1981, four years before Bellah, the feminist literary critic, Nina Baym, made this same claim about American literature, arguing that the myth of America "narrates a confrontation of the American individual, the pure American self divorced from specific social circumstances, with the promise offered by the idea of America" (rpt. 1985, 71). If we in the West define ourselves in the binary terms of self versus society (or the private/public dichotomy) and if narratives reflect ideology (as I contend they do), it is only logical for our fiction to reflect this same ideological split. Myra Jehlen, in fact, finds this split so central to Western narrative that she characterizes the Western (middle-class) novel as "organically individualistic" (1981, 595).[1]

In contrast to our modern Western concept of an "individual" as someone at odds with, or to be distinguished from, society, however, the archetypal Igbo sense of "individual" is closer to the medieval Western meaning of *inseparable*—a difference that leads to differences in our fiction. Vernon Dixon, for example, describes what he considers to be the basic differences between the Euro-American worldview and the African worldview. Although Dixon can surely be faulted for eliding all differences among African cultures, I want to cite his distinctions, less as a way of characterizing a monolithic "African" concept than as a point of comparison to our modern Western view of individuality. The Western view he describes is similar to the one I have sketched out earlier, emphasizing the separation of individuals from each other and from the natural world (1976, 55).[2] In contrast to the modern Western worldview, in what he insists (for heuristic purposes) on calling the "'pure' Africanized world view [sic]," he finds that essentially "there is no gap or separation of man, nature and supernature" (1976, 61).[3] In striking contrast to what we in the West hold to be true, in the African system that Dixon describes, individuals are seen as human only if they are "part of a social order" (1976, 63).[4] So fully integrated with their society are these individuals that their identities would be virtually inseparable from it. While Dixon's definition purports to speak for all African cultures and may therefore misrepresent as much as characterize the concept, it does seem to mesh well with what Chieka Ifemesia has to say of traditional Igbo cosmology, a cosmology to which Emecheta has been direct heir. Ifemesia writes that "in Igbo cosmology, nothing is absolute. Everything, everybody, however apparently independent, depends upon something, upon somebody else" (1979, 67). Elechi Amadi goes so far as to suggest that a human being "thrives best in the type of social setting that exists in Nigeria. Extreme individualism only generates despair and antisocial behaviour" (1982, 110). As Williams himself puts it, in most non-Western societies, "the community would be the axiom, and individual man the derivative" (1961, 77).[5]

Given these different views of the relationship between the individual and society, it is not surprising that the European novel undergoes considerable change when an African writer like the Senegalese novelist Sembene Ousmane or the Ghanaian Ayi Kwei Armah adapts what historically has been a genre of individualism to a more communal ethos, when the public/private split is no longer at the heart of fiction. In order to make this Western form more acceptable to their own African ethos, many African novelists have, for example, changed the kind of protagonists we are accustomed to seeing in fiction. Dan Izevbaye describes a typical African hero, for example, as someone "who embodies the essential traits of his society or as the type of man so highly regarded in his society that it would seem that his fate ... is that of the society itself." At other times the novelist makes "the shift from an epical hero to a group of heroes, a device made familiar by [Ousmane's] *God's Bits of Wood*" (1986, 126). Or sometimes the novelist uses the "device of the plural voice as narrator" as found in Armah's *Two Thousand Seasons* (127). As far as Izevbaye is concerned, the two central issues facing African novelists today involve "the question of commitment and propaganda, as well as that of the individual and the community. Both are problems with which the novel form will have to cope" (134-35).

There are still other narrative differences. Izevbaye suggests, for example, that "the world of fantasy" is not one that African novelists have been much interested in, regardless of their "concern with the past" (1986, 117). He attributes this lack of interest to the novelists' preoccupation "with the problem of re-creating contemporary reality" and coping with current political issues (118). Authors who set their stories in the present tend to write in a more "realistic mode," therefore, leaving the romantic mode to those few who write about the past (119). But Izevbaye thinks that African writers differ from American writers even in their attitudes toward the past, as they tend not to romanticize the landscape. In contrast to their American (male) counterparts, who seem to feel that the land has been theirs to name and subdue, African writers feel as though their ability to name and subdue was stolen from them by the European colonialists. Unlike the Americans, they cannot look back to a time when the land was theirs and they were the land's. What interests them, therefore, is the need to transform the landscape, to make it their own. The drama in their fiction, therefore, primarily "takes place in the consciousness of the characters" (123). This description seems to have implications for the private/public dichotomy that informs so much Western fiction. If action takes place inside the characters' heads instead of in the landscape, there seems to be little possibility of a split between the private and public arenas. Because of these differences between Western and African fiction, Irina D. Nikiforova is willing to suggest the possibility that "a substantial number of African authors took from the West only the very idea of the novel, its key situation (the depiction of man's fate in complex social conditions), but not its concrete forms" (1987, 425). Nikiforova further observes that in a great deal of contemporary African fiction, "the fate of individual characters is relatively subordinated in status, while the author's attention is concentrated on the destiny of his entire country" (432). Izevbaye concludes his essay by noting that the novel, while more adaptable than other genres, is still "closely bound to reality which nourishes and shapes it"—a central point to the argument I am making myself about Buchi Emecheta's fiction (134).

Instead of being informed by the opposition between an individual and society, therefore, an African novel seems more typically informed by intercultural conflict: individuals clash because of different tribal or national backgrounds. As a result, one of the most significant themes of contemporary African literature is how romantic love cannot surmount the deep-seated differences between Africans and Westerners. Though the protagonists of these novels seem to have overcome the color bar readily enough, much as they try, they cannot overcome the cultural bar. The results can be tragic, as in Mariama Bâ's 1981 *Scarlet Song* (rpt. 1985b), where the heroine, daughter of a French diplomat, is literally driven insane by her marriage to an African. Their marriage and her sanity crumble because neither Mireille nor Ousmane is capable of seeing the world through the other's eyes. Though Mireille has already lived for several years in Africa, once she marries her Senegalese lover, she finds it impossible to adapt to his traditional customs. Her adjustment is made more difficult by the hostility shown her by her mother-in-law and by her husband's stubborn insistence that she accept the ways of his people. "Of what uncompromising dogma had he set himself up as the apostle," the text inquires near the end, "in the land where the water-pitcher passes from hand to hand and from mouth to mouth without repugnance?" (Bâ 1985b, 165). Because Mireille and Ousmane are able to maintain a passionate relationship with each other for years *before they get married*, the novel seems to invite the Western liberal explanation that cultural differences reside less in individuals than in social institutions—that society corrupts their love once they formalize it in the institution of legalized wedlock. But it must not be overlooked that Ousmane himself fails Mireille in the land of sharing: once they make their forbidden love "official," he becomes less tolerant of her and more insistent on the ways of his people. In short, though he has tried to ignore his ties to society, he cannot exist apart from it—even for love. The example Bâ's novel provides seems to have application to our project, as it implies that all of us (authors and readers alike) are bound to our cultures.[6] If Ousmane and Mireille cannot find enough common ground to sustain their love across cultural differences, perhaps we readers cannot find enough common ground with Bâ's or Emecheta's texts to really understand them. We will be especially disadvantaged in this attempt if we fail to foreground our own cultural prejudices.

Because we start from a philosophical premise that valorizes individualism, while remaining deeply skeptical of society, we Western readers come to these women's texts ill-prepared to understand them. If we hope to understand this literature, then, we must at the very least acknowledge intellectually (if not emotionally) that there is more than one way to conceptualize the relationship between an individual and society. We must be willing to accept the fact that societies are not by definition harmful or hostile to individuals, that indeed individuals can be inseparable from their societies. In short, we need to read these novels in the language of perspicuous contrast. Failing to do this will lead us to the ethnocentric conclusion that Senegalese or Nigerian ways are somehow inferior to our own. Rather than understanding these African texts, we will resist them in preference to our own superior way of life.

I want now to look briefly at the relationship of African artist to audience, a relationship that is foreign to most of our Western experiences—and one that has much to teach us.

ART FOR ART'S SAKE?

In his 1981 essay "Modernity Versus Postmodernity," Habermas describes a rough tendency in Western thought over the past 200 years that suggests an increasing autonomy "in the definition and practice of art" (9). (This trend may be detected on the continent of Africa also, but I want to argue that it is being more fiercely resisted there than it has been in the West.) What we in the West have known as the project of cultural modernity was inspired in the eighteenth century by the division of substantive reason into three specialized autonomous spheres: science, morality, and art (8). Theoretically, each of these separate spheres, through the institutionalized efforts of its practitioners, was to make a contribution to the Enlightenment project of emancipation and enrichment of everyday life. As part of this institutionalization, during the mid-nineteenth century "an aestheticist conception of art emerged, which encouraged the artist to produce his work according to the distinct consciousness of art for art's sake" (9). At its inception, the idea of a separate aesthetic sphere seemed a promising development, because it freed the artist "from the constraints of routinized cognition and everyday action" (9). But the more one strain of art increased its isolation from everyday life, Habermas argues, the more it fed the surrealists' conviction that they needed to forge "a reconciliation of art and life" (10). The blind spot in the surrealists' movement, on Habermas's view, was its failure to cross over all three spheres, science, morality, and art. Though they were able to muster incredible intellectual and imaginative resources in the revolutionary cause of reconciling art and the life-world, they ultimately failed to achieve the primary goal of emancipation because their revolt was waged on only the aesthetic front, an oversight that left the scientific and moral spheres intact and still distant from everyday life (10-11). The alternative that Habermas offers to the surrealists' failed rebellion is the unique example of a group of German workers who in 1937 waged their own successful, but limited, battle against artistic alienation (12). Though his example, gleaned from Peter Weiss, is a compelling one, it is apparently a singular one. Far better, then, it would seem to me, to look outside European society at the remarkable and enduring Igbo phenomenon of *mbari*.[7]

Like many other Africans, Chinua Achebe firmly believes that art is, and has always been, "in the service of man" (1975c, 19). As evidence of his claim, he points to the ancient Igbo tradition of mbari, which he views as "a profound affirmation of the people's belief in the indivisibility of art and society." Celebrated every few years among the Owerri Igbo, mbari called upon several members of the community to help "prepare a festival of images" in honor of the earth goddess, Ala. The men and women chosen to participate in the ceremony "moved into seclusion in a forest-clearing and under the instruction and guidance of master artists and craftsmen began to build a house of images" (21).[8] In this custom, the people are not presented with a finished work of art that someone else has made in their behalf, as occurs most often in the West. Instead, they actually help to create the work of art themselves. Because mbari emerges from within the community itself and is neither autonomously developed nor imposed on it from above, it would seem to offer a promising resolution to the modernist dilemma of how to reunite the autonomous sphere of artistic expression "with the life-world out of which [it] emerged" (Jay 1985, 132)—a resolution more promising than that of the surrealists and one that improves on the ad hoc solution of the German workers. Without being fully autonomous, mbari does nonetheless stand apart from the ordinary activities of the Igbo life-world: it is a discrete artistic activity that only a select few people, representing the community at large, participate in at specific times.[9] The question remains open, of course, as to whether such a ceremony, were it adopted by the West, could increase the emancipation effect of the other two autonomous spheres of morality and science. But at the very least, it offers us an alternative to our Western view of art.[10]

As we might expect from this account, while there is some interest in an art-for-art's-sake movement among contemporary African writers, the idea of a self-referential, highly individualized art generally enjoys little credibility on this continent, where audience participation has traditionally been the norm and where colonization has only recently left its legacy of cultural modernization. Though this European legacy should have meant the division of the lifeworld of African society into three separate spheres—cognitive/scientific, moral/ethical, and aesthetic/expressive—the latter, a specialized autonomous aesthetic sphere, does not seem to have taken hold particularly well (nor has the European cognitive sphere entirely replaced the various African styles of cognition). So close are artist and audience in the African oral tradition, in fact, that Aliko Songolo suggests it has been "sometimes . . . difficult to distinguish one from the other" (1977, 126). Ngugi goes so far as to argue that even if today's novelists try to be disinterested, they will be unable to dissociate their art from society because "literature is partisan: literature takes sides" (1981, 6). Chinweizu and his colleagues agree, attacking what they call "the airs of an artistic elect who must keep their works unsullied by the political concerns of their fellow citizens" (1980, 251). In a memorable phrase that serves as one of the epigraphs to this section, Achebe seems to echo J. P. Proudhon[11] when he expresses the disdain many Africans feel for the aesthetic consequences of cultural modernization when he asserts, "Art for art's sake is just another piece of deodorised dog-shit" (Achebe quoting himself, 1975c, 19).

What these African intellectuals find particularly objectionable about Western art can be seen in *A Question of Power*. Here, in a classic scene, Head mocks Western aesthetics, when an insufferable Danish woman brags that the culture in her country has become so "complex" one needs "a certain level of education to understand our novelists. The ordinary man cannot understand them . . ." (ellipses in original). In a wry aside, the narrator comments that it has never dawned on this woman "that those authors had ceased to be of any value whatsoever to their society—or was it really true that an extreme height of culture and the incomprehensible went hand in hand?" (1979, 79). In "Decolonization and the Ideal Speech Community," John O'Neill warns of the dangers when "exceptional individuals" are permitted to assume this kind of sole responsibility for a society's "cultural activity" (O'Neill 1985, 65). When this occurs, he argues, "thought degenerates into verbalism, and action is misled into activism." In contrast to the divisiveness of representative speech, what O'Neill refers to as "true speech" has the beneficial effect of holding "thought and action together; it speaks in order to alter the world, to move men and women and to be moved by them in true dialogue" (67). I believe that African writers are able to provide us with models for this kind of dialogical exercise by showing us new ways for art and society to intersect. Certainly, the tradition of communal aesthetics is rooted deeply in the Igbo psyche, as we saw in their custom of mbari. Such communally based activities help demonstrate what we in the West can learn from a study of Achebe's and Emecheta's shared African culture.

ARTISTIC COMMITMENT—TO WHOM AND TO WHAT?

But what is the status of the African artist today, in this post-independence, post-European Enlightenment period? As we have already seen from Achebe, Ngugi, and Chinweizu et al., there is a transcultural tendency among African writers to retain (or recover) the traditional pre-colonial relationship to their community. In a collection of interviews, Phanuel Akubueze Egejuru quotes the aesthetic principle of the Algerian writer Mohammed Dib that all writers are the "voice" of their people; for "it is through the writer that the people express themselves" (1980, 23). For Chinweizu and his Nigerian colleagues, the role of African artist as the people's representative must be maintained as part of Africa's own emancipation project; they charge contemporary writers to remember that the "artist in the traditional African milieu spoke for and to his community" (1983, 241). Because of this heritage, they insist that artists today accept "a sense of social commitment" (252). This commitment involves helping African peoples see and understand their own cultures—including what needs to be preserved and what needs to be changed (253). Although Chinweizu et al. emphasize continuity with the past, they clearly also have an agenda for the future. Simply stated, it is the absolute decolonization of the African continent. But this agenda would appear to require a different role of the artist. Where once the artist spoke in concert with the community's values and traditions, today the artist must speak against them whenever they are supportive of a colonialist or neocolonialist mentality (a task made more difficult when artists must use the language of their former colonizers). By standing outside the community, of course, the artist risks losing the African audience altogether (not to mention entering the autonomous artistic sphere of the West); because communal values are no longer represented in such writing, the seamless web between artist and audience has been broken. In short, as O'Neill warns, such a situation would be ripe for the separation of thought and action from "genuine praxis" (1985, 67).

As my discussion of mbari suggests, it seems unlikely, historically speaking, that precolonial Igbo peoples suffered from the kind of cultural alienation I have quoted O'Neill as deploring. But his worries are not without merit, given the kinds of concerns expressed today cross-culturally by African writers themselves. The South African writer Ezekiel Mphahlele, for example, agrees with Chinweizu that a writer should have "commitment" and "inform his public" (Egejuru 1980, 115). Unfortunately, the very identity of this "public" has become problematic for many African writers. Though Chinweizu et al. maintain that "the proper primary audience [for African writers] is the African audience" (1983, 264), Mphahlele is no longer so certain of this position. Commenting on the difficulties facing an African writer, he admits that he cannot be "sure of the audience that reads his novels, and he has no way of tuning into the mind of his audience" (Egejuru 1980, 102). In "The Writer, the Audience and the Critic's Responsibility," Aliko Songolo argues that traditional audience participation in African society has become problematic because the community may find the work "eccentric or too audacious," or it may simply be created in such a way that not everyone will find the work "accessible" (1977, 127). One form of inaccessible art is the novel itself, which is a genre that does not permit the same kind of audience participation (such as call and response) as traditional storytelling. Cynthia Ward argues, for example, that the "value of the oral tale" lies not just "in the tale itself but, perhaps more significantly, in the discussion it generates after it is told" (1990, 88). The cultural alienation permitted (or even encouraged) by novels, in contrast, is partly attributable to the fact that one reads them in private, alone, away from the community. More specifically, the novel is also inaccessible to many Africans because of the relatively high illiteracy rate still extant in many countries—a problem of which Emecheta is well aware. Economics is also a factor, as she informs an interviewer: "A hardback is $17 which is often a person's income for a whole month. It would be silly to buy a book with your salary" (Topouzis 1990, 69).

Though Emecheta clearly longs to speak to her own people (no doubt in her own native languages), she seems resigned to the fact that she is also dependent on a Western readership. In this she is no different from most other post-independence African novelists who explain tribal customs and terminology to their non-African readers. To what extent African novelists should assist Western readers—if at all—is a point of some contention. The problem writers face, of course, is how to explain their African customs without boring or insulting their African readers. Though it might appear to be merely a technical problem, the solutions have direct bearing on the novels' meaning. John F. Povey suggests, for example, that an awareness of "a dual audience and the need to appeal to an English publisher may effect some change in the nature of the novelists' work even before submission" (1970, 27-28). Different writers have chosen different strategies to assist their Western readers. One fairly common strategy is to introduce a specialized African term in the narration and then almost parenthetically define it. Another is to explain a custom as part of the dialogue, by having one character describe the custom for another. Variations on this narrative strategy are used by the Nigerian writer Flora Nwapa in *Efuru* and *Idu*. When Ajanupu, one of Efuru's friends, asks her if she is going fishing, Efuru reminds her that it is Orie—a statement that means nothing to Western audiences, so Nwapa explains it by having Ajanupu confess her absentmindedness: "It is true. I talk as if I am a stranger. I forget that today is Orie day and that all worshippers of the woman of the lake go on a special diet . . ." (1966, 120). In *Idu* we are informed about the community's values by statements such as these: "[T]hat's not how our people behave. It is an abomination. I have never heard anything like that before" (Nwapa 1987a, 31). The problem with the technique Nwapa uses in *Idu* is how quickly it becomes repetitious and how readily it begins to look like the people involved know nothing about their own traditions. At the same time, as intrusive as it becomes, this technique does emphasize how community pressures help to reinforce traditional behavior among the people.[12] A third strategy is to confine all specialized explanations to footnotes (Soyinka 1965), endnotes (Bâ 1985a, 1985b), or a glossary (Achebe 1959).

Emecheta solves the problem by incorporating explanations as much as possible into the body of the narration. Though these explanations are noticeable, they generally do not interrupt the flow of her narrative very much, nor are they particularly jarring to Western readers.[13] Emecheta's ability to explain one culture in terms of another has probably been enhanced by her years of living and working in England, just as her interest in Western readers probably stems from the fact that she began her writing career in England with British publishers.[14] Her sympathetic reception in England was apparently countered by indifference from Heinemann, the world's most influential publisher of African and Caribbean literature. According to what Emecheta reports in her autobiography, when her agent tried to interest Heinemann in publishing *The Bride Price*, she received no response. As a result, she "rewrote [it] for non-Nigerian readers" (1986, 184). If Western readers are, at least sometimes, her primary audience, we would appear to have a special obligation to try to move beyond our own parochialism and learn to speak (read) in a language of perspicuous contrast. This does not mean that we will find no fault with Emecheta's culture or her novels. It does mean we may find fault with our own, no longer able to enjoy what Charles Taylor calls the "luxury of ethnocentricity" (1985, 130). This obligation to listen to Emecheta and learn to speak the language of contrast is even more crucial when we recognize that she—like Armah, Nkosi, and Ngugi—is fully committed to using her art to effect social change. In fact, I think it is possible to argue that Emecheta is attempting to *write* in the language of perspicuous contrast (I discuss this idea more fully in chapter 5). She is, after all, utilizing and modifying what has been historically a Western literary form.

But is she really writing these novels in the English with which we are familiar? This question brings me to a discussion of the wide-ranging debate that continues to rage over the language(s) of African literature.

DIALOGIC HETEROGLOSSIA: WHOSE ENGLISH IS IT?

First, Emecheta's views on the subject. That she must write in English does not seem terribly problematic to her, though she is certainly aware of the political irony involved. She acknowledges, for example, that she must use "a language that belonged to those who once colonized the country of my birth." But she then says that she is glad she "mastered the language" because otherwise she would have been "telling [her] stories only to those women and children in Umuezeokolo, Ibusa" (1986, 242).[15] Achebe overcomes his reservations by asserting that he writes in a Western language that has been Africanized: the English he uses "will have to be a new English, still in full communion with its ancestral home but altered to suit its new African surroundings" (1975b, 62). Nkosi notes that "modern African writing has its origins in the politics of anticolonial struggle and still bears the marks of that struggle" (1981, 1). But he also argues that this writing "presents to us the aspect of a cultural hybrid in which African and European concerns are inextricably mixed through the twine and woof of a common language." Like many, he finds it bitterly ironic that African writers have had to wage war "in the same languages that were used to enslave them" (2). Though Chinweizu et al. insist that under ideal conditions "African literature should be written in African languages," they are still willing to concede that the political realities that currently "compel African nations to use Western languages as their official language also compel African writers to write in them" (1983, 242).

Ngugi, however, has not felt so compelled.[16] In an impressive act of political and artistic courage, this Kenyan writer has recently vowed to forgo English and write instead in Gikuyu, his native language. Having himself once written in English and given it up (for imaginative works in 1977 and for criticism in 1986, with the publication of *Decolonising the Mind*), Ngugi echoes Achebe's haunting phrase by assessing the situation in terms of "'the fatalistic logic of the unassailable position of English in our literature'" (1986, 7). Where Nkosi reluctantly acknowledges that "the best of African literature [is a hybrid that] reflects a former colonial dependency" (1981, 2), Ngugi more simply refuses to recognize this fiction as African at all. Claiming that language is, indeed, "a carrier of culture," he refers to literature written by Africans in English or French as a transitional "hybrid tradition" (13). On Ngugi's view, virtually everything today that constitutes the African literary tradition should more properly be designated "Afro-European literature" (26-27). Basically, I agree with Nkosi and Ngugi that this fiction is a cultural hybrid (Emecheta's surely is). But I want to argue that what Nkosi regards as a "common language" is only a myth. The novels of Buchi Emecheta may be written in English, but it is not the English most Western readers know. Nor could it be.[17] Contrary to what most critics have assumed, in speaking the so-called "same" language as Emecheta, we have not yet attained, in *Gadamerian terms*, the "common language" we need in order to converse with the text and begin to understand its subject matter (Gadamer 1989, 378-79).

In *The Dialogic Imagination*, Mikhail Bakhtin makes a distinction about language that I, as a Western reader, find essential for negotiating the treacherous waters of Buchi Emecheta's fiction. Bakhtin conceives of language as "ideologically saturated," of always reflecting a worldview (1987, 271). Because languages are situated in particular times and places and are reflective of their social origins (272), Bakhtin finds that "there are no 'neutral' words and forms—words and forms that can belong to 'no one'" (293). He argues further that "any concrete discourse [is] shot through with shared thoughts, points of view, alien value judgments and accents" (276). This argument is particularly applicable to our understanding of Buchi Emecheta, who speaks three African languages and has chosen to write her novels in English. Not only is her English "shot through" with the alien accents of these other languages, but it is also shot through with her African worldview, a worldview, as I argue in the following chapters, that is alien and often antithetical to our Western worldview.

In contrast to Bakhtin, Gadamer has described the transparency of language, stressing its "self-forgetfulness" and arguing that the "more language is a living operation, the less we are aware of it" (1976c, 65).[18] It would seem to me that, rather than accepting Bakhtin's views on language, most Western readers of African fiction have tacitly accepted Gadamer's views and assumed that the English they encounter in this fiction is, indeed, transparent to them— just as it would be transparent in the Western fiction they have read all their lives.[19] But I would argue that Emecheta's English is not transparent to us— though it would be more transparent to her Nigerian readers (particularly those who share her other languages). I would argue further that our Western English is more transparent to her (than hers is to us) because she, like so many other African novelists, has been educated in the West. Invoking Bakhtin here, I would also argue that Emecheta's English is a reflection more of her worldview than our own—even though we seem to recognize most of the words in her texts.[20] Rather than assuming her English is transparent to us, we ought to admit that it is often opaque. If we fail to acknowledge its opacity, we will surely fail to see what Bakhtin would call the "dialogized heteroglossia" of her fiction—the dialogic exchanges of the novel's different languages (272). And missing the heteroglossia, we also misunderstand the alien worldview. The "common language" (in Nkosi's terms) that might help to ensure a mutual understanding among her Anglophone African readers, therefore, runs the very real risk of ensuring a misunderstanding among her Anglophone Western readers. The textual explanations Emecheta provides, while seemingly designed to bridge the gap between her English and ours, have the paradoxical effect of increasing the novel's heteroglossia by calling attention to the fact that we do not understand the words as she is using them. The more explanation of terms that is offered, the more the text calls attention to its competing language systems and to the fact that it contains concepts that are quite foreign to our experience and worldview.

In a 1962 essay, in which he admonishes Western critics for their ignorant hubris, Achebe musters a similar argument, warning his readers that no one can hope to "understand another whose language he does not speak (and 'language' here does not mean simply words, but a man's entire world view)" (1975b, 48). He goes on to argue that Africa is more than a geographical location; "it is also a metaphysical landscape—it is in fact a view of the world and of the whole cosmos perceived from a particular position" (50). Because we (white Western feminists in particular) do not speak Emecheta's many languages, for the most part, we have been blind to her "metaphysical landscape." Though we might wish otherwise, the (standard) English of Buchi Emecheta's novels is not the (standard) English that we know.[21]

EPISTEMOLOGY AND NARRATIVE FORM

Not only do we in the West not have the Africans' languages, but most of us do not have their traditional literary forms.[22] Because we are familiar primarily with Western (white Anglo-American or European) novels, we have been inadvertently trained (virtually sentenced) to read Emecheta's fiction as though it were classic European realism.

Let us look briefly at this "classic European realism," the (largely middle-class) form that provides us with the standards and patterns I contend are so epistemologically ill-suited to an understanding of African fiction. Though they may seem self-evident, actually determining the formal characteristics of realism is more than a little problematic—as the debates among the German Marxists remind us. In his 1938 debate with Ernst Bloch, for example, Georg Lukács, no friend of modernism, attacks the German Expressionists for not using language referentially and for moving away from realism (1986, 29). In describing his model of what constitutes a great realist writer, Lukács idealized Thomas Mann for his ability to express "how thoughts and feelings grow out of the life of society and how experiences and emotions are parts of the total complex of reality" (36). The goal of realism for Lukács is "to uncover the deeper, hidden, mediated, not immediately perceptible network of relationships that go to make up society" (38).[23] In his review essay of *The Meaning of Contemporary Realism* (1958), however, Adorno criticized Lukács for naively insisting that art reflects reality, arguing instead for a mediating role for art and, more famously, that "[a]rt is the negative knowledge of the actual world" (1986, 160). Though the German Marxists and their Anglo-American successors have not been able to agree on a definition of realism, they are able to agree on its aesthetic and political value.[24]

Rather blithely ignoring the practical problems one might encounter in an attempt to define the poetics of realism for a particular culture, Raymond Williams, for example, has described the term almost rhapsodically. For him, thinking about "the realist tradition in fiction" evokes an image of a novel that "creates and judges the quality of a whole way of life in terms of the qualities of persons." What he finds so crucial to this tradition, so rare and valuable, is the "balance" it achieves in portraying the worth and importance of individuals and "a society that is larger than any of the individuals composing it" (1961, 278). It is exactly this balance between individual and society that he finds absent in contemporary fiction (but could find, I think, were he to have looked, in much recent African literature).[25] What he does not find in contemporary Western literature but does see in traditional realism is a merger of "idea into feeling, person into community, change into settlement," which is essential to us today (287). He concludes his essay, therefore, with a plea to reestablish this balance. Recognizing how difficult the task is, in these contentious times, he argues nonetheless that "a new realism is necessary, if we are to remain creative" (289).

If we stopped with these Marxist perspectives, quarrelsome as they are, "realism" would be a fairly accurate term to describe what Buchi Emecheta achieves in her African novels, since she is ever-mindful of the interdependence of the individual and society. Seen in this light, in fact, realism would seem more suitable as a vehicle for Emecheta's communitarian philosophy than for Western individualism. Seen in this light, realism could certainly function as an agent for positive social change. But not everyone is as enamored of realism as the Marxists. Barthes, for one, is deeply skeptical, arguing that "the most 'realistic' work will not be the one which 'paints' reality, but which . . . will explore as profoundly as possible the *unreal reality* of language" (1972, 160). Catherine Belsey is also wary of realism, regarding it not as an agent of change but as an instrument of political repression. In fact, she seems determined to reverse the Marxist views altogether.

In the nineteenth century, Williams tells us, realism was often described as "'startling,'" because of its "attention to the unpleasant, the exposed, the sordid." Realism was thus revealed to be "a revolt against the ordinary bourgeois view of the world" (1961, 275). But Belsey argues to the contrary that "[c]lassic realism is characterized by *illusionism*, narrative which leads to *closure*, and a *hierarchy of discourses* which establishes the 'truth' of the story" (1980, 70).[26] On her view, because the novels of classic realism move inevitably "towards closure," they "cannot foreground contradiction" (82). Belsey's definition thus dismisses the possibility, acknowledged by Brecht, Williams, and Jameson, that realism originally had a subversive purpose. In contrast also to Lukács, Belsey argues that realism itself is an expressive genre and has its critical corollary in the "expressive attitude," whereby the "text is seen as a way of arriving at something anterior to it: the convictions of the author, or his or her experience as part of that society at that particular time" (13). Missing in this scheme, according to her, are all the lessons about language we have learned from post-Saussurean linguistics—including the idea that authors themselves are constructed discursively (54).

Rather than casting my lot with either Belsey or Williams, I want to argue that, read from a Western/positivist perspective, Emecheta's novels do seem to lead to closure, but, read from a non-Western Africanized perspective, they challenge a bourgeois view of the world. What I am trying to convey here is how fatally easy it is for Western readers to read these African novels as traditional European realism—and how totally inappropriate this reading is. As I am incapable of becoming an African reader of Emecheta's fiction, defined as I am by my Western prejudices, the best I can probably do is to offer a thoroughly self-conscious Western reading that has been informed by knowledge of Emecheta's African culture and customs—a reading that highlights the differences between my own Western texts and cultures and those of Emecheta. This observation brings me to the usefulness of Belsey's ideas to my project. Belsey offers the explanation that "[r]ealism is plausible not because it reflects the world, but because it is constructed out of what is (discursively) familiar" (Belsey 1980, 47). She further suggests that the "experience of reading a realist text is *ultimately reassuring*" to us because the world we encounter there is one we already know, with similar "patterns of cause and effect, of social relationships and moral values" (51; emphasis added). Annette Kolodny would expand Belsey's judgment to encompass all literature, not just realism, arguing as she does that "insofar as literature is itself a social institution, so, too, reading is a highly socialized—or learned—activity" (1985, 153). Taking a Gadamerian angle on interpretation, she goes on to argue that "we read well, and with pleasure, what we already know how to read; and what we know how to read is to a large extent dependent upon what we have already read" (154).

Having familiar patterns reassuringly confirmed is exactly what can happen when Western readers encounter Emecheta's novels. I know. It happened to me. When I read these books for the first time, I thought they pretty much confirmed the patterns of the world that I already knew. It is with some embarrassment that I confess what I (thought I) found there. But, in the spirit of

Louis Althusser, "as there is no such thing as an innocent reading, we must say what reading we are guilty of" (1987, 14). Because Emecheta's novels were written in English and looked a lot like the fiction I already knew, I thought I understood them quite well (as have apparently many other Western feminists). Because the protagonist of her first two novels was a woman who was mistreated by her altogether despicable husband, I read them as I was reading Anglo-American feminist fiction of the time: as disturbing briefs on man's inhumanity to woman. Though African men were the villains here, the feminism seemed to be familiar. In short, I found pretty much what I expected to find. Or, in Nkosi's words, I saw pretty much what my ideology had equipped me to see (1981).

But if we can agree with Belsey and Lukács that ideology is somehow inscribed in the *form* of the novel, we can at least begin to see why I misread Emecheta so willingly. Irrespective of any cultural and nationalistic prejudices, I misread her because I thought she was an Anglo-American realist. I was so sure she was speaking my language, writing my realism, expressing my values and worldview, that I insisted she was. What I failed to notice, in my eagerness to be reassured, was all the incidental evidence the texts amassed that would counter a Western interpretation. In short, I ignored the plurality of her texts; I tuned out their heteroglossia. I took Buchi Emecheta's African novels and—through the magic of interpretive criticism—turned them into Western fiction. In addition to its other projects, this book, then, is also an attempt to show what can happen when plurality and heteroglossia are invited back into a consideration of Emecheta's fiction. The result, in part, will be to argue that Emecheta is already writing the kind of "new realism" Williams envisions. Read as a kind of African realism, based in traditional Igbo culture, Emecheta's novels will be seen to challenge those three divisions so central to our Western thought: (1) between individual and society, (2) between humanity and nature, and (3) between men and women. In short, her novels will interrogate three of our most cherished ideas and ideals—and will reveal them to be nothing more (or less) than linguistic social constructions.

NOTES

1. I discuss Jehlen's ideas in more detail in the next chapter.

2. Similarly, Alison Jaggar argues that traditional Western liberalism conceives of rationality "as a property of individuals rather than of groups." On this view, metaphysically speaking, "human individuals are the basic constituents out of which social groups are composed. Logically if not empirically, human individuals could exist outside a social context" (1988, 28-29).

3. There is some similarity between the Igbos' African worldview and that of Western feminists, a similarity that is evident in current feminist science fiction, such as

Sally Miller Gearhart's 1979 novel in which the women are able to commune with nature and with each other telepathically.

4. See also Harding 1986b.

5. Clifford Geertz reminds us that the "Western conception of the person as a bounded, unique, more or less integrated motivational and cognitive universe . . . is . . . a rather peculiar idea within the context of the world's cultures" (1979, 229; see also 1973 and 1983.) Marcus and Fischer inform us that the "Samoan language has no terms corresponding to 'personality, self, character'; instead of our Socratic 'know thyself,' Samoans say 'take care of the relationship'" (1986, 65). According to Alasdair MacIntyre, in "many pre-modern, traditional societies it is through his or her membership in a variety of social groups that the individual identifies himself or herself and is identified by others" (1984b, 33). "This conception of a whole human life . . . is something that ceases to be generally available at some point in the progress—if we can call it such—towards and into modernity" (34). For further discussion of the ill effects of modernity on the self, see Bellah et al. 1985, 80-84.

6. For an autobiographical account of the cultural differences faced by an African American woman and her Nigerian husband, see Golden 1983. See also Harris 1992. But compare these with the platonic relationship between a white Western man and an African woman in Bessie Head's 1974 novel, *A Question of Power* (rpt. 1979).

7. See also Asante's complaint about the Eurocentric arrogance of the Frankfurt School (1987, 4-5).

8. For additional discussion of mbari, see the interview with Achebe in Rowell 1990.

9. Ngugi describes a similar interpenetration of art and society: "Drama in precolonial Kenya was not . . . an isolated event: it was part and parcel of the rhythm of daily and seasonal life of the community" (1989, 37). Soyinka reports that "[m]uch African writing is still rooted in the concept of literature as part of the normal social activity of man, but one which is nonetheless individual in its expression and its choice of areas of concern" (1990, 67).

10. For another alternative to modernism, that found in the black vernacular tradition, see Gilroy 1993, who proposes that "we reread and rethink this expressive counterculture not simply as a succession of literary tropes and genres but as a philosophical discourse which refuses the modern, occidental separation of ethics and aesthetics, culture and politics" (38-39). Gilroy claims further that the musical forms of the black Atlantic disguise their "anti-modernity" as a "premodernity," which "seeks not simply to change the relationship of these cultural forms to newly autonomous philosophy and science but to refuse the categories on which the relative evaluation of these separate domains is based and thereby to transform the relationship between the production and use of art, the everyday world, and the project of racial emancipation" (74).

11. Pierre Bourdieu quotes from Proudhon's *Contradictions economiques* (Paris, 1939): "Art for art's sake, as it has been called, not having its legitimacy within itself, being based on nothing, is nothing. It is *debauchery* of the heart and *dissolution* of the mind" (Bourdieu 1984, 49). For yet another critical account of this movement, see, Onoge 1986b, 50-63.

12. Ernest Emenyonu claims, however, that "There is not one false tone . . . in the voices of these characters" (1975, 31).

13. In contrast to my reading, Emenyonu argues that in *The Bride Price*, Emecheta permits her "narrative to degenerate into anthropological digressions" (1987, 132).

14. This has led Elaine Savory Fido to suggest that "Emecheta's work, influenced as it is by her British experience, is characterized by a greater element of what one might call Western style feminism than is true of other African women writers in Nigeria" (1986, 226).

15. See also Topouzis 1990, 68.

16. On this subject, see also Mlama 1990.

17. Ngugi, I think, would agree with me. See, for example, his discussion of the three aspects of "language as culture" and the effects of colonization on the minds of African children as they were forced to learn new languages (1989, 13-16).

18. He continues, "What is said in it constitutes the common world in which we live and to which belongs also the whole great chain of tradition" (Gadamer 1976c, 65).

19. Again let me say that I do not intend by this to engage in the Afrocentric debates about language.

20. I also acknowledge, of course, that Emecheta herself has been influenced by her exposure to the West. As before, I am not arguing for a complete absence of cultural correspondence or connections, only that we not be too quick to assume them (see Ward 1990, 87).

21. The question of language as a patriarchal construct is also at issue here. One might even be tempted to say that an African woman writer like Buchi Emecheta is doubly inscribed by patriarchal language: the hegemonic language of the (Christian) West and the patriarchal language of African tradition—the Voice of the African Fathers. To a certain extent, I think this is true. But I also intend to argue in my discussion of Emecheta's novels that the language of the African Fathers offers a significant challenge to the "master narratives" of the West.

22. For a discussion of the oral tradition in Emecheta, see Ward 1990. For the literary connections between Africa and African American culture, see K. Holloway 1992. For a discussion of the relationship between form and content in African fiction, see Gikandi 1987.

23. Stressing the importance of the formal characteristics of realism, Lukács maintains that "the more closely we combine an examination of the ideology informing a writer's work with an examination of the specific form given to a specific content, the better our analysis will be" (1971, 83). Brecht, however, faulted Lukács for his absorption with formalism, arguing that realism "is not a mere question of form" (1986, 82).

24. For Jameson, the "originality of the concept of realism . . . lies in its claim to cognitive as well as aesthetic status." For him "the ideal of realism presupposes a form of aesthetic experience which yet lays claim to a binding relationship to the real itself" (1986, 198).

25. Miller's criticisms of Gugelberger notwithstanding.

26. Barthes's distinction between the "work" and a "text" is relevant here (see 1979, 74, 76).

3

Life as an Emigré

... in Igbo cosmology, nothing is absolute. Everything, everybody, however apparently independent, depends upon something, upon somebody else.

Chieka Ifemesia
Traditional Humane Living Among the Igbo (1979, 67)

... in all our knowledge of ourselves and in all knowledge of the world, we are always already encompassed by the language that is our own.

Hans-Georg Gadamer
"Man and Language" (1976c, 62)

A DOUBLE MARGINALITY

When Buchi Emecheta first tried her hand at writing fiction, she turned to what she knew of traditional Igbo culture and wrote what was eventually published as *The Bride Price*. There was a considerable gap, however, between the initial composition of this novel and its eventual publication since Emecheta's husband burned her only copy of the original manuscript (an event she later fictionalized in *Second-Class Citizen*). This spiteful act confirmed Emecheta's decision to leave him, although doing so meant disregarding the traditional ways of her African people. Emecheta began her writing career in earnest shortly after her divorce from Sylvester Onwordi was final, when she was motivated primarily by the need to support her five children and apparently driven by a desire to come to terms with the disappointments she had experienced since leaving her homeland. Rather than returning to *The Bride Price* and trying to reconstruct it, therefore, Emecheta decided, first of all, that she would write about her life in England and her failed marriage; she completed *In the*

Ditch in 1972 and *Second-Class Citizen* two years later, reworking *The Bride Price* in 1976. Already at least partially alienated from Nigerian society by virtue of her emigration (and alienated from much of the expatriate Nigerian community by virtue of her divorce), Emecheta found life in England much more difficult than she had anticipated. Though she was able to find work easily enough, she was simply not prepared for the widespread racism she and her family encountered. She thus found herself in the unexpected position of living on the margins of British life, far from home and estranged from many of her own people. But this marginality has served Emecheta well as an artist, allowing her the distance necessary for what Herbert Marcuse calls the "Great Refusal—the protest against that which is" (1964, 63).[1]

As part of her larger social protest, Emecheta consistently questions what Rachel Blau DuPlessis calls the construction of gender, joining other twentieth-century women writers from Woolf to Lessing in rupturing the narratives that would define and enslave us (1985, 4). But Emecheta, like other African women writers, such as Nwapa, Head, Bâ, and Aidoo, also questions the effects of colonialism on the African mind[2] and, in so doing, shares the philosophical positions of many of her African male contemporaries, such as Soyinka, Ngugi, Achebe, Awoonor, Armah, and others. The apparent conventionality or simplicity of her plots, therefore, should not blind us to the fact that her work celebrates a plurality of protest. Nor should we be misled by the objectivity she is capable of bringing to her writing as a trained sociologist. She may give us a factually accurate account of what it is like to be an African woman, but having suffered herself, she obviously has a psychological stake in the fates of her heroines. She is, in short, clearly a political writer. Her politics, of course, are what make her so appealing to Western readers. But ironically enough, the politics of her writing are what can most confuse us. Because her narrators do not unthinkingly embrace everything about their Igbo tradition, dozens of passages in her fiction tempt us Westerners into what I have suggested is a very familiar ethnocentric rejection of Nigerian culture. What I hope to do throughout this study, therefore, is demonstrate that Emecheta's politics are more sympathetic to her African heritage than most Western (and some African) readers have heretofore thought.

In the Ditch (1972)

INTELLIGIBILITY AND THE (SOCIAL) CONSTRUCTION OF RATIONALITY

In the Ditch is a novel about how a young Nigerian woman learns to cope with the British welfare system by becoming part of a community of women on

Life as an Emigré   53

the dole. When the story begins, Adah Obi has just separated from her husband and is trying to finish her education, keep her job, and take care of her five children.³ Her problems are compounded by the fact that the landlord, himself Nigerian, wants to evict her. Although one might expect him to behave compassionately toward a fellow emigré, he seems to do just the opposite, even charging her double the normal rent. In her description of this particularly venal man, Emecheta seems to implicate all Nigerian men (or at least all Nigerian expatriates) when she claims that the landlord, who knows the hardship she faces "was, *of course*, taking the best advantage of the situation" (1979a, 8; emphasis added). Once Adah's landlord realizes she will not leave the flat willingly, he treats her with such hostility that she is fearful he would poison their food if she left it in the communal kitchen. In short, although the bulk of the novel focuses on the problems Adah has in dealing with the British welfare system, it opens with a bitter criticism of how Nigerians mistreat one another when they live abroad. By portraying a Nigerian man as the cause of Adah Obi's problems, the novel seems to be inviting Western feminists (most particularly) to align ourselves with the heroine and to tempt us into making false generalizations about Adah's patriarchal culture.

The misgivings that Adah has about her own people are perhaps best expressed in the scene where the landlord finally employs juju in an effort to drive her away. Although this scene may appear to be a minor one, it raises several important questions for cross-cultural understanding, primarily because of its emphasis on magic and Adah's lack of fear when her landlord tries to practice it on her. Adah is scornful of her landlord for stooping to witchcraft, but, to her own surprise, she is not frightened. Back home in Nigeria no one would doubt the juju's effectiveness, but here in England she finds it virtually unthinkable that such an ordinary man dressed in a filthy leisure suit could ever be "a medicine man" (9). Being in England seems to have given Adah the strength to withstand what would otherwise be a seductively compelling perspective. I want to look more closely at the pattern of thought Adah Obi follows here, but first I want to comment on the sociological truth that Emecheta is describing: the power of the group to enforce its view of reality on individuals. Peter Berger and Thomas Luckmann address this sociological issue by arguing that our everyday reality is largely a social construct that we experience through and with others (1967, 23). Because our reality is constructed through our interaction with others, it stands to reason that once Adah Obi moves to England, the power of the juju would wane.

But let us look further at the role—and significance—of language in this context, since it is not only reality but we ourselves who are created in language. In an essay first published in 1967, Gadamer seems to lend reinforcement to Berger and Luckmann's ideas when he observes that language is "the reservoir of tradition and the medium through which we exist and perceive the world" (1976a, 29). But, for Gadamer, language "is by no means simply an instrument," as it puts it in "Man and Language"—it is the way we know ourselves and the world (1976c, 62). He thus concludes this second essay by arguing that we achieve our humanity through language, which is "a realm as indispensable to human life as the air we breathe" (68). Gadamer's view of language here informs my own sense that just as Adah Obi takes her own African language(s) into England—and thus, by necessity, takes her African worldview with her—Emecheta has brought her African language(s) and African worldview into the so-called Western novels she has written. But because we human beings are constantly in the process of creating ourselves, we cannot help but revise our subjectivity as we encounter the language (and thus the worldview) of another culture. It seems significant, therefore, that Adah Obi no longer fears the juju. Though she might retain many African ideas, she has apparently on some level decided to reject this one. In Bakhtin's terms, she has chosen, in this instance, the language of Western rationality. As Bakhtin puts it, the ideological aspect of becoming human is largely a matter of choosing the correct words—by carefully "assimilating the words of others" (1987, 341). In moments like this, Bakhtin would argue, someone else's discourse defines for us the boundary conditions of our own behavior; in other words, it functions both "as authoritative discourse" (coming from without) and as "an internally persuasive discourse" (coming from within) (342). I return to this concept of authoritative discourse in subsequent chapters, as Emecheta's other heroines grapple with the question of which discourse—African or Western—carries more weight. Living in post-colonial Africa, these women are continually faced with deciding which is the "true" discourse, that of their own internal discourse, that of their African fathers, or that of their Western colonizers. It is a question not just of culture and tradition but also of narrative forms: which story will be authoritative. It is also a question of power, which affects not just Emecheta's heroines but also her readers. For Adah, it seems clear that the authoritative discourse of Western rationality has supplanted the traditional authoritative discourse of her African upbringing. That is, Western rationality has become internally persuasive to her. This scene suggests, in other words, that Adah remains immune to juju in England because she has successfully adapted to (at least part of) her new country's view of reality.

But it also raises another question: how do we Western readers respond to the invocation of magic? Because Adah is able to disregard the landlord's efforts, we are not directly faced with whether or not we believe the juju could be effective. But Adah does strongly imply that it would still work in Africa. Can we be so sure that she is wrong? In other words, how should we read the claim that juju is efficacious, even if only in Nigeria? The philosophy of the social sciences can help us address this question. In an essay first published in 1962, Alasdair MacIntyre asks whether understanding religion is compatible with believing in it. The example he poses is the culturally internal one of Christianity, comparing how modern-day skeptics understand religion to how pre-seventeenth-century Christians understood it. What he seeks to discover is, how is it possible "that what appears intelligible in one social context can appear not to make sense in another?" As part of his answer, he provides three general reasons for unintelligibility: (1) in some cases a concept works if "certain questions are not asked about it"; (2) in some cases "incoherence and intelligibility are to some extent manifest to the users of the concept," but the concept is so central to their life that they are willing to put up with a certain amount of incoherence; and (3) in other cases the concept can lose its coherence when patterns of social behavior undergo fundamental change (1984a, 72). Emecheta's novel seems to provide a fourth case, which is a kind of variation on examples two and three. That is, when a concept itself is transplanted from one culture to another and thus deprived of its sociocultural raison d'être, it can lose its intelligibility. In Adah Obi and her landlord's case, without the supporting presence of their African tradition, the concept of juju becomes incoherent. Where a certain amount of incoherence within the concept or practice of juju might be tolerable to believers in Nigeria, it proves to be a fatal flaw in England. In effect, in being transported to England, juju has been secularized and thus loses its power—a point that brings us back to MacIntyre's discussion.

If non-believers are to understand religion, he ultimately concludes, they must be able to eliminate the current "social context" and "supply" the missing one (76). If we regard Adah Obi as a skeptic or even as a kind of informal cultural anthropologist, it seems pretty clear that she would be able to supply this missing context because she herself had once experienced it. So, even though she herself no longer believes in juju, she understands how someone else living back home in Nigeria might believe. But the question still remains whether we Westerners can understand its power. To borrow from MacIntyre, is it possible to "understand [only] what makes sense to us already?" (69). His answer is equivocal. He argues, for example, that as we strive for understanding, we "cannot avoid invoking [our] own criteria," that is, those of our own society. He also contends that we must grasp the operative criteria that determine "belief and behaviour" in the alien society. Our task is completed only when we have "filled in the social context so as to make the transition from one set of criteria to the other intelligible." The hard part, of course, lies in making the transition from one system to another. If we detect "incoherence" in the alien system we are studying, MacIntyre argues, it means, no doubt, that "we have already invoked *our* standards. Since we cannot avoid doing this it is better to do it self-consciously" (71). He then enumerates the three kinds of situations I have described in which a belief or practice loses its intelligibility (72) and concludes that, indeed, those who (today) *understand* Christianity cannot believe in it "because its peculiar invulnerability belongs to it as a form of belief which has lost the social context which once made it comprehensible" (76). He is thus in a position to argue that "sceptic and believer do not share a common grasp of the relevant concepts" (77). I read this to mean that, in the case of the juju in

Emecheta's novel, we in the West cannot share a common understanding with Adah Obi, for there is simply too much social context we are unable to supply. Adah Obi's understanding involves belief, in other words, and ours cannot.

In this cross-cultural encounter, as Peter Winch would remind us, what is at stake is the notion of rationality itself: the different *"criteria of rationality"* that separate our culture from Adah Obi's (1964, 317). Where Adah's African culture could provide criteria that would make the practice of juju rational (and thus efficacious), we in the West who are wedded to a concept of rationality that is virtually indistinguishable from scientific instrumentality are unable (not to mention unwilling) to provide similar criteria. The best we can probably do, therefore, is acknowledge the different kinds of rationality that inform our different understandings—and in acknowledging them, avoid arguing for the self-evident superiority of our own.[4]

A DIFFERENCE IN VALUES: THE INDIVIDUAL AND THE COMMUNITY

The scene describing Adah's problems with her landlord is important not just because of what it reveals about the different criteria for rationality but because similar scenes appear throughout all of Emecheta's work. Emecheta often uses scenes like this, for example, to question constructions of gender, as her heroines face the dilemma of whether to rebel against, or conform to, society's expectations. Whatever they decide, their actions graphically illustrate how a given society acts to enforce its view of reality on individual members. By showing the absolute interdependence of a society and its people, these scenes also convey an unmistakable Igbo philosophy. Because of their reliance on Igbo values, scenes like these make reading Emecheta's fiction difficult for Western readers to understand.[5] Independent women may well be the heroines of Emecheta's novels, but her fiction is no paean to rebellion. More than is obvious at first glance, her novels are a reaffirmation of her received African concepts of community. For example, although Adah considers her immunity to juju a sweet victory, she is not as free of her Nigerian culture as she thinks she is, as the rest of the scene with the landlord demonstrates. Feeling secure in her newfound freedom, she mocks the landlord in her mind by comparing him with the stereotype of a tipsy "television Red Indian." Then she tries to imagine what her white neighbors see in the situation, deciding that the landlady resembles "the pictures of black devils [which whites] knew from their childhoods" and the landlord himself looks "like the Devil's servant." But no sooner has she gazed scornfully at these Africans through white eyes than she realizes that she herself "was part of the picture" (10). This realization forces her to change perspective once again: "Blast these illustrators!" she thinks. "Who told them that the Devil was black?" (10-11). Having thus reclaimed a racial loyalty, she remains silent when the white milkman tries to help her by finding out what is going on (11).

This scene takes up virtually the entire first chapter, and its plurality of meaning establishes the mode of the entire book. Though it concludes with Adah's loyalty to her Nigerian landlord, the scene is not altogether a defense of African ways. Like Emecheta herself, Adah Obi is a woman caught between cultures. On one hand, she has fled her African homeland (as we learn in *Second-Class Citizen*) because her father has implanted an almost sacred vision of Great Britain in his daughter's imagination; and in leaving Africa, she has sought to escape the limitations of a patriarchal Igbo culture that would subordinate her needs to those of her husband and his family. On the other hand, she has found England to be less than the Promised Land about which her father dreamed. Though she is shocked by the dreadful living accommodations Africans are forced to accept in England, she nevertheless learns to deal with her disappointment and soon gets a job as a librarian. Her husband, however, is almost immediately defeated by the prejudice and passively accepts his second-class status. Bitterly disappointed in Francis, Adah sees little to admire in him or the other Igbo men who have immigrated to England.

In another key scene, the one concluding the book, Adah reflects on her attitude toward African men. Her best friend, a white woman also on the dole, has just confessed that she is pregnant by an Igbo emigré. Whoopey, the friend, is delighted to be pregnant and thinks she and he might marry someday. Although Adah has never met the man, she is furious since she knows he will never marry a woman with two children (125). Not wanting to ruin Whoopey's optimistic plans, Adah says nothing, but silently "she cursed all African men" for mistreating women (127). This statement implies that all African men behave as badly toward their women as Francis has behaved toward her (again, inviting Western feminists to make sweeping generalizations about the sexism inherent to Igbo society). Yet this statement, too, is followed by a rather poignant admission, where Adah acknowledges that she should not "rebuff men of her own race; they were more sensitive than others." Again comparing her attitudes at home with those here, she realizes that in Nigeria she would have ignored a stranger who addressed her, but if it is a black man in England who speaks, she always responds because he "needed to have his morale boosted" (128).

It is significant, I think, that Emecheta opens and closes her novel with two scenes so full of ambivalent feelings toward the people of her homeland. Even more significant is the fact that virtually all the ambivalence is directed at men. In part, because of how I interpreted these two scenes, I initially missed the novel's plurality of meaning. Because Emecheta's narrator had so strongly criticized the way Nigerian men treated women, it seemed simple enough to assume that this novel, like those written by Western feminists in the early 1970s, was a critique of the worldwide phenomenon of sexism. Although these two scenes certainly provide a kind of (Western) feminist frame for the novel, I no longer think their inclusion is so simple. I would argue strongly against any kind of extrapolation vis-à-vis Emecheta's attitudes toward her Igbo heritage. The rest of the book may also have a feminist perspective, but it is not in the service of attacking patriarchal Nigerian traditions. Its feminism lies rather in how it praises and encourages solidarity among women. It is Africanist in its reflection of fundamental Igbo values. But it is often difficult for (white) Western feminist readers to sort out these two controlling themes. In part, I think the difficulty arises because we have generally failed to distinguish between reading Emecheta's novels as reflections *of* Nigerian culture (an approach I would discourage) and reading them as reflections *on* this culture (an approach I endorse). This distinction, while still allowing her texts to function as a kind of (displaced) ethnographic documentation of Nigerian customs, has the added virtue of reminding us that hers is but one voice among many and represents (as do the voices of others) an interested or invested perspective. But even as we maintain this distinction, we must not fail to interrogate ourselves and what we bring to the cross-cultural reading experience.

As I suggested earlier, one of the aspects of Emecheta's fiction that Western readers find so puzzling is her characters' loyalty to the community. I think there are both formal and cultural reasons for our failure to understand this loyalty. It will be recalled, for example, that Myra Jehlen has described the Western (middle-class) novel as "organically individualistic." On her view, the novel is structured around "the unitary self versus the others"; it is additionally "about the generation, the becoming, of that self" (1981, 595). If Jehlen is correct in her assertion, this would certainly help explain the difficulty we Westerners face in reading novels that fail to endorse this individuality—that seem, in fact, to refute it, or worse, be utterly indifferent to it. I have already discussed how important the concept of individuality is to Western thought. But not all Westerners, of course, value the individual to the same degree. Alison Jaggar, for one, has posited a more attractive alternative to the liberal conception of human nature in her description of socialist feminism (1988). Other feminist theorists have suggested a basic difference between what men (are taught to) value and what women (are taught to) value. In short, men value independence, autonomy, and abstract principles of just behavior, while women value relationships and community.[6] But there is a significant difference, I think, between sharing the values of the dominant culture (as occurs in Igbo women's attitudes toward the community) and sharing the values of an oppressed subgroup (as occurs among women in Western society). Here is a case where it is clear that the prejudices we bring to a text can fundamentally determine how we (mis)understand it. If we assume, as most Western readers have, that Emecheta's novels are about the generation of an independent heroine, we see Igbo society in negative terms. If we recognize, on the other hand, that traditional Igbo culture values community in much the same way we feminists do,[7] we can perhaps begin to rethink our own relationship to society at large and not be so judgmental. What makes it difficult for us to see the commonalities, however, are the alien customs in Emecheta's fiction that seem to us (if not their practitioners) so self-evidently to disadvantage African women—polygamy, bride prices, and clitorization, for example.[8]

Not only do the differences between Igbo and Western customs complicate our reading, but they complicate the novels themselves, contributing to their plurality of meaning.[9] For the community, important as it is to Buchi Emecheta, does prescribe certain limitations on women that in real life she herself has soundly rejected. Emecheta discusses this conflict in *Head Above Water* when she explains that the rebellious autobiographical heroine of *The Bride Price* has to die at the end because she had challenged tradition: "I had realized that what makes all of us human is belonging to a group. And if one belongs to a group, one should try and abide by its laws" (1986, 166). In real life, of course, the even more rebellious Buchi Emecheta does not die, but, in her fiction, she continually reaffirms the value of community. If we Westerners are to read African novelists from an ethical standpoint, therefore, it is imperative for us to foreground our own fundamental belief in the primacy of the individual and approach this fiction interactively—invoking the language of perspicuous contrast. Having done so, we will soon discover that reading this literature is an enormously rewarding but fundamentally disturbing experience, an experience that will change us far more deeply than if we had approached it as a variant of our own Western literary forms. The experience that awaits us, in other words, is parallel to Adah's encounter with the landlord. When we inhabit the world of African fiction, we are invited to experience an alien view of reality. Whether we are able to resist the juju of "superiority and arrogance" (Achebe 1975b, 5), therefore, largely depends on whether we are willing, like Adah, to accept the tenets of an alien worldview.

RETAINING AND TRANSLATING A CULTURAL HERITAGE

The tensions that conflicting cultural traditions generate are also evident in the structure of the novel itself—but they are displaced in an unexpected fashion. Where the first and last scenes have to do primarily with Adah's disappointment with Nigerian men (who presumably should share her cultural values), the body of the novel describes the love and support Adah receives from a community of British women. Ironically enough, the Nigerian men betray their heritage of humane living while the British women honor it, for the values they live by are remarkably African. The two men, the landlord and Whoopey's lover, seem to have accepted in full the Western liberal idea that the individual comes first. The landlord, knowing Adah's problems, takes advantage of them, while Whoopey's lover simply uses her as a comfort in his time of loneliness. In short, both have been corrupted by their stay in England. Having lost touch with their own ethical system, they seem to have learned only the worst of the West's ethical alternatives.

According to both Ali Mazrui and Elechi Amadi, the loss of a cultural heritage is not an uncommon pattern among Africans. For example, Mazrui describes six colonial forces that have helped destroy the traditional values of community by fostering a Western-style individualism among African peoples. These forces are Christianity, which weakened tribal custom; Western liberalism which emphasized "the right to privacy and personal choice"; urbanization, which weakened "the constraints of collective village life"; Western capitalism, which taught the "pursuit of personal profit"; "the rules of western [sic] education and science," which stress individual accomplishments; and, finally, "the rules of western [sic] art," which punish plagiarism (1983 66-67). Amadi also attributes the problem to the effects of colonialism, arguing that the "imported religions, namely Christianity and Islam, do not have the same powerful hold on the people as the traditional religions, so their use as ethical instruments is not as effective" (1982, 6). If the loss of ethical instruments was a danger faced by colonized Africans who remained in Africa, it is conceivably even more of a danger for those who left the continent altogether. Trying to counter this loss, Amadi concludes his account with an eloquent defense of traditional Nigerian ethics; urging his people to cling to their "cherished social graces, no matter what the pressures of modern living may be," he reminds us that "life is more real, has more meaning, when we interact very closely with other human beings" (110). But in Emecheta's novel, it is the British women who befriend Adah, who themselves have certainly never been in Africa, who nevertheless live by the values that Amadi describes. The cultural differences that might otherwise have kept the women apart and in conflict, Emecheta writes, had been forgotten "in the face of greater enemies—poverty and helplessness" (71). Thus, the selfish independence shown by the men is answered by the selfless interdependence exhibited by the women, and traditional African values are reaffirmed.

Chieka Ifemesia argues that the fact that the Igbos have survived for thousands of years means that they necessarily "had to show empathy, and consideration and compassion for human beings" (1979, 31). Ifemesia reports, for example, that the "training and discipline of children was [sic] . . . both an individual and a communal responsibility" (58). As part of this process, the community taught its children how "to be at once independent of and dependent upon one's family" (67). The key to Igbo thought was the concept of interdependence, "exhibited now as duality or reciprocity, now as ambivalence or complementa[r]ity" (68). These are exactly the same values affirmed by Emecheta's first novel. Contrary to what the (feminist) frame suggests, this novel is not an attack on (patriarchal) Nigerian culture but an affirmation of it— displaced into British terms. Without ever stating it outright, this novel shows how even British women living in the ditch can benefit from traditional Igbo values. Emecheta responds to the aesthetic problem Nkosi describes (1981) by focusing on an individual who must learn to integrate herself into her new culture even if this culture is sometimes hostile to her. If Adah Obi is to survive, she must learn to translate her old African values into her new Western environment.

Her task is made difficult because, the women on the dole notwithstanding, the two cultures are quite different. One difference that Emecheta stresses in this novel involves child raising. Though Winch does not identify it as such, I would think that the practice of raising children would qualify as one of his fundamental human ideas that he calls "limiting notions" (1964, 322). In the case of Emecheta's novel, the understanding works in two directions—as Adah and her readers learn about each other's culture. Adah has trouble, for example, accepting the fact that parents should talk to their babies, regarding the custom as both foreign and strange. When she talks to her own baby, she does so in secret so none of her Nigerian friends will think that she is some kind of "a witch, talking to something that did not answer back" (14). This, however, is a rather harmless cultural difference. A potentially more serious one is what happens to the children when Adah goes to work. Unaware that it is dangerous to leave five young children home alone, Adah has been doing just this. She is therefore quite surprised when the Family Adviser tells her it is not permitted (30). Though our first (ethnocentric) response might be one of horrified disapproval (that Adah Obi would leave her children alone without adult supervision), from this we can also deduce that children are more valued in Africa since they would not be harmed if they were left alone. Implicit here is also the fact that the children would be seen as belonging to all of the community and not just to their parents. Thus, Emecheta's novel provides us with the opportunity to rethink (or defamiliarize) many of own cultural practices and prejudices.

I have said that the understanding works in two directions: Adah Obi must learn to understand the West, and we must learn to understand her. Thomas McCarthy discusses a similar proposition. Drawing on the work of Horkheimer, Winch, and Habermas, McCarthy suggests that in situations where cultural differences and rational disagreements predominate, the only "nonarbitrary" route to take is that of a "symmetrical" discussion that weighs "the pros and cons of the divergent outlooks." For McCarthy, this means that not only will we try to see things from *their* point of view, but, conversely, so neither side maintains a discursive advantage, they will be expected to try "to see things from *our* point of view" (1988, 84). But, having set up his own version of a Habermasian ideal speech situation, McCarthy acknowledges that historically the West has dominated the conversation, and the "alien cultures" in question have been allowed to speak only insofar as they have learned the language of the West—that is, they, in effect, have had to "become 'modernized'" (85). He goes on to describe situations in which the conversation and thus the learning may fail to achieve symmetry, such as those that involve people who hold "magico-mythical worldviews" (87). In this type of situation, where people are themselves unable to conceptualize alternatives to their own worldview, the very fact of being exposed to our Western alternatives would, on his view, irremediably change these people, thus calling into question whether symmetry in conversation leads to equitable results.

Given the scenario that McCarthy plays out, I think we can return to the scene with Adah Obi's landlord and ask if, indeed, the juju would ever work for her again, even if she were to return to Africa. My guess is that it would not. Having been educated in the West and fully exposed to its view of rationality (including the split between the cognitive and non-cognitive spheres), Adah Obi, it would appear, cannot unlearn this lesson. Since the juju never works in the novel at all, we ourselves are given no alternative model to learn. In the area of child care, however, the conversational situation might actually achieve more symmetry, for I do think that Emecheta does a reasonably effective job of showing how silly some of our Western customs can be. It just might be preferable—or at least instructive—to think of children, for example, as belonging to the community rather than belonging to individual parents. But even Adah learns to rethink some of her views about raising children. As a sign of her own willingness to enter a cross-cultural conversation, Adah resigns her job at the British Museum and goes on the dole so she can stay home with her children. At first she is bitter to have lost her financial independence. Yet by going on the dole, she finally is accepted as part of the community (33). In short, she becomes more Western by obeying its rules for raising children. But at the same time, paradoxically enough, she is returning to the humane tenets of Igbo living: in joining the community of single mothers at the Mansions, Adah finds meaning, strength, and even "joy in [their] communal sorrow" (61). This new alliance helps her to fend off some of the racism of her adopted country, the racism that helped to destroy her husband and would keep her apart from other people. In many respects, then, this decision to go on the dole becomes a victory for Adah, for up to this point she has been reluctant to submit herself emotionally to this new culture because of the racial snubs she has endured.

Although Adah takes considerable comfort from the friendship of these women, she still misses her own country and never quite feels that she is good enough to be accepted on her own terms (74). One reason she feels this way is that she continues to encounter racist attitudes. At one particularly low moment in her life, Adah longs for her own country, thinking that at least in Nigeria there would be people to hold her hand. Then she remembers that many of her people met tragic deaths as they fled for their lives during the Biafran War and concludes that there is "no safety anywhere, really" (112). No safety anywhere. This statement could almost stand as the epigraph to all of Emecheta's fiction, for it represents the kind of isolation experienced by her heroines as they struggle to find a place for themselves in a world that is often hostile to their dreams and ambitions.[10] For Adah, however, the struggle has a relatively happy ending when she aligns herself with the disfranchised working-class women whose generous behavior puts to shame that exhibited by the functionaries of the welfare state. In portraying this alignment, Emecheta seems to be joining the ranks of other African socialist realists, like Ngugi, who claim that the future of Africa lies with the masses. She also graphically portrays what it means to be poor, black, and female—in England and in Africa—and thus begins to envision the parameters of what Jameson would call a "new realism" (1986, 212).[11] By their own behavior, some of Emecheta's heroines also suggest, in Onoge's terms, that even though the world is not safe, it is "changeable" (1974, 36). The change, it would appear, lies in the direction of cross-cultural understanding: a melding of African and Western values.

Second-Class Citizen (1974)

LOVE, MARRIAGE, AND NARRATIVE CONSEQUENCES

If I initially had trouble reading *In the Ditch* because of my ignorance about Igbo traditions, I had even more trouble with *Second-Class Citizen*, which describes the breakup of Adah Obi's marriage. It was a matter not only of cultural ignorance, however, but also of critical bias, since I continued to read these African novels from the perspective of a white Western feminist (as do many other of Emecheta's critics).[12] Because Adah's situation gives feminist readers a lot to be angry about, I only too readily sided with this abused woman as she struggled bravely against a hostile (male-dominated) society. Her marital situation seems so grimly hopeless, in fact, that most Western readers are likely to long for the moment when she finally gets up the gumption to leave her worthless husband.[13] But longing for this moment ignores what divorce would mean to a woman like Adah, who was raised to believe in traditional Igbo values. For, as necessary as this separation might seem to us in the West, the failure of her marriage signals a tragic rupture in the very community that should have nurtured her. In leaving Francis, she is leaving her own people in some respects—but she does not renounce all her culture or even most of it, nor is the novel as critical of the Igbo tradition as it might seem. Because Emecheta is so effective in gaining sympathy for her heroine, however, it is almost too easy for Western readers to miss the sympathy she expresses for her culture. It is easy, in other words, to miss the novel's multiplicity of meaning.

The desire to have our values reconfirmed by a text is so compelling that I am almost tempted to argue that Western readers willfully overlook Emecheta's defense of customs alien to our own. I, for one, completely overlooked the complexity of the first two chapters, in which Emecheta explains the nuances of her

African culture. These chapters seem to reflect Emecheta's own ambivalence, as she is apparently both accepting and skeptical of what she has been taught. They also provide a backdrop to the bleak conditions of African emigrés in England, descriptions of which provide the setting for the rest of the novel. The racial prejudice that Adah experiences in England forces her to evaluate the good and bad in both cultures. Because of our predisposition to favor our own culture, however, it is difficult for Western readers to hear the voices in this novel that defend African culture. When I first read the book, for example, I thought that Adah's traditional Igbo heritage had completely failed her. Assuming that the novel reflected some of Emecheta's own disillusionment, I also thought that she found virtually nothing of value in her patriarchal African culture—that she had set out intentionally to expose its sexism.[14]

Certainly, a Western feminist critic would find much to deplore in Adah's upbringing. From the very beginning of her life, for example, Adah's family was so disappointed that she was not a boy that they failed to record her birth (Emecheta 1983a, 7). This kind of disappointment, of course, is not limited to African cultures (which might provide us with another of Winch's limiting notions: the relative value of female children versus male children). Seen in the context of other information, however, this passage can look as if Emecheta were specifically censuring her own Igbo people for how they treat females. When Adah's father dies, for example, Adah is expected, like other female orphans, to become a "servant" for her uncle's family (17). Even though Adah longs for an education, the family decides to send her younger brother to school instead. Because these customs seem pretty harsh, it is easy to overlook the fact that Emecheta herself (or at least her narrator) finds value in them. This is why it is so crucial to notice that for every narrative attack on custom there is a counterattack—that is, a passage in which Emecheta explains or defends her Igbo tradition (see also Solberg 1983, 252). For example, in the matter of Adah's servitude, the narrator pointedly warns us not to impose our own ethical system on hers. It would be easy, she says bluntly, to think "that Africans treated their children badly." But as far as Adah and her people are concerned, it is simply "the custom" and nothing to be concerned about. Lest we think custom is not sufficient, the narrator continues to explain that all children, but young girls especially, "were taught to be very useful," a system that "had its advantages." Fully aware of the ramifications of her situation, Adah is grateful that her uncle has given her a chance to survive and does not "waste time thinking about its rights or wrongs" (18). Eventually her family does allow Adah to stay in school because they realize that the more educated she is, the bigger bride price she will command (17).

Not insignificantly, once Adah gets married, the problems she faces with her patriarchal culture seem to intensify—as do the problems Western readers have in perceiving the text's sympathetic treatment of African culture. In part, these interpretive problems arise because of the differences between Western and African concepts of love and marriage—and, in part, they arise because of the narration itself. While the theme of love between individuals is central to an entire tradition of Western literature, Irina D. Nikiforova, for example, finds it is "almost totally unexplored in African literature" (1987, 427). When it does appear, it often serves the political purpose of cultural conflict, as in Head's and Bâ's fiction. But most Western readers coming to Emecheta for the first time will bring with them the tradition of *Western* love stories, a tradition that can actually interfere with our understanding. It must also be said that Emecheta's novels seem almost to invite misreadings because they do focus on marriage and love relationships. They do have brave, independent heroines, many of whom long for the perfect husband and with whom we are invited to sympathize. In short, although the heroines are Africans, they seem, by our Western standards, to be very familiar already. This so-called familiarity with characters and themes would help explain why Western readers confuse these African novels with the social or classic realism they are accustomed to. But as familiar as these characters and themes might seem, they do not have the same significance as they would have were they to appear in Western fiction. This difference has largely to do with how we express feelings of love.

Joseph Okpaku explains, for example, that the "African believes in implicit or understood love while the Western man's love is explicit and dramatized." Aesthetically speaking, then, Africans would regard displays of Western love as "superficial and melodramatic." The Western reader, in return, would think the African "callous, unaffectionate and cold" (1970b, 20). This difference certainly helps explain our reaction to Francis Obi, who certainly does not meet our expectations for a romantic hero. Though he may, indeed, love Adah, we see no affection in his demeanor. To us he is cold, selfish, and uncaring. Our unsympathetic response is compounded by the fact that Adah herself, perhaps because of her British education and her exposure to European novels, seems to want Francis to behave more like a Western husband. When he tells her she must stay in Africa, for example, she remarks that her husband is thoroughly "African," while a "more civilised man" would break the news to his wife more gently (28). Later, the narrator even tells us that had Francis been English, the marriage would have lasted, and Adah would have been content to stay at home (163). At these moments Western readers, invoking their own cultural biases, are only too ready to side with Adah. But in so doing, I think we tend to forget that this is Emecheta's (fictional) meditation on her culture—and not an objective ethnographic document. I think we also fail to realize that the standards of behavior we are invoking are not necessarily appropriate to Francis's cultural upbringing—or even to the novel itself, Emecheta's political investments in her heroine notwithstanding.

For, if we look more closely, we will see that the Obis' entire relationship has been little more than a business transaction—one that gives Adah the freedom to continue her education and gives Francis access to her scholarship money. The Western concept of love plays no apparent part in the exchange. The entire courtship ritual, such as it is, is condensed into three short sentences: "In short, Adah had to marry. Francis was a very quiet young man who was reading to be an accountant. Adah congratulated herself on her marriage" (23). The account of their wedding is confined to six brief paragraphs.[15] It would thus appear that Adah is not quite the victim of circumstances and a loveless marriage as we might think. It may very well be the case that Emecheta, in trying to get us to sympathize with her (highly autobiographical) heroine, actually invites us to invoke the romantic expectations for love and marriage that we Westerners have inherited from our own literary tradition. But in inviting our sympathy, she seems inadvertently to have made it more difficult for her Western readers to understand how Adah can remain loyal to the culture she has come from—and thus made it difficult to understand the novel.

Our interpretive dilemma is exacerbated in other scenes. The same six paragraphs that describe the Obis' marriage, for example, also describe the African custom of the bride price, where the husband pays the bride's family for the privilege of marrying their daughter. According to Amadi, in "ancient Nigeria a wife was regarded as the husband's property. The man paid a certain amount as bride-price, and the woman became his" (1982, 75). In some respects, this situation seems not much different from that of many Western women before the passage of the married women's property acts—though in Adah's village the custom is still honored in the middle of the twentieth century. But then we learn that her relatives refuse to attend the wedding ceremony when Francis is unable to pay the bride price (24). They are angry because they had allowed Adah to stay in school only to increase her value, and, in effect, they are not getting the proper return on their investment. Western families, of course, also boycott weddings—but not because the bride has not been paid for. In fact, we would find the whole notion of payment repugnant whether Francis's family made it or not. Thus, it is almost impossible for Western readers to identify with anyone in these passages except the poor heroine, who has been forced by circumstances beyond her control into a loveless marriage her family does not sanction. Many of us will also recognize and reject the objectification and obvious commodification of another woman.[16] Furthermore, as Westerners who believe in the tradition of romantic love, we would regard it as particularly unfair for society to force Adah into a loveless marriage and then not sanction it. Other comments also tempt us to read the novel as a general critique of Igbo tradition, as when the narrator observes that Adah has been coerced into agreeing to a situation about which "as an individual, she had little choice" (27). With our emphasis on individual rights, we are quick to imagine that these rights have been violated.

Much to our subsequent bewilderment, however, Adah loyally accepts her husband's shortcomings as part of the deal she has made in marrying him, refusing to give up on him until he burns the manuscript of the novel she has written—a transgression even she cannot forgive (170). In the meantime, she sticks it out. Though her reasons for staying are complex, they are primarily cultural ones that Western readers do not share. Emecheta remarks on these cultural differences in a recent interview. What Francis does is not necessarily excused, she explains, but it can be "made understandable by a knowledge of his background." For her, the key to understanding Francis lies in the fact that his mother had "spoiled" him, leaving him vulnerable to the "hard-boiled atmosphere of English society, where he was without the support of his family" (Schipper 1985, 44, 45).[17] But Emecheta herself has done little in the novel to facilitate this understanding, implying through the narrator that African men are uncivilized. Nor is understanding increased when a complete stranger accosts Adah in the street and tells her to beg her husband's forgiveness, and the narrator characterizes the event as "[t]ypical Ibo psychology; men never do wrong, only the women" (155-56).

A DEFENSE OF AFRICAN CULTURE AND CORRUPTION IN THE WEST

But, while Emecheta might be unhappy with her culture's restrictive conventions, I think it an oversimplification to argue that she has the same attitude as her Western readers. There is just too much else in her novel that either cancels out or otherwise balances her criticism of African tradition. For one thing, the relationship that Adah had with her father was a very special one. When she makes it clear that she wants an education, her father insists that she go to the best school available (14). When her brother hears about the problems she is having, he sends his life savings to her so she and the children can come home (an offer she does not accept). Francis behaves so irresponsibly, in part, because England cannot provide him with the same kind of diversions he would have had back home in Nigeria. Cut off from the traditions and customs of their people, Francis is unable to maintain the same level of mental health as men in the home country (156). Another expression of the good that Adah is able to see in her own culture is the fact that her new family is delighted with her and welcomes her into the fold. These are important passages, which are based firmly on Igbo values reflecting the belief that a wife should be embraced and respected by her in-laws. Francis's parents are especially pleased by her, moreover, because she is both a good source of income and very prolific.

Even though the theme of infertility is prominent in several recent African novels, such as Flora Nwapa's *Efuru* (1966) and *Idu* (1970) and Emecheta's own *The Joys of Motherhood* (1979b), it is still hard for Westerners to understand why Adah's fertility is so valued by her in-laws. Filomina Chioma Steady suggests, for example, that the "importance of motherhood and the valuation of the childbearing capacity . . . is [*sic*] probably the most fundamental difference between the African woman and her Western counterpart" as we work to rid the world of sex discrimination (1981, 29). Chieka Ifemesia recalls that historically if someone was infertile, the family ordinarily tried to solve the problem internally. Sometimes this involved the husband taking an additional wife—sometimes even at the bidding of the first wife "because, in accordance with the people's humane view of life, the family must not lack human beings." If the man was infertile, it was not uncommon for the family to arrange for the woman to have another sex partner. As an indication of how highly children are valued, Ifemesia also informs us that there are "no words for 'illegitimate', 'bastard', 'base-born', and such-like terms in the traditional Igbo vocabulary" (1979, 61). Raised within these traditions, Adah realizes that she or any woman could do almost anything if she only had children (26). But even though these passages seem designed to defend Adah's culture, her own dissatisfaction often makes it difficult for us to see the good in African customs.

While she is still living in Nigeria, after hearing that her mother has died, Adah wishes, for example, that she and Francis could start life over in another country surrounded by "new people" (27). Inspired by her father's exaggerated dreams of England, Adah convinces her new husband they should emigrate. But without consulting her, Francis and his family decide that he will leave and she will keep her job in Lagos in order to support him and help to pay for his sisters' schooling. Even though Adah resents the fact that she has not been consulted (27), resentment, as the narrator is quick to inform us, is not Adah's only emotion. In fact, it may not even be the primary one, for she apparently does not care that she has been left in Nigeria with so many responsibilities (25). Our own willingness to accept the good in her cultural background is made more difficult by the direction of the plot, as Adah Obi *apparently* moves away from her African origins, first in leaving Africa itself and then in leaving her husband. But as I hope to suggest later, even when she seems most strongly to criticize her African upbringing, she never entirely rejects it. On one hand, Adah has violated traditional Igbo customs by insisting that she has a right to be educated, even if she is only a girl. On the other, she accepts all the responsibilities her new family heaps on her "even though her bride-price had not been paid" (25). This statement is important because it informs us that, rebellious as she is, Adah still believes in tradition. It is not until much later, after suffering through years of hell with Francis, that she finally repudiates the concept of bride prices (122). Before she reaches this point, she looks back on her time in Africa "almost with nostalgia," wondering "why she had not been content with that sort of life, cushioned by the love of her parents-in-law . . . and respected by Francis's younger sisters" (26).

Once Francis has left for England, Adah convinces her in-laws she would be even more valuable to them if she were to join her husband abroad. But what had been at least a tolerable situation in Lagos soon disintegrates into near chaos once she arrives in London. Though he has not been in England very long, Francis Obi, like Adah's landlord, has already lost most of his African values. The man who comes to the pier to greet his family, Adah quickly realizes, is not the man she knew. In fact, she is "stunned when he kissed her in public" (36). Without the information that Adah is shocked by Francis's behavior, the significance of this scene would be completely lost on Western readers. But even with it, the knowledge is probably not sufficient to convey the full depth of Francis's corruption at the hands of the West. His behavior informs her that he thinks it is fine for African men to "get civilised in England. But that privilege has not been extended to females yet" (37). The first night she arrives, he virtually rapes her and then has the audacity to warn her that he will not tolerate her "frigidity" (40). Because he is studying, he refuses to get a job (42). So even though Adah is pregnant and has resumed her own studies, she herself takes a job as a senior library assistant. Later, hoping to avoid yet another pregnancy, she wears a diaphragm without asking Francis's permission. This act so enrages him that he uses it as his excuse for failing one of his accountancy examinations. Any one of these events would be sufficient to win the sympathy of most women readers. In wretched combination, they help explain why so many Western readers find it so very tempting to treat Emecheta as a Western-style feminist writer.[18]

Through it all, Adah Obi suffers silently, refusing to give up on her husband, even when she realizes that he is having sex with other women. The narrator assures us that Francis is not "bad"—only a victim of an "over-demanding society" (101). Though Francis is certainly under pressure, to Western readers this seems to be an overly generous assessment of the situation. Eventually, Adah herself assumes a less tolerant perspective, when it finally occurs to her that Francis should have shouldered some of the responsibility. In retrospect she finds it amusing that she used to feel "it was her duty" to support her husband (95).[19] Is it any wonder that Western women become enraged at what goes on in this novel? But cultural chauvinists that we are—and I believe that even most Western feminists would defend their own sexist culture against an African one—we cannot see that Francis has been corrupted by his stay in England. If Adah and Francis had stayed in Nigeria, their life would have been less plagued by troubles. When he almost hits her, Adah is horrified by the change in him. Whereas in England, Francis feels free to act out his frustrations on Adah, at home he would not have dared to, since his parents would have forbidden it (39).

A MATTER OF SIGNIFYING AND DIALOGIC HETEROGLOSSIA

In her previously cited essay, Myra Jehlen raises some additional issues about the thematic and formal characteristics of Western fiction that seem to be relevant here. Jehlen suggests, for example, that male characters are defined by their "defiance," while female characters are defined by their "vulnerability." Jehlen further argues that, structurally speaking, the novel, as a form, is built on the same "sexual hierarchy" found in modern (middle-class) society (1981, 595). She then proposes the thesis that the "interior life, *whether lived by man or woman, is female*, so that women characters define themselves and have power only in this realm" (596). In contrast, the "exterior life" of the novel is male (598).[20] With Jehlen's ideas as background, I want to propose that Adah Obi insists on her right to write herself into the external world of the novel. Initially driven by her husband to get a job, Adah soon begins to define herself as an autonomous working woman. She dares to define herself as a "man"—a male character, becoming, in effect, a male impersonator. Back in Nigeria, her status as a working woman was not problematic, to either Francis or his family; on the contrary, her in-laws counted on her income and valued her for it. But in England, other cultural/literary conventions obtain, and Adah must be "punished" by her Westernized husband for daring to write herself male—even though he himself has driven her to this action. But how the female self is defined seems to be changing, as more and more women work outside the home. Mark Poster argues, for example, that change itself is the hallmark of self-constitution in the late twentieth century, change that would appear to have far-reaching social consequences since historically the dominant (white male) culture has been able with some success "to confine self-constitution as much as possible to the activity of work." On Poster's view, "the rise of sexual counter-modalities" seems to "threaten" the dominant culture—a threat that even the African immigrant Francis Obi seems frightened of, perhaps because of his longing to be part of the Western male elite power structure (1989, 68). In Foucauldian terms, Adah's most disruptive and daring act of self-definition as a male impersonator is to write a novel herself (write herself as novel). That is, unhappy with how she has been interpellated as a (female) subject, she actively participates in the reconstruction—the rewriting—of her own subjectivity, becoming, as it were, a female hero.[21]

Alasdair MacIntyre would suggest that, on the surface, there is nothing particularly daring in Adah's behavior, since it is "natural" for people to think of themselves "in a narrative mode" (1984b, 206). While it may be natural (or at least not uncommon) to *think* this way, writing ourselves as narrative can be a self-assertive (and potentially threatening) gesture. In MacIntyre's terms, Francis may well be threatened by Adah's writing because it reflects her attempt to author her own life—to eliminate his role as co-author of her narrative. "Only in fantasy," MacIntyre reminds us, "do we live what story we please" (213). Perhaps the element of fantasy helps to explain why Emecheta herself originally gave *The Bride Price* a happy ending; perhaps she was trying to write herself out of her miserable marriage. In any event, *Second-Class Citizen* contains two layers of narrative: Emecheta herself writes a narrative of her own unhappy married life, while Adah writes a novel about a happy (if forbidden) marriage. But in violating her preordained (Western) fictional role by becoming autonomous and functioning in the forbidden male territory of external reality, Adah has, in Jehlen's terms, violated "the very forms and categories of all our thinking" (1981, 600). (Thinking of her "self" as narrative is not the violation; thinking of herself as "male" is.) It is thus a sign of Francis's true corruption into Western middle-class values that he tries to silence Adah by burning her novel. Ironically, had he been a traditional (Western) breadwinning husband himself, she would have been content to limit herself to the novel's interior life.

The rigid public/private division Jehlen finds at the heart of Western fiction seems absent in Emecheta's traditional African culture—as does the related notion of an atomistic self that MacIntyre finds central to modern Western thought. Though men and women had different roles and responsibilities in traditional African communities, the rigid public/private dichotomy would appear to have been imported to Africa by Western colonialists. Evidence suggests, for example, that African women enjoyed much higher status in the community before colonization.[22] Adah Obi, by writing herself into her novel as both working woman and author, has (on Emecheta's and our behalf) called into question both the universality and the necessity of the public/private opposition. She has, in short, shown it to be a social construction that is neither natural nor inevitable. By posing the problem Adah has with her (Westernized) husband in terms of his response to Adah's novel, Emecheta manages to question the public/private division that Jehlen finds organic to Western fiction. Seen in this context, Adah's decision to leave Francis after he burns her manuscript becomes even more significant—as she refuses to remain a character in the Western narrative that would confine her to a subservient domestic role. In portraying Francis as a "domestic" male, who refuses to accept work outside the home, Emecheta has already challenged the traditional nineteenth-century concept of the woman's sphere. Emecheta's African novel thus becomes a gloss on Western novels; in short, her novel is signifying.

In "The Blackness of Blackness," Henry Louis Gates, Jr., employs this African American linguistic trope (signifying or signifyin') to describe the formal and thematic relationship between (or among) African American texts. It is, in short, Gates's (Africanized) version of intertextuality, whereby texts speak to, and indirectly comment on, other texts. Gates finds the origins of this literary technique in the Signifying Monkey, which he traces to "the trickster figure of Yoruba mythology" (1984, 286)—a figure that Emecheta herself would have familiarity with.[23] One of Gates's best-known examples is *Their Eyes Were Watching God*, which he reads as "a signifying structure . . . because it revises key tropes and rhetorical strategies received from such precursor texts as [Jean] Toomer's *Cane* and W. E. B. DuBois's *The Quest of the Silver Fleece*." To Gates it is quite simply self-evident that "black writers read and critique other black texts as an act of rhetorical self-definition" (290). I do not wish to suggest that Emecheta has not been influenced by the African American literary tradition, but I do want to suggest the possibility that because she was trained by British missionaries and educated in England, it is likely here that she is reading and critiquing white Anglo-European realism. Thus, what might appear (to us) to be an invocation of Western feminism and Western realism is more likely what Gates calls "critical signification," a kind of "critical parody, of repetition and inversion" in which Emecheta challenges the hegemony of Western culture—and even challenges the West's own challenger (Western feminism) (294). In short, she is using the West's own literary forms to critique the West itself. Her novel, that is, signifies upon the whole tradition of Western fiction. Emecheta is signifying—with a difference.

As we read her fiction, we can also use Taylor's language of perspicuous contrast to see that she is calling attention to the shortcomings in our own narrative discourse and in our cultural assumptions about sexual asymmetry. In dismantling our narrative conventions, Emecheta shows them to be vehicles for promoting the "false consciousness [that serves] the interests of the ruling class" (Jaggar 1988, 57). But many of the problems Adah and Francis have are also directly attributable to the fact that the British regard them as inferior because of their race (another distortion that serves the interests of the ruling class). One reason they live in a run-down tenement is that the whites refuse to rent to them. This prejudice erodes Francis's self-confidence to the point where he will no longer eat in a restaurant—having convinced himself that blacks do not belong there (58). From this it becomes evident that Francis has also adopted this manifestation of false consciousness as he believes what his oppressors tell him about himself. Although Adah never believes in her own inferiority, she is not unaffected by the hostility they encounter. When she has trouble with the day-minder who takes care of her children, for example, she realizes that she has no one to confide in since, unlike Lagos, "nobody was interested in the problems of others" (66). But just as we begin to suspect Adah's problems might be caused primarily by the whites, the narrator wonders if it were possible that "the real discrimination" might instead be "the work of her fellow-countrymen" (70). In short, the novel expresses a multiplicity of meanings in a multitude of voices—signifying upon Western culture and its African imitators, much the way Wole Soyinka does in *The Interpreters*.[24]

The heteroglossia of her novel is apparent not only in the cultural perspectives that are expressed here but also in several passages where Emecheta draws on Western literature and terminology—sometimes to quite startling effects. After Francis bitterly informs her of her new second-class status, Adah sits on their new settee, defeated, "like the dying Ayesha in Rider Haggard's *She*" (39). What a bizarre and complex comparison this makes. *She*, of course, is set in the heart of darkest Africa; She herself is a powerful mythic white female deity who is destroyed by the man She loves. In another passage, when Adah becomes discouraged by life in England, she says she is carrying "the heavy load of Christian in *The Pilgrim's Progress*" (55). When Francis proselytizes from his Seventh-Day Adventist tracts, he sounds to Adah like a character "in *Quo Vadis*" (101). It is as though Emecheta were attempting to place her own fiction in a Western literary tradition. But the appropriation fails—a failure that reminds us that this is not a European novel but an African one, replete with dialogic heteroglossia. Because all words are "half someone else's," according to Bakhtin, they can be appropriated only if we infuse them with our own "intention" (1987, 293). But not all words readily lend themselves to appropriation; some "stubbornly resist, others remain alien, sound foreign" (294). So it seems to be with these literary allusions in *Second-Class Citizen*.[25] Though the appropriation fails, it serves the alternative purpose of contrasting her fiction with the Western tradition she attempts to invoke—a contrast that is highlighted in the novel's various languages.

In the Ditch is particularly marked by the contrast between the refined language of the educated Nigerian heroine (whose training has prepared her to work in a library like "the British Museum" [88]) and the coarse, colorful language of the working-class British women she lives with in Pussy Cat Mansions. Though the differences in their language seem destined to separate the two classes of women, their common suffering brings them together. At first Adah is "shocked" by her friends' "low language," such as the time Whoopey relates a fantasy she has had about running off to Australia with a handsome man, and her mother wants to know how she will feed her "bloody kids" since her arms are "too fucking rusty" to do the work. But it is not long before Adah realizes that the swearing does not mean much—it is just the way her new friends talk (41). When Adah tries to lodge a complaint about the dogs that are defecating outside her door, she says politely: "You see, these dogs always do their toilets at my door. It's so embarrassing." But her friend impatiently interrupts: "Embarer—what? . . . Don't give him that nice talk" (70). Even though Adah/Emecheta's English echoes that of the British ruling class, her African worldview has not been colonized by this alien language. Even though the fiction Emecheta has written is first cousin to classic Anglo-American realism, her African heritage (and its languages) has left its own distinctive imprint on her novels' form and content. These are not English novels, but African novels written in English and thus part of a different tradition. Unlike the classic European realism that Belsey describes, Emecheta's modern African realism most assuredly is not "constructed out of what is (discursively) familiar" to us Western readers (1980, 47). Nor is the experience of reading Emecheta's fiction one we should find "ultimately reassuring" (51). Reading it is, in fact, (or at least should be) a very unsettling experience.

NOTES

1. Though marginality is theoretically advantageous for the artist, it is not a condition that most of us would choose for ourselves. Strategically speaking, it may be entirely overrated. See Newton 1988 and Hartsock 1987.

2. Her challenge to the social construction of race also puts her in the company of African American women writers, of course. See, for example, Carby 1987, McDowell 1989, and Ogunyemi 1985.

3. The remarkably successful and graceful way Emecheta has managed the difficult feat of raising five children and writing fiction inspired Alice Walker's encomium, "A Writer Because of, Not in Spite of, Her Children" (1983b).

4. Although here I have obviously been influenced by Winch's principle of hermeneutic charity, Winch himself challenges many of MacIntyre's arguments in his own essay.

5. Arun P. Mukherjee argues similarly that the Western critic, having been "trained by the forms of Western literature in which the individual has long held the centre of the stage, is unable to do justice to those works from the new Commonwealth in which community life and large socio-political issues are of central importance" (1986, 347).

6. See Gilligan 1982 Hartsock 1983—and Schweickart 1986, as the difference pertains to reading.

7. I am indebted to Cecilia K. Farr for pointing this out to me.

8. For a view contrary to mine, see Held 1985.

9. For discussion of plurality in Emecheta, see Ward 1990, 87.

10. This passage echoes one in Ngugi's *Weep Not, Child*. During the Mau Mau uprising, the African schoolboys are warned to stay home. The hero's brother, however, tells him "there's no safety anywhere. There's no hiding in this naked land" (1964, 94).

11. On this point, see also Brown 1981, 38-43.

12. I am thinking here most particularly of the work of Nancy Topping Bazin, who has published widely on Emecheta, focusing usually on the feminism in her fiction (1985a, 1985b, 1986, 1989). I am grateful to her, however, because the overt feminism in her approach has helped me see my own work in a different light.

13. Jürgen Martini quotes one reviewer who admits: "I kept shouting at Adah as I read on, leave the bastard. You don't need him" (1986, 230). Rolf Solberg writes that Adah is "fettered to a useless slob of a Nigerian student husband" (1983, 250).

14. In a 1986 essay, Bazin focuses exclusively on the passages that describe how hard it is to be female in Emecheta's culture (35). Apparently unable to see how the narrator defends some customs we find most repellent, Bazin argues of Emecheta's novels that they "reveal the extent to which the African woman's oppression is engrained in the African mores" (36). In contrast, Martini notes that Emecheta "does not judge African society and the subjugation of women by using Western and feminist standards" (1986, 232).

15. Though courtship is missing in *Second-Class Citizen*, it provides much of the plot in *The Bride Price*, a novel that presents similar interpretive difficulties for Western readers—largely *because of* an emphasis on romance.

16. Catharine A. MacKinnon might argue that Adah has become simultaneously alienated and objectified (1982, 539).

17. Emecheta suggests that she could have portrayed Francis "even more scathingly" than she chose to (Schipper 1985, 44-45).

18. Bazin, for example, opens two of her essays with the assertion, "Feminist consciousness permeates the works of four major female novelists from black Africa"—including those of Emecheta (1985a, 183; see also 1989).

19. This theme, ordinarily so alien to Western readers, is central to Anzia Yezierska's 1925 novel *Bread Givers*, where the women in an orthodox Jewish family are expected to support the scholarly father.

20. Jaggar challenges this public/private division, arguing that "the distinction between the so-called public and private spheres obscures their interpenetration and essential unity" (1988, 146).

21. See also Weedon 1987, 21-41.

22. In this context, see M. Z. Rosaldo (1980, 395-96) for a warning of what we will miss if we insist on starting with "the universalizing questions."

23. For commentary on Gates's ideas, see Esonwanne 1992.

24. Perhaps Soyinka's most devastating signifying occurs during the embassy reception when Monica Faseyi, the white European wife of a black African professional, disgraces him and shocks the rest of the company by not behaving European enough (Soyinka 1965, 42-43). Other African male writers who can be said to signify on Western literature include Armah, Nkosi, and Ngugi.

25. For discussion of unintended heteroglossia in Emecheta's fiction, see Eustace Palmer 1982 and 1983.

4

The Sense of an Ending

For all the widely publicized nonnarrative or antinarrative forms of thought that are supposed to characterize our time . . . we remain more determined by narrative than we might wish to believe.

Peter Brooks
Reading for the Plot: Design and Intention in Narrative (1984, 7)

There has been a very widespread retreat from social thinking, rationalized by the formula that almost all good things are done by individuals, almost all bad things by societies.

Raymond Williams
The Long Revolution (1961, 109)

A MATTER OF GENRES

In this chapter I continue to examine the "human constants" of narrative poetics, suggesting most particularly how our understanding of African novels is affected by their resolutions. In the previous chapter I argued that the content of narrative differs from one culture to another, that the theme of romantic love, for example, which is so fundamental to narrative in the West, is largely absent from African fiction. Here I intend to argue that the shape of narratives differs from one culture to another, that what might constitute a tragic outcome in the West is not necessarily tragic in Africa. What I examine, therefore, is narrative *telos*, the direction taken by the plots of these three African novels, with special attention paid to their endings. I work from the premise that all societies are constituted in narrative and that members of a given society share a vision of themselves that helps to distinguish them from members of other societies. This shared narrative vision, which is a form of social mythology, helps give shape and meaning to the narratives of our lives and those of our novels.[1] If, then, as I have been arguing, our Western mythology does not envision the same social good as Emecheta's, it is also true that our narrative telos will not coincide with her own. But because this telos informs the very fabric of our being, it is virtually impossible for us not to invoke it as we read. What I want to illustrate in this chapter, therefore, is how tempting it is for us to apply our own narrative telos but also how inappropriate such an application can be. In sum, the familiar patterns that improve understanding in one interpretive situation may serve to impede it in another.

Writing in the philosophy of the social sciences, Richard J. Bernstein argues similarly that different cultures have different *genres* that are "embedded in social practices, and these genres may not lend themselves to translation in any simple or direct way into those with which we are familiar" (1989, 103).[2] Most commonly, these differences manifest themselves in the debates over rationality and relativism, as cultural anthropologists try to decide how to reconcile alien beliefs in magic with their own Western tradition of scientific instrumentality.[3] Because the categories of science and even religion, for example, are both particularly ill-suited to explain that of magic or juju, we in the West may have to devise new genres or find a way to modify the genres we know "in order to *compare* what may be *incommensurable*. The art here is one of knowing what are the right questions to ask in approaching the strange practices of an alien culture" (103). Bernstein is not describing literary genres here, but his argument is the same as mine: we have been trained to think (and read) in deeply rooted and largely invisible social patterns that are culturally specific. When we are faced with the task of reading the texts of an alien culture, these patterns help shape our understanding without our even being aware of their influence. Once more, then, we are faced with the necessity of foregrounding the expectations we bring to a text—and of asking whether our Western genres (literary and otherwise) can be used as they stand, whether they need to be modified, or whether they need to be replaced altogether.

That narrative functions on a structural level as a system of ideological representations is something most women writers have intuited throughout the twentieth century, according to the argument put forward by Rachel Blau DuPlessis in *Writing Beyond the Ending*. DuPlessis finds, in fact, that a common narrative "project" has united scores of these writers, including Olive Schreiner, Virginia Woolf, Margaret Atwood, Alice Walker, and Doris Lessing—all of whom have used their own work to examine how socially scripted gender relationships have found their way into fiction, where they help determine the narrative's content and its form (1985, 4). On these two narrative fronts—thematic and formal—twentieth-century women writers have attacked the dominant gender ideology of their time. Formally speaking, the most significant challenge to traditional ways of organizing society has occurred in the new kind of endings

The Sense of an Ending

women have devised for their novels (5). DuPlessis argues for the importance of endings because it is at the end of a novel that "the word 'convention' is found resonating between its literary and social meanings" (3). In the nineteenth-century romances that provide the background for her study, the conventional endings for women were marriage and death—marriage if the heroine did what was expected of her, death if she did not. Twentieth-century women writers, having rejected these restrictive conventions, have been faced with the question of how to liberate their heroines from the old stories. The disruptive narrative strategies these writers have evolved constitute the focus of DuPlessis's study. Since the narrative patterns we encounter in fiction can help determine how we organize and define our own lives, the ability to disrupt the old stories is of more than theoretical interest. In effect, by liberating their heroines from the old scripts, twentieth-century women writers have provided us with new models of female behavior. Not only do these models give us new ways of defining ourselves and organizing society, but, in breaking with the past so dramatically, they remind us that social scripts are themselves constructed in language and thus changeable (DuPlessis, 133).

Though I, too, am working from the premise that ideology is contained in narrative, I do not think we should simply slip Emecheta into the list of twentieth-century women writers that DuPlessis discusses. While Buchi Emecheta would probably be sympathetic to their efforts, I doubt she would regard herself as a participant in their Western feminist project. Rolf Solberg, for example, has asked her if "she is a feminist." She replied: "Not in the western [*sic*] sense, no. Because I think our problem is beyond feminism." She goes on to explain that "until [the men] are free you can't really . . . claim to be a feminist" (1983, 260; ellipses in original).[4] In *Head Above Water* she says that she had never even heard of feminism until 1975, when she was invited to speak in celebration of the International Woman's Year. During the conference, the white women in attendance debated such issues as "birth control in the Third World, and how the Third World women were suffering." As a result of having to hear these white women discuss black women's problems with such apparent cultural superiority, Emecheta says she now finds herself "disagreeing on everything suggested by white women" (1986, 190).

Given these remarks, it seems especially important to read her novels aware of the fact that different cultures give rise to different literary conventions and that the feminism in her fiction is not necessarily our own. What particularly concerns me in this chapter, therefore, is how Western readers interpret the endings of these three woman-centered but African-based novels. At the conclusion of *The Bride Price*, for example, the heroine is punished by death for violating custom and taboos. By the end of *The Slave Girl*, the newly freed heroine is utterly content to be enslaved both by marriage and by tradition. In *The Joys of Motherhood*, the heroine, who has chosen to conform to societal expectations, nonetheless dies at the end, unhappy and virtually deserted by her family. Are these endings, as they certainly appear to be, unhappy?[5] Or is this a misreading based on cultural differences? I have already suggested that the conclusion to *Second-Class Citizen* is problematic because it does not have the same meaning for us as it does for Adah Obi herself. In Western terms, the novel seems to rupture the old stories, for once Adah escapes the confines of marriage, she is not punished for refusing the role her culture would assign her; instead, she is apparently free to do and become whatever she wants. By freeing her heroine from social and novelistic conventions, therefore, Emecheta seems to be participating in the same narrative liberation movement as that undertaken by Western women writers. Though feminist readers might applaud Emecheta's ostensible narrative dissent, however, Adah herself recognizes that the end of her marriage is not exactly something to celebrate. If we applaud the separation, are we then transforming an African text into a Western one and thus misunderstanding it? In Cynthia Ward's terms, are we practicing criticism that shores up our own power and influence, by erasing "individual distinction and historicity within and between groups of people" (1990, 85)? Or, in Christopher Miller's terms (1988), are we asking an African text to meet certain Western needs and solve particular Western political problems?

The Bride Price (1976)

NARRATIVE INTENTIONS

Returning to the issue of narrative intention, the question raised by the ending of *The Bride Price* then becomes the following: toward what goal has this novel been oriented? Or, more specifically, what direction do *Western readers* expect this novel to take? Does this expectation help us understand the novel, or does it interfere with understanding? For those of us who were trained to find patterns in literature by Northrop Frye's *Anatomy of Criticism*, I would argue that the tacit assumptions we bring to *The Bride Price* virtually ensure that we will (try to) read it as New Comedy.[6] This mode, according to Frye, is commonly centered on "an erotic intrigue between a young man and a young woman which is blocked by some kind of opposition, usually paternal, and resolved by a twist in the plot." Although the blocking agents initially govern society, a new society emerges at the end "after a discovery in which the hero becomes wealthy or the heroine respectable" (1957, 44). As we can see from the following outline, for most of Emecheta's novel this comic pattern holds true— just long enough for us to expect a happy ending. But, ultimately, the narrator disappoints our expectations: first by failing to redeem the hero, then by killing off the heroine and apparently agreeing that it is best that she die, and finally by reinstating the power of the old society.

When Aku-nna is thirteen years old, her father dies unexpectedly. Following tradition, Ma Blackie takes her two children back to Ibuza to live, where she marries her husband's older brother. Shortly after Ma Blackie's marriage, the community school teacher falls in love with Aku-nna and begins to court her. [Boy meets girl.] Their love is forbidden, however, because Chike is the descendant of slaves. [Outside interference tries to keep them apart.] Though Aku-nna is widely sought after by many suitors, she knows she will be happy only with Chike. Once she becomes eligible for marriage, one of her suitors arranges to kidnap her—which, according to custom, is a legitimate way of getting a wife. [Boy loses girl to outside interference.] To save her virginity after she is captured, Aku-nna tells Okoboshi the lie that she has already had sexual intercourse with Chike. She then finally escapes and runs off with the man she loves. [Boy regains girl.] Her uncle is so enraged by her scandalous behavior that he divorces her mother and refuses to accept the bride price from Chike's father. [Here the comic plot begins to break down.] Aku-nna and Chike love one another deeply, but she never recovers from the fact that her village and family refuse to forgive her. The novel ends when Aku-nna dies giving birth to a daughter whom Chike names Joy. Following Aku-nna's death, the narrator concludes the novel with an extraordinary paragraph, in which she explains that ultimately Chike and Aku-nna reinforced "the traditional superstition" they had been unwittingly challenging (Emecheta 1976, 168). Moreover, she tells us that Aku-nna's death is used by her people as an object lesson to young girls, who are warned not to pick husbands on their own and to make sure their bride price is paid. If it is not paid, they will surely die, like Aku-nna, in childbirth. This cautionary tale, according to the narrator, still carries "psychological" weight today, but why it does is "anybody's guess" (168).

If we have been reading the novel expecting a comic resolution, not only are we astounded by Aku-nna's untimely death, but we are at a loss as to what to make of the narrator's attitude toward it.[7] Are we to mourn Aku-nna and pity her for her foolishness? Is her death tragic? Or is it a necessary punishment for her sins? Should we be glad for her society that its values were upheld? But if, indeed, Aku-nna must die, we expect at least the narrator to be sorrowful over this necessity. When she expresses no sorrow, she challenges us to rethink the genre we have been using to understand the novel. Clearly, the conflict between an individual and her society is more complicated here than we had originally been led (by our own cultural expectations) to believe. A Western reading would assume that tradition had somehow failed Aku-nna because it punished her for being herself. But the narrator's concluding remarks cast doubt on this interpretation. It will be recalled that the first time Emecheta wrote this book, the story ended with Aku-nna and Chike "living happily ever after, disregarding their people" (Emecheta 1986, 166). But Emecheta finally concluded that the community's values were more important than a (Western-style) happy ending. So when she rewrote the story, she created a girl who purposely picked "her own husband because she was 'modern' but was not quite strong enough to shake off all the tradition and taboos" (165).[8] Aku-nna is thus destroyed by the guilt she feels for having disobeyed her mother and uncle. This outcome, justifiable as it might appear to Emecheta, troubles most Western readers, however, because of our predisposition to side with these two lovers, who have become social outcasts.[9] It troubles us, in other words, because the beliefs it is based on are embedded in a tradition alien to our own.[10]

At the same time, an obverse reading to the one just proposed—that Aku-nna fails her people by violating tradition—seems equally questionable since for most of the novel the narrator is extremely sympathetic to this rebellious heroine.[11] Emecheta achieves this sympathy, in part, by narrating the novel from Aku-nna's point of view. The opening scenes, for example, seem calculated to pull on our heartstrings, as we witness first the unusually close relationship between father and daughter—and then see this bond torn apart by the father's unexpected death. In fact, Emecheta's heroines are usually closer to their fathers than to their mothers. Aku-nna's relationship, in particular, seems to symbolize that she would like to take over the role of the father by deciding for herself what she will do. After her father dies, it seems significant that Aku-nna temporarily loses her voice during the mourning rituals. This double loss (father/voice) suggests that in losing her father she has lost an advocate. At the same time, the death of her father can be seen symbolically as the Death of the Fathers; for once she has regained her voice, she "speaks out" against the Will of the Fathers by going against tradition. But hers is an ill-fated rebellion, soon silenced by the Voice of Tradition. What happens here is similar to what Peter Brooks describes as happening in Balzac's *La Peau de chagrin* (suggesting that some European fiction can, indeed, help us understand Emecheta's novels). When the father dies, Brooks argues, "the Name-of-the-Father—the father as prohibition, law, 'morality'—emerges only the stronger, to be submitted to in full abnegation, or else rejected in a total revolt" (1984, 56). Aku-nna's rebellion fails, as we see later, because she is incapable of marshalling the resources needed for the total rebellion Brooks identifies. But before the failure becomes manifest, Aku-nna does seem to be assuming her father's protective mantle.

Once Aku-nna moves to Ibuza, for example, she becomes convinced that she will have to help take care of her mother and thinks she might be able to do so by becoming a teacher. She recalls sadly at this point that her father had wanted her to have more education (66). But this same loving father has named his daughter "Aku-nna, meaning literally 'father's wealth,' knowing that the only consolation he could count on from her would be her bride price."[12] What the narrator means by "consolation" is not entirely clear, however. Does Ezekiel need consolation because he is disappointed that Aku-nna is not a son? Or does he need it because he will lose Aku-nna to another man? Or both? Whatever the meaning, Aku-nna herself is not upset by the arrangement. In fact, she only hopes she will not be a disappointment to him (10). Our sympathy for Aku-nna deepens after her father's death, when we see how ill at ease she is in her new surroundings. Though Ibuza is the village of her ancestors, Aku-nna is so unfamiliar with the customs of her people that one of her young relatives chastises her for her ignorance. Her mother is not much help either. It is not only ignorance but also shyness that makes the transition hard for Aku-nna. Not having been raised in Ibuza, for example, she cannot understand why it is acceptable for men to see her bathing naked in the stream or for her suitors to play roughly with her breasts. These customs are also alien to Western readers, who probably have much the same reaction to them as Aku-nna. Perhaps we sympathize with her as much as we do because she is like us in being unfamiliar—and uncomfortable—with Ibuza customs.[13]

For his part, Chike makes a perfect Western hero. He is a handsome, charming, reformed rake who is absolutely devoted to his new love—treating her with kindness and compassion when everyone else ignores her. Perhaps the most touching scene in the novel occurs when Aku-nna gets her menarche during school. She is in pain and embarrassed, but Chike is so gentle and tactful that she lets him take care of her. After giving her an aspirin, he loans her his jacket so no one can see the blood on her dress; later he brings her a supply of sanitary napkins with a little booklet explaining what to do—all this from a man whose culture still teaches that a menstruating woman is unclean (93). It is no wonder Aku-nna falls in love with Chike. We practically do ourselves. Our sympathy only intensifies when it becomes clear that Chike and Aku-nna will not be allowed to marry because his ancestors were slaves.[14] To us, this is a prohibition that makes very little sense. But the villagers and the narrator insist that for her "to marry the descendant of a slave would be an abomination" (110-11). Class differences we might be able to accept (especially if we were British), but this goes beyond class. Chike, in fact, comes from a wealthier (and better-educated) family than Aku-nna. Nor would we regard marriage to the descendants of slaves as an abomination. Such events occur without censure—or comment—all the time in our culture. In sum, Western readers have trouble anticipating—and accepting—the ending of *The Bride Price* because the narrator focuses so much attention on Aku-nna and Chike's courtship ritual. In watching them meet and gradually fall in love, we ourselves become emotionally involved in their relationship—especially as they have to contend with the older generation's prohibitions. Illustrative of the difference between African and Western readings is Chikwenye Okonjo Ogunyemi's description of Aku-nna and Chike's relationship. Where I as a Western reader enjoy the emotions evoked by their touching love story, Ogunyemi dismisses the "sentimentality evoked by the lovesick couple" (1983, 71). How, then, are we to read this novel? Since our Western comedic genre is not particularly useful, we need to ask if we have any other genres that might do a better job of helping us understand Emecheta's novels.

EPIC OR NOVEL?

Bakhtin makes several distinctions between the epic and the novel that are useful to Western readers trying to understand Emecheta's fiction. The epic he associates with the "absolute past" and the power of tradition because it speaks in the monologic voice of unquestioned authority (1987, 15). The novel, on the other hand, "is determined by experience, knowledge and practice (the future)" (15). Its dialogic (competing) voices speak in "unofficial language and unofficial thought" (20). In short, where the epic is a closed genre reflective of what has already occurred, the novel is open—to the present and the future. As such, the novel is almost by definition a progressive genre. Since we in the West believe that Chike and Aku-nna would do no lasting harm to society by falling in love and marrying, at first glance "epic" seems a more suitable term to describe *The Bride Price* than "novel," as it certainly appears to valorize the past and to reaffirm tradition. Because we value individual rights over community rights and because we cannot take seriously the taboos surrounding the descendants of former slaves, we think Chike and Aku-nna should be free to marry. From our perspective Aku-nna's punishment by death is unwarranted, unmotivated, and implausible. To us, this ending is reactionary, invoking the archetypal endings of an absolute past[15] when heroines were not free to do and become what they wanted.

But if we read the novel from more of an Africanized perspective, the ending, while perhaps not very progressive, does not seem to be particularly reactionary. It is conservative in that it does reestablish the old society, but Aku-nna and Chike's transgressions apparently threaten the very fabric of village life—as is evident in the villagers' response. In revenge for Aku-nna's behavior, for example, the Ofulues destroy all the vegetation on the plantation owned by Chike's father, and Ma Blackie's new husband divorces her. Though we in the West are horrified that Aku-nna must die to reaffirm her people's tradition, the narrative suggests that the sacrifice of this individual rebel is necessary for the well-being of the community. In her death, moreover, Aku-nna signals that she has accepted the importance of tradition. Because these traditions can be quite flexible, Ward argues that it is not necessary for Aku-nna to accept them blindly (1990). But Alasdair MacIntyre, another student of tradition, sheds a different light on the situation when he argues that because an individual is part of an ongoing (narrative) history, she becomes, consciously or not, "one of the bearers of a tradition"—an assertion the novel seems to support (1984b, 221). For even though Aku-nna might have felt initially that her actions were her own and thus of little interest to the community, she soon comes to realize that she herself is the community, that what she and Chike do affects everyone, not just themselves. After trying to make a life for herself, she realizes that she can live only within the community that raised her. Her death therefore becomes a symbol for the fact that she has finally accepted her role as a bearer of her people's African traditions.

But for us in the West to see that the ending of *The Bride Price* is not necessarily so tragic, we have to be able to foreground our own prejudices—and listen to the competing voices that, in Bakhtin's terms, make this more a novel than an epic. Whereas the monologic epic has a "singular belief system," the dialogic heteroglossia of a novel makes for multiple competing belief systems (1987, 334). Bakhtin finds, moreover, a correlation between what a character does and says—with the one informing the other ideologically (334). In the dialogic or competitive environs of a novel, unlike the monologic world of epic, the hero's discourse is constantly being challenged, leading Bakhtin to argue that the "idea of testing the hero" may be the single most important "organizing idea in the novel" (388). Here Bakhtin distinguishes between "authoritative discourse" and "internally persuasive discourse"—which I invoked in my discussion of Adah Obi. Authoritative discourse originates externally in religion, politics, and morality. It is, therefore, associated, like the epic, with the authority of the past and treated like "the word of the fathers . . . . It is akin to taboo." Internally persuasive discourse reflects the ideology of the individual character, but, in direct contrast to authoritative discourse, it carries no status in society (342). Within a novel (but never an epic), these two kinds of discourses engage one another dialogically in the consciousness of a single character, helping to form his or her belief system (343). In what I will then call Emecheta's *novel*, the struggle between Aku-nna's internal discourse and the authoritative discourse of her African fathers can be seen most readily in how the hero/heroine copes with the pressures of tradition. Though Aku-nna listens to her own internal discourse and finds the courage to reject certain traditions, others she dutifully accepts.

Let us first look at the customs Aku-nna accepts, those that have to do with menstruation—the symbol of her womanhood that signifies her marriageability. She begins with a minor rebellion that she is unable to sustain. Because she does not want her family to arrange a marriage for her, she keeps the fact of her menarche secret for two months. She reveals her secret to her friends only when she needs to consult with them whether it will be permissible for her to cross a stream in her "unclean" condition. Far better to tell her friends, she thinks, than to risk being treated forever "as an outcast leper" (108). When Aku-nna finally does cross the stream, she prays "that the god of the stream would be lenient with her for this terrible sin she was committing" (112). This scene at the river suggests the differences between Emecheta's African and our Western attitudes toward nature, a difference that would certainly seem to favor Africa. Though it would never occur to most Westerners that they could sin against a river no matter what the act involved, we might all be better off if we were able to conceive of this possibility, as much of the world continues to use its fresh waterways (and its oceans) as repositories of untreated sewage. But

Aku-nna is a traditional African woman who has been taught by her people the necessity of maintaining the purity of the village water supply. This teaching has been reinforced through myth and taboos to such an extent that it constitutes the very fabric of Aku-nna's being. Rather than reading these taboos as evidence of the sexism in Aku-nna's culture, Western feminists might better ask what is served by such customs. Philomina Chioma Steady argues, for example, that the taboos surrounding menstruation are not as misogynistic as they might seem to Westerners, since semen also "can be seen as polluting" (1981, 32).

Though it simply does not occur to Aku-nna to question her unclean status as a menstruating woman, she does question other taboos—if only implicitly. In Bakhtin's terms, Aku-nna represents a "potential discourse," which is largely unspoken but nonetheless quite evident from her actions (1987, 334). In this novel, the authoritarian, closed language of the fathers (custom, tradition, taboo) is continually being challenged by the unofficial, open language of the daughters—a challenge seen in most of Emecheta's other novels. Though the language spoken by the daughters is not the revolutionary woman's language called for by French feminists, the terms of the battle are quite similar. Emecheta herself clearly establishes the primacy of the fathers' language. As soon as Aku-nna's stepfather, Okonkwo, learns that she has begun menstruating, he tells her she must give up her friendship with Chike, speaking to her in "the voice of authority . . . which was a kind of legalised power. He was telling her, not in so many words, that she could never escape" (116). The discourse of the fathers is so powerful that Okonkwo needs no words to tell Aku-nna she is trapped by tradition. She knows it, and the knowledge destroys her. Because the men hold the women enthralled by the power of the authoritative discourse of the fathers, the daughters must speak another language (an internally persuasive unofficial discourse) if they are ever to liberate themselves. When Aku-nna is kidnapped, it looks for a while as if she just might have the will to speak such a language. She is so sickened by the prospects of being married to Okoboshi that she achieves a mysterious strength that gives her courage to defend herself and "fight . . . for her honour" (136). Significantly, she saves herself by what she says—and what she says is a lie. It is a lie that overturns reality by challenging the legitimacy of the fathers' discourse. Furthermore, it is a lie that insults Okoboshi's manhood. Aku-nna says scornfully that his father is merely a "dog chief," since all he has been capable of stealing is "a girl who has been taught what men taste like by a slave" (138). But hers is a doomed rebellion. Though she successfully defends herself against her kidnapper's sexual advances, she is soon discouraged by the realization that she has nowhere to run. Because she has brought shame on her family, her uncle prevents her mother from intervening and would kill her himself if he caught her. But Aku-nna knows that if she has to stay with her kidnappers, she will not live long since no one violates "the laws of the land and survives" (141).[16] Even after betraying her people, Aku-nna remains a believer, begging Chike, for example, to pay her bride price so she will not die in childbirth. Though Chike's father offers her uncle a large sum of money, Okonkwo refuses to accept it. Determined to kill this girl who has brought such shame on his household, Okonkwo makes a fetish in Aku-nna's image, the purpose of which is to force her to come home (162). Soon Aku-nna tells Chike's father that her stepfather "calls me back in the wind." Though she vows to stay, inevitably she surrenders to the authority of the fathers' discourse—the "voice" that tells her to return to her family (163).

HETEROGLOSSIA AND TEXTUAL PLURALITY

Although Aku-nna's internal discourse is no match for the authoritative discourse of her African fathers and she herself is ultimately silenced by death, the novel itself is a veritable forum of competing discourses. Additional heteroglossia is evident, for example, in statements such as the following one, which describes Ma Blackie's attempts to have a third child by Ezekiel; desperate, she returns to her village in hopes that she can "placate their Oboshi river goddess into giving her some babies" (8). There is no way that this statement can have the same meaning for Westerners as it would for Africans. It is not even clear that it would have any meaning for Westerners, if by this we mean to imply we actually think we understand what has been said. For, at best, we would probably consider it a quaint notion that a river goddess would have anything at all to do with fertility. We certainly would never believe it. What is a river goddess anyway? More particularly, what is an *Oboshi* river goddess? This passage and our questions about it suggest that Emecheta has not forsworn her African point of view, for the narrator never questions the premise behind Ma Blackie's attempts to placate the river goddess. There is absolutely no suggestion that the narrator thinks it is either a quaint or irrational approach to what (most) Westerners would regard as a straightforward medical problem. The question arises, therefore, of how we Westerners are to read Ma Blackie's behavior and informing beliefs. Do we accept her behavior on its own terms and regard it as rational, or do we judge it on our terms and regard it as irrational?[17] At the very least, if we are sincere about trying to make sense out of an alien practice, we might do well to return once more to Peter Winch's advice about understanding Azande magic. It will be recalled from my discussion of his ideas in previous chapters that Winch believes it is wrong for us to try to force the Zande category into our own familiar distinction between science and non-science. Instead, because it is, after all, we who want to understand them, we have the far more difficult challenge of trying "to extend our understanding" of their categories (1964, 319). As we have already seen in our discussion of genres, Bernstein argues that the "primary issue [for Winch] is not whether the Azande make logical inferences according to the same rules that we use." Rather, what is at issue is "how we *classify* what they are doing" (1989, 102).

To return, then, to the practice in question, Ma Blackie's visit to a river goddess. In describing the place of river goddesses in African culture, Elaine Savory Fido reports that such a "deity is usually beautiful, seductive, powerful," whose actions "can vary between malevolence and protective good nature" (1986, 235). This description, however, does not offer much help to us Western readers who are still not quite sure how to categorize the concept of a river goddess. What we want to know is, how does placating a river goddess compare, for example, with our Western notion of prayer? How does it compare with soliciting advice from a medical doctor? Or are both these categories insufficient for understanding what is going on here? Is there a genre somewhere between faith and medical science that might be more useful to us in coming to terms with Ma Blackie's pilgrimage? Moreover, have the attitudes of Igbos themselves toward their own river goddesses changed significantly over the years? How would these or other African readers today interpret Ma Blackie's behavior? Would they find the behavior quaint and outdated? Or would they find real value in what she is doing? Unfortunately, Emecheta's novel remains silent on these questions—and in so doing reminds us of the differences that separate us.

Other examples of heteroglossia (which lead to similar problems of classification and interpretation) can be found in the African terminology that Emecheta includes—terms that also reflect a worldview alien to that of the West. As a child, Aku-nna gets sick every time an illness goes around; she is sick so often that Ma Blackie often implores her daughter to make up her mind if "she was going to live or die." This seems relatively clear. Any distraught Western parent might say the same thing. But then the text continues with the information that Ma Blackie could not tolerate "a 'living dead', an *ogbanje*" (9). Emecheta does not stop to explain just what the term "living dead" means to these people. It does not mean what Westerners mean by it. It is not the same as a zombie. An ogbanje is a baby or small child who refuses to stay alive or dead: to torment its parents, it keeps getting born and then dies soon thereafter. In other words, if a family has three or four young babies die, it is the same ogbanje being born over and over again.

Ezekiel's response to his wife's infertility is another classic example of the heteroglossia in this novel, as it moves from one worldview to another in a single sentence. Keenly disappointed by the fact that he has only one son, he reminds Ma Blackie how unfair it is since once he had "paid this heavy *bride price*[,] he had had their marriage *sanctified by Anglicanism*" (9; emphases added).[18] Ezekiel's funeral is a more extensive example of heteroglossia, as its components are created out of a melange of the old and the new (29). When it comes time to decide who gets to stay beside the body, Ezekiel's friends are faced with a real problem since the choice of mourners will determine where he goes after death. The men want him to join his father in the earth, but the more rebellious Lagos women "preferred Nna to go to heaven," attracted as they are to the exotic "imported" religion (40, 42). In making the distinction between the old and the new, the narrator unexpectedly describes the old way as "pagan"—thus raising the question of whether she shares the Christians' negative perception of indigenous African religions (40). This question is raised in another passage when the narrator, having been a kind of advocate for her culture, suddenly takes the viewpoint of an outsider (who seems to have her own problems with classification). It is relatively easy, the narrator notes, for a visitor to see that Ibuza is an Igbo village. It is harder, however, to decide "whether to classify the people as Christians or pagans" (100). As much as the term "pagan" sticks out here, it is also not clear what the term "Christian" means to people who believe in river goddesses, bride prices, and ogbanjes. Certainly, it does not quite mean what it would to a Western Christian. Other terms that are familiar to Westerners also have a different meaning in this African novel. The concept of "father" is extended to those male relatives who take care of children (18); "and in Ibuza one's brother-in-law was also given the title of husband" (46). Some children might have such an abundance of "mothers" and "fathers" that they "may not see much of [their] true parents" (37). The fact that the narrator explains these customs at all, of course, suggests a Western influence—for African readers (or at least most Nigerian readers) would already know about them and not need to have them explained.[19]

In sum, in *The Bride Price* there is, indeed, a rich and complex dialogic relationship between the voices of tradition and those in rebellion against tradition—the very dialogic heteroglossia that helps qualify this text as a novel. But even though Aku-nna's unofficial challenge to authoritative discourse helps open the text to many interpretations, Aku-nna herself eventually does allow the Voice of the Fathers to overwhelm her internal voice, graphically reminding us of how dependent we are on others for our sense of self and our sense of reality.[20]

COMPETING DISCOURSES AND THE CONSTRUCTION OF REALITY

In *The Social Construction of Reality*, Berger and Luckmann describe a dialogic relationship between the individual and society that is similar to the one Bakhtin describes. Though objective and subjective reality can be characterized as basically "symmetrical," on Berger and Luckmann's view, there is always more objective reality than an individual can internalize (1967, 133-34). Because we simultaneously experience ourselves as a part of, and apart from, society, the status of the relationship between external and internal reality, then, is always being negotiated; in short, it is dialogic and dialectical (134). The "instrument" of our socialization, moreover, is language itself (133) as it has been incorporated in "moral instruction, inspirational poetry, religious allegory and whatnot" (69). At the same time that the maintenance of external reality is dependent on our conversation with others, the maintenance of an individual's subjective reality is also dependent on our various language systems (152). In sum, language defines us as human and saves us from the terrors of isolation (102).[21] As Emecheta's novel convincingly illustrates, because of our (discursive) interdependence, even the simplest challenges to everyday reality are hard to maintain without some sort of group support. In most cases of individual rebellion, according to Berger and Luckmann, the heretic surrenders to the superior strength of the community with very little fanfare. In extreme cases, however, when someone seriously threatens everyday reality, society takes more active measures to protect itself by trying to re-educate the rebel. In effect, the rebel is talked out of her heresy through the therapeutic maneuvers of the analyst's couch or the confessional. If this relatively benign persuasive route fails, society labels the heretic insane or criminal and, if necessary, incarcerates her for either her own or society's good. African societies may be less threatened by heretics, may try to call them back to the fold by the informal intervention of relatives or friends, but the principle remains intact: individuals must fit into their social roles. The person who fails to be socialized, according to Berger and Luckmann, "is socially predefined as a profiled type—the cripple, the bastard, the idiot, and so on" (165). Such predefining has the socially desirable consequence of denying both plausibility and permanency to any heretical self-definitions that the individual might dream up (166).

So it is in *The Bride Price*. For whatever reason, Aku-nna does not accept all teachings of her people's authoritative discourse as her own. But in rejecting one of her people's most fundamental tenets, she fails to find enough external support to sustain her rebellion. Though Chike clearly adores her, his love is not enough to counter the overwhelming influence of what Bakhtin calls tradition "sacred and sacrosanct" (1987, 16). Though the discourse of *The Bride Price* is not to be *equated* with that of an epic, therefore, the ideals of the past are justified and reconfirmed here in a process that is *similar to* what occurs in an epic. Tradition is not only how things were done but how they are still done. When Aku-nna's father dies, for example, even though Ma Blackie is still alive, her people treat Aku-nna like an orphan. Even in modern-day Nigeria, the narrator observes, a family without a father is "in fact a non-existing family. Such traditions do not change very much" (28).[22] In Berger and Luckmann's terms, therefore, we might say that Aku-nna has been socially predefined as an "orphan"—or, at the very least, she has been allowed to forget that she is a child of the community and must abide by its conventions. Chike is by birth socially predefined as an outcast. When they fall in love and break a taboo, therefore, they are simply acting out the outsider status they seem already to have. Because they are outsiders, their actions can have no validity or merit. Chike is doomed to social approbation and isolation because of his ancestry, but Aku-nna must be reunited with her people, if only in death—for tradition must be honored. Because this is a novel and not an epic, however, the ideals of the past are also shown to be vulnerable to challenge—a vulnerability that we have already seen in the text's abundant dialogic heteroglossia.

Though, indeed, Aku-nna herself fails the heroine's test and is ultimately silenced by death, neither side achieves narrative hegemony. The fathers fail to silence the heroine's internal discourse (Aku-nna never does go home), and the heroine fails to overthrow the fathers. Complicating the issue for Western feminist readers, however, is the fact that the fathers' language represents traditional African values, whereas the daughter's language, in some respects, represents almost a Western alternative to these old ways.[23] Lest we think that the novel's meaning lies only with the daughter's voice, however, it is important to remember that the narrator speaks in yet another voice—one that is richly complex and full of contradictions (see Slomski 1986).

In *The Bride Price*, as in all of Emecheta's fiction, the narrator functions as a kind of mediating voice between the fathers' and daughters' discourse—and between an African and Western discourse. Because Emecheta's narrator mediates between cultures, we might even suggest, adapting an idea from Marcus and Fischer, that she is functioning as an ethnographer. Envisioning the ethnographer as positioned *outside* the alien culture, however, they suggest—borrowing themselves from Clifford Geertz—that an ethnographer juxtaposes the alien culture's "experience-near or local concepts" with those "experience-far concepts that the writer shares with his readership" (1986, 31).[24] For my purposes I want to reverse the stance and suggest that the writer (narrator) in Emecheta's case is more likely to share the experience-near or local concepts with her subjects and, as a consequence, is frequently not speaking in terms familiar to her readers.[25] Though we, as Western readers, may be tempted to see the narrator as speaking primarily in experience-distant concepts (our own), I think it is a temptation we must work to overcome. This shift cannot help but remind us that much of what we read is truly alien to our Western experience and not easily accommodated within our own horizons. Only by accepting these differences, after all, do we have any hope of seeing ourselves anew. This is not to say that we are so locked into our own language game that we cannot understand anything in the alien culture; it is to say that it is more difficult to understand than we might wish—or think. For Marcus and Fischer, when we attempt to understand across cultures, the ethnographer functions for us "as mediator between distinct sets of categories and cultural conceptions that interact in different ways at different points" (1986, 31). From this I infer that we can expect some interactions to be relatively painless while others will be almost unbearably difficult. Clearly, there is much in Emecheta's fiction I feel confident I understand. But I am equally confident that much of this confidence is misplaced.

Following the passage cited previously in which Okonkwo has told Aku-nna to break off relations with Chike, for example, is this statement: "He walked away, leaving her standing there by the egbo trees, *for he must not come near or touch her now when she was unclean*" (116; emphasis added). What is unclear in this sentence is whose point of view the italicized part represents. It immediately follows Okonkwo's authoritative statements and could represent his thinking. Yet it is contained in a paragraph that expresses Aku-nna's point of view and internal thinking. We can be certain that Okonkwo, the Voice of the village Fathers, would *share* the perception that she is unclean. We can also be pretty certain from what occurred at the stream that Aku-nna shares the same perception. But we cannot tell whether the narrator joins them. In short, though we know who *could* be speaking, we are not sure who *is* speaking. According to Barthes, a text's plurality reveals itself in our inability to decide who is speaking—in fact, the "more indeterminate the origin of the statement, the more plural the text" (1974, 41). The more plural the text, we might add, the more difficult our interpretive task of understanding. While we might simply be content, in this postmodern age, to enjoy the novel's plurality and let it go at that, if we accept Emecheta's texts as ethnographic documents (as they perforce must be accepted, at least to a certain degree), unthinkingly embracing their plurality seems a facile solution to a problem of "translation" that deserves more careful attention. At other times, however, submitting to the plurality of Emecheta's texts seems the "right" thing to do. Since the people who inhabit Emecheta's novel are, for the most part, not plagued by what Bernstein calls Cartesian anxiety, submitting to the plurality of her texts certainly seems an African thing to do.[26]

The Slave Girl (1977)

NARRATIVE TELOS

In *The Slave Girl*, Emecheta turns to the events of her mother's life for inspiration—seeming to affirm in the process a renewed respect for her own African heritage. As we might expect from her previous fiction, however, the loyalty Emecheta expresses for her African legacy has been somewhat tempered by her Western experiences. In several passages, for example, the narrator seems to reflect Emecheta's more modern perspective. But, overall, this same narrator seems fundamentally sympathetic to African culture. Even so, she is fully aware that her narrative is set in a time of incredible change, the transitional period of early colonization when the old Igbo ways were yielding to the "glamorous" new ways of the British conquerors and their handmaidens, the Evangelical Christian missionaries. The uncertainty and upheaval of this transitional period are evident in the novel's dialogic heteroglossia, as the two cultures blend and clash in virtually every scene—and the heroine is caught smack in the middle.

Emecheta elsewhere describes her mother as being "doubly culturally-enslaved," so it is not surprising that the heroine of *The Slave Girl* is even more conservative than the timid heroine of *The Bride Price* (1986, 5). Though Alice Ojebeta Ogbanje enjoys a few successful moments of minor rebellion, unlike Aku-nna she never represents a dangerous threat to her people's central traditions. Because hers is a story of someone who moves willingly from one master to another, the potential discourse that she represents is an internally persuasive one that very closely corresponds to the external, authoritative Voice of the Fathers. As a result, the ideology she expresses is very much in keeping with that of her people. She is so obedient, in fact, that the elements of Western culture she does adopt seem more to strengthen the hegemony of her African fathers than to challenge it. But because the narrator expresses an extraordinary ambivalence about her heroine's desire to remain enslaved to tradition, Ojebeta's unyielding social conservatism serves unexpectedly enough to enrich the plurality of meaning in *The Slave Girl*—thus trapping readers between cultures. But the narrator offers us no guidance out of this trap. In fact, she seems almost to have set it herself. As is often the case with Emecheta's fiction, however, the complexity of meaning is lodged within a fairly simple narrative framework.

Alice Ojebeta Ogbanje is a very special little girl because her parents, who already have two sons, have wanted a daughter for years. Because Umeadi's female babies have never before lived beyond infancy, Umeadi and her husband take extra precautions with this one, adorning her with elaborate charms to prevent her from returning to the land of the dead. Ironically, when Ojebeta is six years old, her parents themselves die from the influenza epidemic that is sweeping the globe—and her second brother, Okolie, sells her for eight pounds to Ma Palagada, a powerful trader at the Onitsha market. This woman teaches Ojebeta how to sew and sends her to the C.M.S. (Church Missionary Society) school to be educated with the other slaves. After Ojebeta has been a slave for several years, she meets Ma Palagada's son Clifford, who proposes marriage to her. Shortly thereafter Ma Palagada dies, her trading empire breaks up, and Ojebeta decides not to marry Clifford, choosing instead to return home to her people in Ibuza. There she starts a profitable business for herself selling palm oil. Not long afterward she meets and marries Jacob, a conventional, tradition-bound local man. Even though Ojebeta is married in church, she is still technically the property of the Palagadas. When Clifford Palagada asks to be reimbursed for his mother's purchase, therefore, Jacob willingly gives him the eight pounds in order to keep his marriage from being cursed. Once the debt is repaid, Ojebeta, kneeling in front of Jacob, thanks her "new owner" and admits to feeling "free in belonging to a new master" who hails from her hometown (Emecheta 1977, 179, 178). When Clifford and her brother joke about spending money on women, Ojebeta giggles in delight: "For had she not been rightly valued?" (179).

Are we to take these quoted passages at face value, or can we read them as examples of what Bakhtin calls "hybrid construction"—that is, statements that seem to emanate from one person but in reality convey "two semantic and axiological belief systems" (1987, 304). It is certainly tempting to argue that Ojebeta's own words are being used by the narrator to critique her willingness to accept enslavement. But whether we are right is another matter altogether, as the novel concludes even more ambiguously: "So as Britain was emerging from war . . . and claiming to have stopped the slavery which she had helped to spread in all her black colonies, Ojebeta . . . was changing masters" (179). First of all, the question arises of why the status of the British Empire is included in a summary of Ojebeta's fate. If Christianity is, indeed, Ojebeta's "greatest enslavement," as Emecheta claims in *Head Above Water* (1986, 204), this might answer our question. But I am not sure the novel itself supports this interpretation—since the custom of ownership that is in question throughout the novel is one of Africans enslaving Africans. To ensure his own and his wife's happiness, Jacob is, after all, purchasing his wife from Clifford Palagada, who owns her only because her brother has sold her for his coming-of-age dance, transactions that involve African and not Christian tradition. It is true that Ojebeta's Christianity modifies some of her African beliefs (in polygamy, for example), but it fails to supplant them altogether. When Jacob repays Clifford, in fact, both Christian and native traditions are invoked to sanctify the proceeding. In short, the novel leaves us with more questions than answers.

Like the plot of *The Bride Price*, the plot of *The Slave Girl* appears to head in a direction Westerners can understand and accept. But at the very end, once again, we are stumped by what our reaction should be. Though we are horrified when Ojebeta is betrayed by her own brother, we are pleased by her escape from slavery and her subsequent success as a merchant.[27] Because the narrative is apparently celebrating Ojebeta's independence, it seems at this point to be following a familiar Western success story—the sentimental novel, where an orphan girl escapes indenture, strikes out on her own, and eventually is brought back into society by marriage to a respectable, hardworking husband. But Emecheta's novel does not end with Ojebeta's marriage. It shows us what a real marriage can be like. In so doing, *The Slave Girl* seems to be signifying on Western sentimental novels by showing us the reality behind the romantic myths. So, then we think perhaps the novel is a feminist critique of marriage—an interpretation that still allows us to maintain our identification with Ojebeta. This identification is brought to an abrupt halt, however, when we see how honored she is when her husband buys her from the Palagadas. Though the novel does end in a reconfirmation of her marriage, this is certainly not the happy ending we had in mind for her. So we are faced once more with the problem of deciding if Emecheta intended the ending to be happy or ironic. But discovering the attitude of the narrator is no easy task in this novel. I also think that many feminist readers will intentionally or unintentionally discount the ambiguity in the novel so we can claim that the narrator unequivocally condemns her culture for sexism. Some of us, including me at one time, want a guilty verdict so much, in fact, that we are able to find one even when it is not there.[28] But this reading is based more on ethnocentric compulsions than it is on a genuine understanding of the text. For *The Slave Girl*, like the rest of Emecheta's fiction, is notable for the open-mindedness of the narrator. Clearly, this narrator is not in the business of condemning either Ojebeta or her culture. But she has included just enough of a Western perspective to tempt us into this interpretation.

A MÉLANGE OF CUSTOMS AND HYBRID CONSTRUCTIONS

First, let us look at the question of Ojebeta's name. After she leaves the Palagadas and returns to Ibuza, Ojebeta attends the Protestant C.M.S. church and follows current fashion by adopting a European name (Alice). While this change might be quite significant to Ojebeta herself, the narrator reports it almost dismissively (156).[29] Although her friends willingly call her "Ojebeta Alice" (159), the narrator refuses to adopt the new name—a refusal I find somewhat puzzling since I regard the narrative voice as a refraction of Emecheta's voice; and Emecheta, I would certainly think, is more Westernized than Ojebeta's friends. Perhaps the narrator hopes to remind us that, whatever the Western trappings her heroine has assumed, Ojebeta is still African, and her story is to be understood as an African narrative. This interpretation is given support when we learn that Ojebeta has taken "the *extra title* of Mrs Okonji, which *her people translated to 'Missi'*" (173; emphases added). The italicized portions of this sentence call attention to the fact that Ojebeta does not simply take the title "Mrs."; she takes the *extra* title—the alien title, the Western title. By including the Ibuza pronunciation of missus, moreover, the narrator calls attention to its alien source and tarnishes some of the luster Ojebeta hoped to gain by employing it.

Something similar occurs earlier when Ojebeta has first returned to her village. Having been taught by the Westernized Palagadas to use the terms madam and sir, Ojebeta calls her aunt Uteh "Ma'am" when she greets her. But Uteh is offended by Ojebeta's address because she hears "Ma'am" as "Mah," a sound she associates with goats, and "Sir" as "Sah," a sound she associates with scaring off a snake (151). By interpreting these polite forms of Western speech as nothing more than rude noises, the aunt, in effect, defamiliarizes them—a defamiliarization of Western language and custom that occurs elsewhere in the novel. For example, when Ma Palagada tells the slave girls to make themselves

Western-style gowns out of muslin, they call the dress a "gam" and the material "Mossulu" (108). The effects of this defamiliarization are manifold. One is to remind us of the differences between African and Western culture. Another is to undermine or mock the colonialists' (and the Western readers') implied self-importance by Africanizing the language they use. Finally, the defamiliarization of English words adds to the novel's heteroglossia as the alien pronunciation gives ordinary words new meaning. This may be especially the case with the origins of "oda." After saving the life of a district officer (D.O.), Ojebeta's father gets the coveted job of court messenger. When the people in the native court get rowdy, Okwuekwu simply shouts out "'Oda!'" Even though the D.O. had repeatedly tried to teach him the phrase "Order in the court," Okwuekwu fails to see why he should bother to learn "a lot of meaningless sounds" when a single word is enough (15). Not long after this, he becomes known as Okwuekwu Oda. Thus a Western phrase becomes an African name—and in the process almost completely loses its original meaning for us. In still other passages, Emecheta incorporates African terminology into English sentences, as occurs in the statement that some of the men left home for what they called "'*olu oyibo*', white men's work" (80). At other times Emecheta uses an English translation without the original Igbo words, referring to Ojebeta's brother as her "'little father'" (56). By setting the term in quotation marks she calls it to our attention and reminds us that she is using the English word "father" to mean something different from what we are accustomed to.

Much of the heteroglossia of the novel and the ambiguity of the narrative voice can be seen in the text's many hybrid constructions, which are especially evident in the first chapter. Of the events that led to Okwuekwu being appointed court messenger, the narrator recalls, for example, that he had been fortunate to find work for an ailing district officer who "had been sent to the *troublesome town of Ibuza*" (14; emphasis added). Though no quotation marks enclose "troublesome," clearly the narrator is quoting the opinion of the white colonialists in the italicized phrase. The very next paragraph utilizes a more complex hybrid construction. It opens by revealing that Okwuekwu has little sympathy for Europeans and makes no meaningful distinctions among them. Then it reads: "the people of Ibuza—at a time [1] *when it was glorious to be an Englishman*, when the reign of the [2] *great Queen Victoria's son* was coming to its close, when the [3] *red of the British Empire covered almost half the map of the world*, when colonialism was at its height, and Nigeria was being taken over by Great Britain—did not know that they were not still being ruled by the Portuguese" (15; emphases added). This paragraph has begun by describing Okwuekwu's view of whites. But the sentence I have quoted clearly contains information that Okwuekwu is not privy to, as is evident by the information that appears outside the dashes. So whose point of view is being represented here? Though most of the material inside the dashes expresses the narrator's point of view, it does not appear to be limited to her discourse. In the first example [1] the clue is "glorious." Though the word is not set off by quotation marks, it would appear from what follows that the narrator is not of the opinion that it is ever "glorious" to be an Englishman. Similarly, in the second example [2], the clue is "great." This is a word the British would use to describe their monarch; it does not seem to be the narrator's opinion. In the third example [3], the clue is "red." But this clue itself is double-voiced; that is, it carries two simultaneous meanings. If "red" is understood to be a royal color and/or a major color in the British flag, it belongs to the British perception of themselves. But if it is understood as "blood," it belongs to the narrator's perception of them.

Like the funeral of Aku-nna's father (in *The Bride Price*), Ojebeta's wedding is also a mix of African and Western customs. The narrator comments indirectly on this uneasy commingling of cultures by reporting the misgivings the Ibuza people have about the Western aspects of the ceremony. After it is over, they ask her why she bothered with a Christian ceremony with its "strange foreign words" since "all the necessary sacrifices had been made," and "the bride price had been paid" (173). Though the phrase "strange foreign words" no doubt expresses the villagers' judgment and not the narrator's, the overall effect of the passage seems to be that of challenging Western custom. Because she folds the entire description of Ojebeta's wedding into the villagers' hostile interrogation, the narrator herself seems to question the purpose of a church ceremony. This perception is reinforced by the observation that "Mrs Ogbanje Ojebeta Alice Okonji" was "confused" herself as to why she wanted a Christian ceremony (173). To their queries she can only reply that it serves the same purpose as "a man cutting a lock of a girl's hair." But in contrast to this African custom, a Christian marriage means that the husband can have only "one wife" (173). The heteroglossia in this passage is manifested first in Ojebeta's full name. In her very essence, this passage seems to suggest, Ojebeta expresses the awkward commingling of two cultures that seems to sit well with no one: characters, narrator, or reader. Even the heroine, who had insisted on a white church wedding, is confused about what it will accomplish. She explains its usefulness in African terms but then suggests it will include the Western advantage of monogamy.

Her people continue to represent the traditional Ibuza perspective when they ask her what will happen if she has no children in this Western-style marriage. To this she has no answer, but the narrator provides one parenthetically in a passage that contains four key statements. First, she tells us that [1] "*years later Nigerian men solved the problem*" on their own. A man could marry a woman in church and give her a ring as simply [2] "*as a piece of string can be put round a man's cattle*" to identify it as his own. On the other hand, [3] "*[w]hat if he [could] afford more wives, or if the first one . . . had no child?*" In this case, a man could marry as often as he wished. [4] "*But only a stupid woman would *expect her husband to remain married to her alone."* After all, the narrator continues, isn't she *"only a woman?"* (173; emphases added).

These four italicized statements present us with several problems. The first statement [1] seems to be a straightforward-enough explanation that the narrator is providing her readers, though there is some problem with the phrase "years later," which at the very least separates the narrator from the chronological time of Ojebeta's wedding. The second statement [2] is somewhat more complex, as it is not entirely clear whose metaphor is being invoked. Do the men themselves regard a church wedding as nothing more than branding cattle? Or does the narrator impose this metaphor on them as an explanation for their behavior? Or, less likely, does she herself regard a church wedding as branding? Whatever the answer, the second statement casts a certain ironic light on the first, as the observation "Nigerian men solved the problem" seems now to be accompanied by the unspoken subtext of *"to their own advantage."* The exact source of the third statement [3] is also unclear. Though the men in question are never specifically identified and never directly speak for themselves, they could be the source of this rhetorical question. But, then, so could the rest of the Ibuza community, as evidenced by the questions they have already asked Ojebeta. Finally, we must ask who the source is of the fourth statement [4], which characterizes women as "stupid" for wanting a monogamous mate. According to the context, the men would probably think this. But do the women themselves? Would the women of her village think a woman stupid for wanting to monopolize her husband? Given their problems with the Western customs, the answer again is probably yes. But would the narrator think a woman stupid for wanting this?

The answer to that is not as simple as it might seem. On the face of it, the answer seems to be no. Statements [1] through [3], after all, can be reasonably used as evidence of this. But why, then, does the narrator seem to side with the villagers in mocking Ojebeta's church wedding, and why does she refuse to call her Alice Ojebeta? Why, if she does not think a woman stupid for wishing monogamy, does she not set off the phrase "stupid woman" in quotation marks to make her position known? Why does she allow the paternalistic attitudes about women in the passage to go unremarked? The enigma deepens in the next paragraph. Here the problem of Ojebeta's potential infertility becomes moot with the birth of her first two children. But then the narrator remarks that it is pointless and irrelevant to the Okonjis' situation to ask if they lived happily ever after, as a loving, caring couple (173). Though the extensive explanation proffered about Nigerian marriage customs was provided in response to a question asked by Ojebeta's people, they have not asked if the Okonjis' marriage will be based on a happy, loving relationship. Apparently, then, the narrator, functioning here as a kind of ethnographer-cum-mediator, is responding to a question she thinks Western readers would be asking. Even though she raises the question only to dismiss it, by raising it at all she does momentarily include a Western perspective, which, of course, increases the heteroglossia of her novel. But I think it can be argued that she steps out of her own experience-near *context* primarily to help her Western readers see that their experience-distant *concepts* would not be particularly helpful in explaining the situation. In short, though we can use one of Taylor's human constants here (marriage) we must not invoke our Western sense of marriage if we want to understand Ojebeta's. Clearly, we are being warned off from imposing our own sense of a happy ending on this narrative: do not ask if this couple lives happily ever after, the narrator bluntly admonishes us, almost as if she were able to read our minds. At best, such questions are irrelevant—at worst, they lead to misunderstandings.

But the narrator continues the passage by calling attention to the bond between this man and woman, which has been formed "*maybe* by centuries of traditions" and, more recently, by "Christian dogma." Then she employs the imperative and in so doing blurs any distinctions between slavery and marriage since the husband is everything to and for his wife: "Slave, obey your master. Wife, honour your husband" (173). Because of these traditions, Ojebeta cannot disentangle herself from her husband, cannot function as an individual in her own right. But, the narrator assures us, she is fortunate because even though her husband is "a jealous man," more important is that he is a "Christian" (173). In this extraordinary passage, Emecheta finds analogies between African tradition and Christian teachings, analogies that seem to reveal the subjugation of women to the Voice of the Fathers. But she introduces these comparisons with a word that undermines her daring claims when she says the bond was produced "*maybe*" by these combined forces of tradition and dogma. Why maybe? Is this a reflection of Emecheta's own doubts about challenging the Voice of the Fathers? As an ethnographic narrator, where is she standing? Is she speaking as an African or as a Westerner? Or is she speaking as both at once?

Though she might have reservations about whether she should be challenging tradition, she manages to challenge it somewhat when she notes that Ojebeta does not have much opportunity to express herself as an individual—an observation that is surely more Western than African in its origins. She never says in so many words that Ojebeta should have the right to her own individuality and feelings, but to Western readers the implication seems to be there. This inference is strengthened by the narrator's remarks about how fortunate Ojebeta is that her husband is a Christian. But the reason Ojebeta should be regarded as lucky is puzzling to Western readers (at least this Western reader). How Jacob's Christianity is supposed to balance out his jealousy (and presumably his beatings) is simply not made clear. Is this intended as a kind of sop to the Western reader, who presumably might be more sympathetic to Jacob if they shared common religious ideals? Or is Ojebeta fortunate to have a Christian husband because it means that she and he share common religious ideals?

Whatever its purpose, for most Western readers this statement fails to mitigate what we see as the evils of her enslavement.

QUESTIONS OF ENSLAVEMENT, PROLOGUES, AND ENDINGS

The fact of Ojebeta's slavery is certainly stressed throughout the novel. It is most certainly suggested by the title and by the narrator's many references to women's perennial enslavement, which give readers the impression that slavery is the African woman's permanent condition. But the enslavement seems less a Christian effect than an African one—even though, it will be recalled, Emecheta calls Christianity Ojebeta's "greatest enslavement" (1986, 204). Situations like the one faced by Ojebeta lead Florence Stratton to suggest that we can find in African women's fiction threads of an archetypal pattern of "living burial," where the heroines "are enclosed in the restricted spheres of . . . a male tradition" (1988, 147).[30] Though I cannot go as far as Stratton in seeing an archetypal pattern of "living burial" in this novel, the Ibuza women Emecheta portrays are regarded (at least figuratively) as having been sold into slavery if they marry a man who does not even speak their own language (34). The Palagadas' other slaves, moreover, seem content enough with their status; one even wishes she could tell Ojebeta to accept her fate quietly (63). At one point the narrator reports that, in one way or another, all women are subject to men—either as their daughters or their wives or their slaves (112). Only those outcast women who have violated tradition are free (157).

Though the narrator frequently identifies Ojebeta's particular situation as enslavement, she is also careful to point out that Ojebeta is happy with her fate—and incapable of changing it. In marrying Jacob, for example, Ojebeta has been reunited with her people, something she longed for throughout her time with the Palagadas (see pages 95 and 107). Being submissive does not bother her, nor does "an occasional beating" since that is how she was raised (174). When Clifford comes to collect his money, Ojebeta is struck with how young and handsome her former suitor still looks, but her heart goes out to her husband. She is, in fact, delighted "to belong to Jacob body and soul" (176). Perhaps because of scenes like this, Lloyd W. Brown notes that though "women are slaves as a matter of status," it can also be said that women "are accomplices to their own enslavement" (1981, 58). Concurring with other critics that the novel uses the image of a slave girl as "a symbol of the woman's universal condition in her society," Brown goes on to argue that Ma Palagada contributes "to the female status quo" (59). He concludes, moreover, that "[w]omen like Ojebeta are their own worst enemies" (60).

Echoing Brown's reservations, the questions Western readers raise in response to Emecheta's novel include, should Ojebeta be content with her marriage? Should she be happy to be beaten, if only occasionally? What does it mean that she has been taught to expect such behavior from men? Does the narrator intend this evidence to be a criticism of Ojebeta's culture or just an explanation for her contentment? Or, more subtly, is it a criticism of the effects of colonization on her culture? The narrator does tell us quite bluntly that one reason Ojebeta loves her situation is that she is incapable of imagining anything else. "What was the point of speculation?" (177). Though Ojebeta cannot imagine another kind of life for herself, it is clear that the narrator can. But again we are faced with wondering whose rhetorical question is being posed here. Since it has never occurred to Ojebeta that things could have been different, it seems unlikely that she asks the question. If the narrator asks it, however, it seems to mean that she shares Ojebeta's fatalistic outlook on life. But happy as Ojebeta professes to be, something seems to be missing in her life.

As I have tried to indicate in the preceding discussion, much of the plurality of *The Slave Girl* originates in its narrative voice. But in addition to the kinds of heteroglossia we have already seen, this novel has a narrative voice that highlights the differences between the present and the past. As we have already noted, though this narrator is often sympathetic to a more modern or Western perspective, she also continues to speak in the language of her African people. The story of Alice Ogbanje Ojebeta is preceded, for example, by a Prologue in which the narrator offers a brief history of the origins and customs of Ibuza—a time beyond the "then" of the story.

The history begins by observing how central the Eke Market is to life in Ibuza. It then moves quickly to the legend of how Ibuza was founded by a young prince after he had been banished from Isu for killing an opponent in a wrestling match. When Umejei leaves Isu, his father sends him away with a calabash that contains protective medicine and the instructions to make their home where the gourd falls to earth (9). The narrator recounts this history without any modern or Western commentary that might call its details into question.[31] After describing how perfect their new home was for Umejei's people, the narrator adds parenthetically a description of what we would see were we to make this trek, invoking our participation through the use of second-person pronouns (10). The contrast between the past and present is particularly evident when the narrator informs us that a road now runs through an area that once was so dense with vegetation that it afforded Ibuza a safe haven from outsiders. Not only are we drawn into the narration, but we are drawn into its account of the past as though we, too, should be familiar with the landscape of ancient Africa. For it is the route of the past we are invited to traverse and not the route of the present. I would suggest that this use of the second-person pronoun is Emecheta's attempt to adapt a Western art form to the traditional storytelling techniques she had observed her aunt employ when she was a child in Africa. In *Head Above Water*, she admits that her greatest wish has been to recite her own "stories from [her] own home," as her relative "used to tell her stories in her very own compound" (1986, 242). By inviting her readers to enter the landscape of legend in this fashion, she is therefore fulfilling Chinweizu's dictum that contemporary African writers must remember that the "artist in the traditional African milieu spoke for and to his community" (Chinweizu, 241).[32] But Emecheta's community is not the cohesive, homogeneous group that gathered in her aunt's compound. It is, instead, a fractious, heteroglot group of strangers who probably have very little in common beyond Emecheta herself. In this respect, Emecheta's audience reflects her fiction, as it, too, speaks in a cacophony of competing voices.

The Prologue moves on to a description of the town of Ibuza, which is subdivided into several smaller villages. The village of Umuisagba, for example, has the Eke Market running through it which gives it a role of central importance in Ibuza and encourages the residents to have a somewhat inflated opinion of themselves (11). The Prologue concludes by remarking how even the girls of Umuisagba are independent and rebellious, a conclusion that makes it sound as if we are about to read a story in which the daughters rebel—an expectation that is not borne out in the novel itself (which makes for a kind of structural heteroglossia, as the relationship of this preface to its text is not the conventional one of signifier to signified).[33] For as we have already seen, Alice Ojebeta Ogbanje is a disappointingly conventional heroine. This expectation brings us back to the question of genres and whether the novel has a happy ending.

Though the plot does not conform to Frye's description of the comic mode, it does move the heroine from being an indentured orphan slave girl to being a happily married housewife and mother. In this respect, the novel has a conventional Western happy ending. In the traditional terms of her own culture, Ojebeta also realizes a woman's greatest satisfaction in finding a good husband and having children. Why, then, if the heroine is indeed happy, does the narrator continue to insist that Ojebeta is a slave, was a slave, and as a woman will always remain a slave? Perhaps there is no Western literary genre that can satisfactorily explain the ending to us. Perhaps we are too committed to our Western conception of selfhood to recognize that, for Ojebeta, being married to Jacob is true happiness, enslavement or no. Much as I might try to see the ending in this light, however, I still feel as though I am locked into my Western point of view. As far as I am concerned, the ending meets neither my comedic nor my feminist expectations. Much as I, in an unresisting moment, might like to accept Ojebeta's happiness as representative of an old-fashioned happy ending, I find it will not work: I am incapable of accepting either the submissiveness or the beating as part of this happiness. Conversely, if I read the novel as a feminist, I am still gravely disappointed by the fact that the narrator seems so reconciled to Ojebeta's enslavement. As a feminist, I want the narrator to *name* this marital enslavement a wretched ending. But the narrator remains silent on the question of where she stands.

The uncertainty she leaves us with, however, characterizes the entire experience of reading *The Slave Girl*, as we are never quite sure what cultural values the narrator subscribes to. For expressing this uncertainty, Ogunyemi faults Emecheta and criticizes her fiction, claiming that her "ambivalence reveals an English strain in her attitude towards life, a strain in conflict with her innate Africanness" (1983, 65). I would like to offer an alternative reading. Rather than seeing these conflicting narrative attitudes as evidence of bad writing or psychological strain, I think here is a case when we would do well to accept the novel's complex plurality of meaning and remember Macherey's dictum that novels are, by necessity, multiple in meaning and that "to explain the work is to recognise and differentiate the principle of this diversity" (1978, 78). While politically I might want the attitude of the narrator made more clear at the end, I find the argument for plurality compelling in this case. That is, if my appreciation for the plurality of Emecheta's text results from a close reading during which I self-consciously measure my prejudices and expectations against what the text offers, then it will have been a true cross-cultural reading experience. Perhaps, then, this intellectual appreciation for the plurality of Emecheta's narrative can help loosen the grip my Western perspective has on me while I read. Perhaps, in Winch's terms, I can reach a more "charitable" understanding of Ojebeta's situation if I can simultaneously hold in my mind its good and bad aspects—as, I assume, her author was able to do. Perhaps there is no such thing at all as a happy ending. Perhaps (as many Western women novelists are at pains to show us) it is only a figment of our (literary/cultural) imagination. Perhaps it is a direction we need to steer our plots away from. It is true that Emecheta's novel does not offer the kind of prototypical (Western) ending Du-Plessis describes. But by describing the true conditions of Ojebeta's so-called happiness, does this novel not challenge traditional happy endings themselves? Though Emecheta does not break the sentence by writing beyond the ending, she does question what it means for women to be "sentenced" to happy endings. For Ojebeta it means finding happiness in submission, enslavement, and beatings. But in whose terms is she "enslaved"? Why does marriage for Ojebeta involve enslavement? As we see in our discussion of *The Joys of Motherhood* the advent of colonization and the Christian missionaries that debased the status of traditional African women. Is it not likely that the heteroglossia of *The Slave Girl* helps remind us that the West itself was largely responsible for the changes in African culture that turned more egalitarian, polygamous marriages into monogamous institutions of female enslavement? Is it not possible that Ojebeta's church wedding symbolizes more what is wrong with marriage as it is defined in the West than what was wrong with it in traditional, precolonial Ibuza villages? Among the questions we are left with, therefore, is this crucial one: against whom is the challenge of this novel addressed? Is it a challenge to African cultural traditions? Or is it a challenge to Western traditions? Or a challenge to both? Or neither?

The Joys of Motherhood (1979)

HUMAN CONSTANTS AND DIALOGIC HETEROGLOSSIA

Similar unanswered questions haunt readers of *The Joys of Motherhood* as we are forced to decide whether the narrator reads her heroine's life story as one of tragic disappointment or self-fulfillment. This novel, certainly Emecheta's most controversial, opens in 1934 in medias res with the heroine, Nnu Ego, trying to kill herself because her baby has just died. The narrative then returns to the story of Nnu Ego's parents—Ona and Agbadi—and the unusual circumstances of her conception. With its larger-than-life characters and wonderful events, this part of the novel reads very much like a legend, though the narrator gives no hint that it is to be understood as anything other than factual. Like the Prologue in *The Slave Girl*, it fails to anticipate the direction the rest of the novel takes, providing us with a romantic love story that contrasts markedly with the pedestrian experiences of the heroine.

Ona is a fiercely independent woman who is nonetheless so devoted to her father that she refuses to marry the man who loves her. Content to remain Agbadi's mistress, she lives in her father's compound, hoping to conceive a male child (by Agbadi) whom she can present to her father to raise as his own.[34] In this duty she fails, giving birth, instead, to a daughter who is conceived at the same time Agbadi's senior wife is stricken by a fatal illness. During the funeral, the slave who is buried alive with Agbadi's wife promises to return as a legitimate daughter. Nine months later Ona gives birth to Nnu Ego. After Ona herself dies, Agbadi takes over the responsibility for raising his daughter. When she wishes to marry Amatokwu, her father blesses the union with a lavish dowry—but Nnu Ego fails to conceive and soon returns home to her father. Agbadi arranges for her to marry Nnaife Owulum, who is working in Lagos. Nnaife may not be as glamorous as Amatokwu, but he does make Nnu Ego a "real woman" by giving her children (Emecheta 1979b, 53). The first baby dies, but seven others survive, keeping the family financially strapped. Nnu Ego takes comfort in the fact that her children will take care of her when they have grown. But they are too modern to fulfill their familial obligations, and Nnu Ego, old before her time, dies alone on the roadside. Nnu Ego's eldest son gives her an elaborate second burial and builds a shrine in her honor. Though many ask her help in getting pregnant, Nnu Ego never helps. "Poor Nnu Ego [the narrator remarks], even in death she had no peace!" Even so, it is clear to virtually everyone that Nnu Ego "had given all to her children. The joy of being a mother was the joy of giving all to your children, they said" (224). The novel ends with the following three questions (the second and third of which appear to be rhetorical): "And her reward? Did she not have the greatest funeral Ibuza had ever seen?" For this reason, the villagers "failed to understand why she did not answer their prayers, for what else could a woman want but to have sons who would give her a decent burial?" Its final line reads: "Nnu Ego had it all, yet still did not answer prayers for children" (224).

How are we to interpret these remarks? Whose point of view do they express? From her own actions, I think it is likely that Nnu Ego believed she had it all. I think her community thought so, too. The people of Ibuza, after all, were the ones who taught Nnu Ego to value her sons more than herself. But does the narrator believe that Nnu Ego had it all? Is Emecheta saying Nnu Ego should have rebelled, as most Western readers assume? Or is the novel a measured defense of a traditional way of life that has been virtually wiped out by modernization?

Then there is the problematic statement attributed to the villagers that the "joy of being a mother was the joy of giving all to your children." Given what happens to Nnu Ego, is this supposed to be the narrator's ironic commentary on motherhood? Or is it a statement the narrator would endorse? The novel, after all, has been dedicated to "all mothers." Yet in her autobiography Emecheta informs us that she equated the joy of motherhood in this novel with "a beautiful funeral" (Emecheta 1986, 239). Surely this comparison is meant to be ironic. Most readers understand the title to be ironic also. But is it? Readers agree that the title comes from Flora Nwapa's 1966 novel, *Efuru*, where it appears twice and never ironically. After a year of marriage, Efuru has not yet conceived, but she "did not despair. 'I am still young, surely God cannot deny me the joy of motherhood,' she often said to herself" (23). Though Efuru eventually does have a child, it soon dies, and Efuru fails to conceive again. She is, however, honored when she is chosen by the goddess of the lake to be one of her worshippers, and the novel ends with Efuru's dreaming about this beautiful, happy woman who lives at the bottom of the lake: "She gave women beauty and wealth but she . . . had never experienced the joy of motherhood. Why then did the women worship her?" (281).

The question is not a trivial one, since much of the plot of *Efuru* pivots around the question of Efuru's own childlessness. Before she has her little girl, to some people in the community, "Efuru was [seen as] a man since she could not reproduce" (23). Shortly after the baby is born, her husband begins to neglect her and soon deserts her completely. When she fails to give her second husband a child, they agree he should take another wife since it is "a curse not to have children" (207). But if childlessness is regarded as such a curse, why do the women worship the childless Woman of the Lake? Carole Boyce Davies suggests that the "Woman of the Lake and Efuru's adherence to her reaffirm her belief in herself and her contributions to society and provide a societal alternative to motherhood for women" who are barren (1986b, 252). Do the women then worship the Woman of the Lake out of their own unspoken feelings of rebelliousness—out of their need to reaffirm themselves as persons in their own right? It is not a question I can answer—nor is it one the text seems to answer unequivocally either.[35]

But these passages in Nwapa's novel do shed light on why it is so important to Nnu Ego to have children. Without them, she will not be a woman at all—a conviction she holds as strongly as any of Efuru's villagers. This conviction returns us once again to Charles Taylor's concept of human constants. What does it mean to be a woman? What does it mean to be a mother? What does it mean to be married? How do the answers to these questions differ between Africa and the West? Remarking on the difference, Barbara Christian notes that for most women in "traditional societies . . . there is no worse misfortune . . . than being childless" (1985b, 216).[36] Though individually, many Western women would also surely regard childlessness as the worst possible misfortune that could befall them, most feminist critics would agree with Christian that motherhood is not as deeply valued in the West as it is in Africa. Because of these fundamental cultural differences, the attitudes toward motherhood that are expressed in African women's novels can help us historicize—or even anthropologize—the myths of our own culture. But if we are to use Emecheta's novels to anthropologize the West, we must be able to move beyond our own ethnocentricity. We must find enough value in her Igbo culture to carry us beyond the sheer alienness we discover there. At the same time, we must avoid the temptation of romanticizing the alien culture—of blinding ourselves to its weaknesses. In a novel as complex and demanding as *The Joys of Motherhood*, it has not always been easy for Western readers to achieve this balanced interpretation. Though we are usually in full sympathy with Nnu Ego, we have generally been antagonistic to the culture that spawns her. Or, perhaps it is more accurate to say that *because* we are sympathetic with her, we have judged her culture too severely.

Of all Emecheta's heroines, Nnu Ego seems most capable of generating sympathetic support from Western feminists.[37] The reasons are not hard to come by. Like Aku-nna, she seems to be an innocent victim of a harsh and uncaring society. In some respects she is even more innocent than Aku-nna since she obediently lives her entire life according to the dictates of Igbo tradition. Dutiful to father, husband, and patriarchal custom, she nonetheless is neglected and rejected by her family. Her husband rewards her loyalty by taking several other wives and blaming all his disappointments on her, and the male children put their own needs and desires before hers.[38] In short, as I suggested about *The Slave Girl*, *The Joys of Motherhood* seems almost to invite Western feminists to rally around its mistreated heroine.[39] Seeing in Nnu Ego yet another hapless female victim, we read the conclusion of this novel as a tragic commentary on the status of women the world over who sacrifice themselves to paternalistic customs. Because we so dislike its ending, Western readers have tended to treat the entire novel as a bitter indictment of African tradition. Nor is this interpretation limited to Western critics. Eustace Palmer (of Sierra Leone), for example, sees in Emecheta's novel evidence "of the female point of view registering its disgust at male chauvinism and its dissatisfaction with what it considers an unfair and oppressive system" (1983, 39).[40] But is this reading fair? Does it do justice to the novel's plurality of meaning? At one time I would have argued that, indeed, it is fair—and dismissed the question of plurality as irrelevant. At one time I read the title and the ending as strictly ironic. As far as I was concerned, there were no joys in Nnu Ego's motherhood: she trusted custom and tradition to take care of her and was left with nothing. In other words, because I thought its author was already in agreement with me (was herself a Western-style feminist), I thought this novel had nothing good to say about African traditions and nothing new to teach me about my own Western traditions. Today I am no longer so sure of this reading; today I prefer to treat the novel as more of an anthropological exercise in which we compare human constants by highlighting the novel's dialogic heteroglossia.

The heteroglossia that is so evident in *The Slave Girl*'s narrative voice, for example, seems to have shifted here to the characters themselves, a shift commensurable with Bakhtin's theories in which "each character's speech" is said to "[possess] its own belief system" (1987, 315). In *The Joys of Motherhood* the plot is carried forward by a much larger group of central characters whose voices constitute a veritable chorus of heteroglossia. Even Nnu Ego, for all her submissiveness to tradition, is willing to question the role of women in her society, thus making her less a silenced victim than we might at first think. Christian sees Nnu Ego, for example, as a "victim who has yet to articulate her victimization" (1984, 243). But I would argue that the point of the novel is not one of successful feminist rebellion. After all, the daughters' speech does not seem intended to silence the Voice of the Fathers. More to the point is the fact that the novel allows the daughters to speak in their own voice even as they adhere to the tenets of patriarchal tradition. Just as the Fathers are given voice, so, too, are the daughters. By setting up this kind of dialogic heteroglossia, the narrator seems almost content to let the characters themselves battle things out.

CHRISTIANITY AND THE ROLE OF NIGERIAN WOMEN

The story of Nnu Ego's mother is a prime example of a woman asserting herself *within the tradition* that would contain her. Significantly, the chapter that describes her life is called "The Mother's Mother," thus calling attention to Ona's more co-equal status with the fathers. Though the text does not explain how she achieves this status, it seems to imply that in becoming no man's wife, Ona achieves an independence most mothers do not enjoy. By remaining single, however, she remains subordinate to her father. As Christian notes, even though Ona expresses some rebelliousness, "her story is set within the context of a firmly held belief that a woman's primary function is that of being a mother" (1985b, 229). But the narrator is quite clear that Agbadi is fascinated by Ona's independence and regards her more highly than his submissive, more complaisant wives. There are apparently historical reasons for his preference. When Agbadi was young, according to the narrator, a woman was expected to fight for her honor; if she gave in to a man without a fight, she was not respected. Valuing a woman for submissiveness was an idea imported by Christianity (10). Unlike the other women in Agbadi's compound, Ona is both stubborn and arrogant and, therefore, much loved by Agbadi (11).[41] After Agbadi has been wounded in an elephant hunt, he confesses to Ona that he needs "a heartless woman" like her to nurse him back to health (16).

If we accept DuPlessis's argument that the conventions of a culture's ideologies converge in the heterosexual couple,[42] what I have just summarized takes on additional significance. Seen in this context, the passage provides insight into the deleterious consequences of colonization. In pre-colonial times the women in Nigerian villages were expected to be productive and self-reliant members of the community, but colonialism and Christianity undermined the status of these women by encouraging them to become quiet, submissive, and subordinate to men. But the changes brought by Christianity have not been limited to the women. Ali Mazrui contends, for example, that all colonized Africans, men and women alike, were encouraged to adopt the "feminine virtues of Christianity—the softer ideals of love, gentleness, tenderness, forgiveness and patience." At the same time, the "harder warrior values of Africa—courage, endurance, manhood, and even purposeful ruthlessness—were discouraged." In short, both men and women lost touch with their African heritage as they were transformed into colonial Christian subjects (1983, 52). Kofi Awoonor describes the effects of Christianity in virtually the same terms, arguing that by appealing to social misfits and insisting on "personal and individual salvation as against the group or communal salvation enshrined in the laws and ways of the land," the Christian missionaries undermined the Africans' traditional values and moral codes (1975, 24). This, in turn, "subverted the solidarity and integrity of the African society," making it vulnerable to Western influence and control (23). Christianity, in short, taught the Africans "docility, humility, and unquestioning obedience to authority" (25).

Though Emecheta does not specifically discuss the process of Christian colonization, she offers more than one example (as we see later) of how Western culture has corrupted traditional African values. Florence Stratton finds this pattern of corruption common to a great deal of African women's fiction, suggesting that these novelists illustrate how contact with patriarchal colonizing cultures has adversely affected women and, according to some, led to "the suppression of once-powerful feminine values" (1988, 144). Elaine Savory Fido would agree, arguing that the missionaries repressed women by "waging a war on the remnants of pagan cults . . . which seemed to give [women] greater power and freedom than Christianity was willing to permit" (1986, 230). In her description of the admirably independent Ona, Emecheta, for example, gives us a hint of what has been lost to women—and, by implication, what has been lost to Africa itself. Agbadi's loving but submissive wives cannot help him regain his warrior's strength; only Ona, the woman who fiercely battles all attempts to subdue her, can bring Agbadi back to full manhood. The desirability of correlating Africa with masculinity might be questioned here, but it can probably be forgiven in light of what Mazrui argues. It should also be remembered that this "masculinity," as harmful as it can be, is located here in a culture that historically has been based on far more communal values than any Western culture. Thus, the traditions of the Igbo exhibit what in the West are regarded as the feminine values of community, cooperation, and closeness to nature. Though Agbadi wants to humiliate Ona "in her burning desire," I think it would be a mistake to argue that returning Agbadi to his full manhood works in the novel to reinscribe paternalistic thinking (20). There is no doubt that it reinscribes male sexuality. But because Agbadi loves Ona for her independence, I think it is wrong to suggest that he represents quite the same Voice of the Fathers we have seen elsewhere in Emecheta's fiction.

Because he loves her so much, when she gives birth to Nnu Ego, Agbadi implores Ona's father to accept a bride price. But Umunna rejects his suit. Somewhat surprisingly, given her fierce independence, Ona herself expresses regret that, according to custom, she must remain her "father's daughter" (26). After her father dies, however, she still refuses to be "intimidated" by Agbadi's power or to move into his compound (27). Only when her daughter becomes ill does she agree to live with Agbadi, so Nnu Ego can be near her *chi* (that is, her personal god).[43] On her deathbed, Ona urges Agbadi to let Nnu Ego live her own life and even find "a husband *if she wants one*" (28; emphasis added). Thus the self-assertive woman dies, ironically asserting the right of her daughter to choose a traditional woman's life.[44]

Ona's story seems to serve at least two purposes in the text. The first is to provide a compelling example of how African women were at one time respected in the community for their spirit and independence. Other post-independence African novels make a similar point.[45] In Flora Nwapa's novel, for example, after Efuru has been chosen by the goddess of the lake, the dibia[46] reminds her that the town's larger buildings have been built mostly by "women who . . . have been worshippers of Uhamiri" (1966, 192). Though she has no children, Efuru is also respected for her financial successes—as is Idu, the eponymous heroine of Nwapa's 1970 novel (rpt. 1987a). In his 1986 novel, *Estrangement*, Elechi Amadi suggests that more modern African women also continue to enjoy considerable status in their villages. When Amadi's hero returns from the Biafran War, he is furious with his wife (Alekiri) for being unfaithful to him. Instead of complaining through the proper traditional channels, however, Ibekwe brutally attacks her. When his mother does nothing to stop the fight, the village women express outrage at her callous behavior. Upset at the thoughts of losing "a married woman in Kenke village," they decide to "summon Ibekwe and his wife to a hearing and effect a settlement. This kind of peacemaking was usual and was in fact an important function of Omirinya" (92).[47] Ibekwe does not want to attend the hearing, but his mother forces him to because she knows that he will need the other women to help bury her when she dies.[48]

In *The Slave Girl* Emecheta similarly illustrates the power wielded by the successful Igbo women traders at the Onitsha market. Though Ojebeta legally belongs to Pa Palagada, it is Ma Palagada, a formidable businesswoman, who buys her. During her lifetime, Ma Palagada establishes quite an empire for herself. But after she dies, the business collapses. When the British tried to tax Ma Palagada's historical counterparts in 1929, the women rioted, successfully waging what became known as the Women's War.[49] In short, though their responsibilities were different from those of the men, historically, Nigerian women have been considered important members of the community—a status, as we see later, that declined with the advent of the British missionaries and the colonial administrators. Van Allen reminds us, for example, that women once enjoyed considerable political power, based on their cooperative efforts and "expressed in their own political institutions—their 'meetings' (*mikiri* or *mitiri*), their market networks, their kinship groups, and their right to use strikes, boycotts and force to effect their decisions" (Van Allen 1972, 165). Igbo women lost their clout, however, when the British missionaries and administrators failed to recognize the important political roles the women played in the community—preferring instead to shore up the power of the men (166). Kamene Okonjo agrees, arguing that "[c]olonial rule in Nigeria in the first decade of this century marked the beginning of the end of equality of the sexes in village as well as in national politics" (1976, 55).

This brings us to what is perhaps another purpose behind the account of Ona's independence in *The Joys of Motherhood*: her status in Ibuza provides striking contrast to the unhappy life of her displaced daughter in Lagos. Though Ona never marries, throughout her life she enjoys a privileged position that her daughter knows only while she remains in her father's household. Once Nnu Ego leaves Ibuza, her status in the community and her quality of life fall off dramatically. In Lagos, the little status Nnu Ego manages to acquire is achieved only through the birth of her sons (see also Ward 1990, 94). Unlike her mother's status, her own has nothing at all to do with any intrinsic value she might have. Though village life for women in Ona's time was certainly not perfect, it seems to be preferable to what Nnu Ego experiences in modern Lagos. The contrast is not without complications, however, since Nnu Ego is rejected by her first husband when she seems to be infertile. But, in the main, Ona's life has an air of romance and excitement about it that is completely missing in the drab circumstances Nnu Ego endures. Though the passages that describe Ibuza are not utopian, they seem more than idyllic, suggesting that

Ona represents the very real losses African women suffered when their people became colonized.

If we insist on placing Ona's and Nnu Ego's experiences in a Western context, however, we will only find fault with their culture. As independence-loving Westerners, we are particularly critical of the fact that Ona is expected to stay home with her father to compensate for the fact that he has had no sons. Believing as we do that children belong to their parents, we are shocked that she might have to give up her sons for her father to raise as his own. Deeply committed to the nuclear family, we are also horrified at the prospects of polygamy—and question the wisdom of a culture that would dissolve a marriage because the wife cannot get pregnant. But does the novel share our judgments? I think not. In fact, I would argue that it invites us to place these customs in their proper context and see what function they serve there.

THE COMPETING VOICES OF TRADITION AND MODERNIZATION

Though life in Lagos is a virtual hell for Nnu Ego, she clings to her conviction that back home in Ibuza she, as senior wife, would have had more status and been treated better (137). Some of this is evidence of Nnu Ego's romantic nostalgia, to be sure. But at the same time, it was in close-knit villages like Ibuza that the unwritten laws of her people were designed to ensure the welfare of both women and men.[50] The way things are working out in Lagos, it seems reasonable for Nnu Ego to believe that all she gets out of her rural heritage is "the responsibility" without the benefits (137). Because only the men are expected to hold jobs in Lagos, she and other women have lost much of their usefulness (81). In short, at least some of the bad things that happen to Nnu Ego come not from indigenous, patriarchal Igbo customs but from living in the city—the city that has been designed to meet the needs of the white administrators. This view is supported by Van Allen's findings that "Igbo men have come to dominate women economically and politically" (1976, 82).[51] According to the narrator, the kinds of problems that come between Nnu Ego and Nnaife are typical of those that plague other couples in Lagos. In some respects their problems seem to have been occasioned by the customs of the white colonials that force men and women to live in "a different world" (52). Niara Sudarkasa lends support to this interpretation by amassing evidence that the notion of separate spheres was a concept imported to Africa by the West. During the precolonial period, according to Sudarkasa, in both the "state societies" (of the Yoruba and Asante) and the "non-state societies" (of the Igbo), the private and public spheres were intertwined. "Power, authority, and influence within the 'domestic sphere' was *de facto* power, authority, and influence at certain levels within the 'public sphere'" (1981, 52). At one time "the important economic roles of women in traditional West Africa" were thoroughly integrated into the "domestic roles of wife, mother, sister, and daughter," and their economic responsibilities gave the women crucial roles to play "in the 'public sphere'" (54). More recently, the widespread exposure to Western ideas and values has begun to seriously undermine what remains of these traditional socioeconomic patterns. As a result, young West Africans, in their efforts to become more "modern," are embracing Western definitions of what constitute "suitable occupations" for women (and men); adopting these Western-style occupations has the further effect of weakening "extended family ties which were the traditional bases of personal identity and social security" (61).

These ideas are also supported by Kristin Mann's study of the effects of colonization on members of the Yoruba tribe. Mann argues that the Europeans imported standard middle-class ideas about the proper roles of men and women, describing "husbands as economic providers and wives as mothers and homemakers"—a division of labor that was in conflict with traditional Yoruba customs (1985, 45). The combination of colonization and increasing "international trade," Mann goes on to argue, had a negative effect on West African women since men came to control "the production and trade of lucrative new export crops, even in areas where women played an important part in agriculture" (78).[52] Though women were given "new legal rights" by colonial governments, they often were unable to "obtain access to the colonial courts." In summary, Mann argues much like Stratton that "Christianity and Western education spread ideologies that undermined women's personal autonomy and economic independence" (78). Mann also describes how Victorian missionaries "demanded that educated Africans conform to English marriage practices as an outward sign of inward religious and cultural conversion" (1985, 43). We see some of this European influence in Nnaife's consternation that Nnu Ego has become pregnant before they have received the church's blessing; he is worried that his white mistress might even fire him (50). Less Westernized than her husband, Nnu Ego is sickened by the fact that this "shrivelled old woman" has such influence and power over him (50). Nnu Ego admits to herself, however, that she would not feel half so bad if her husband had been worried about the opinions of his master rather than his mistress. That Mrs. Meers is able to intimidate him in this way is further evidence to Nnu Ego that her husband is only a slave and not a man at all.[53] Other losses to Nnaife's manhood are more subtle—but sadly widespread—as in the fact that he, like most men in Lagos, has lost a sense of "family awareness" still found in "the illiterate farmer" (52). This statement suggests that Nnaife's subsequent indifference to his family is not so much a character flaw in the man himself as it is a consequence of leaving Ibuza.[54] Also missing in the city are the opportunities for romance, where men can "sit and admire their wives' tattoos" and beguile their women with "tales of animals nestling in the forests," like the farmer inviting his "favourite wife . . . to make love" under the open sky (52).[55]

When Nnu Ego loses her first baby and tries to kill herself, she is roundly chastised by another Igbo woman, who remarks bitterly that once people leave their villages, they begin to "forget the tradition of our fathers" (62). This helps explain why Nnu Ego has such difficulty adjusting to her new role of senior wife when Adaku arrives on the scene. The status she would have had in Ibuza is virtually meaningless in Lagos (118). Rather than graciously accepting Adaku, therefore, she bitterly resents her. Because most Western women would shudder at the thought of their husband taking on another wife, we find it easy to side with Nnu Ego's views in this matter—a response that makes it difficult for us to accept the possibility that some benefit might actually accrue to both the women involved. Among Africans themselves there is considerable disagreement about the merits of polygamy. In her 1980 interview, Emecheta herself claims that "in village Africa you still need this tradition" (Solberg 1983, 260).[56] And Leith Mullings reports that even though many Ga women, for example, "find monogamous marriage and nuclear-family relationships preferable in many ways, these new arrangements curb independence" (1976, 253). Joseph Okpaku argues that polygamy was "acceptable to African females because it was based on the idea of the wives sharing the husband's love"; he sees the extended family as an example of this sharing (1970b, 19). Filomina Chioma Steady offers a different defense of the practice by arguing that the communal social arrangement led to "socioeconomic security and cooperation," which freed women from "absolute male dominance" and helped ensure that men would take care of their children (1981, 17). In contrast, Sembène Ousmane, in his satirical 1974 novel *Xala* (rpt. 1983), describes the jealous infighting that arises when an African tradesman announces that he is taking a third wife. Though polygamy itself is not the object of Ousmane's satire, its dark side is mercilessly exposed when a beggar curses El Hadji with *xala* or impotence, making it impossible for him to consummate his latest marriage. Traditional African women might have been resigned to their husband's polygamy, but modern African women, including several of Ousmane's characters, question its necessity. In Mariama Bâ's powerful 1980 novel (rpt. 1985a), *So Long a Letter*, we see the financial and emotional hardships that women can suffer under polygamous conditions.[57]

In Emecheta's novel, if Nnaife had treated his wife more positively, we might have an easier time accepting his polygamy. But he, too, has lost touch with his people's principles of humane living. In fact, he seems to behave very much like Francis Obi in picking and choosing whatever customs will benefit him the most. Without consulting Nnu Ego, for example, Nnaife visits Ibuza after Adaku's departure[58] and returns to Lagos with a sixteen-year-old girl whose bride price has cost him the exorbitant sum of thirty pounds. Not surprisingly, Nnu Ego is furious—but as a dutiful wife and daughter, she can do nothing about (what we regard as) her husband's foolish behavior.

Nnu Ego may occasionally nurture heretical private thoughts, but she chooses to honor tradition by what she does—and says. In fact, most of the time she is very traditional. A classic illustration of how she thinks occurs when Nnaife is put on trial for trying to murder the Yoruba man their daughter wishes to marry. Trying to establish Nnaife's dedication to his family, the defense attorney asks him who pays his children's school fees. Nnaife says he pays them. But when the prosecuting attorney asks Nnu Ego the same question, she says she pays them. When he reminds her what Nnaife has said, she says yes, he pays them. Amid much laughter from the courtroom, he asks her to explain this contradiction. She says that her husband owns her "just like God" does; therefore it is accurate to say that "he pays" (217). In effect, Nnu Ego has testified that she exists only through her husband. But it is significant, I think, that the words of her testimony name her enslavement. Given an opportunity to separate herself from this man, she chooses not to. Although she occasionally has moments in which her internally persuasive discourse challenges the Voice of the Fathers, in this scene in particular what she thinks corresponds exactly with her culture's authoritative discourse—a discourse that has demanded and received her "unconditional allegiance" (Bakhtin 1987, 343).[59] So strong is her fundamental allegiance to this external discourse that she cannot understand why people were laughing at her testimony.

Though Nnu Ego is not herself modern, she is nonetheless the victim of her people's modernization. In fact, it very well might be that she is victimized *because* she herself is not modern. Having been raised to define her value entirely through her children, she could not possibly have known how fundamentally "the values of her country, her people and her tribe" would change in her lifetime (219). Because Nnu Ego cannot live up to the feminist attitude promised in her isolated moments of rebellion, Western readers like me have tended to see her as a victim. If she cannot be a new kind of heroine who throws off the shackles of the past, we see her as a casualty in the war between the sexes. I want now to propose an alternative reading. Rather than seeing the novel as an account of the war between the sexes, might we not see it as a war between the past and the present—between the voices of tradition and those of modernization. Might we not see it, in short, as a war between Igbo and Western values? For Nnu Ego is not alone in clinging to the old ways. Other voices of tradition are powerful and suasive in this novel. Making it hard for Western readers to see the value in these traditions is the fact that most of these voices are male.

The dominant male voice is that of Nnaife Owulum himself, though what he says is often narrated in free, indirect discourse. When Nnu Ego first arrives in Lagos, for example, Nnaife realizes immediately that he is disappointing to her. But he knows there is nothing either can do about the situation. The men see it as amusing that women imagine Lagos as a place "where they would not have to work too hard" and where they will get "a handsome, strong figure of a husband. . . . Women were so stupid!" (43). Passages like this do not exactly endear Nnaife to us. On the other hand, it does summarize Nnu Ego's expectations pretty accurately. The question must be raised, therefore, does any of this passage reflect the narrator's point of view? Other passages suggest that Nnaife does have some legitimate complaints about his wife. These complaints are usually so entangled with other sexist attitudes, however, that it is almost impossible for Westerners to respond positively to him. During one quarrel when Nnu Ego acts particularly insubordinate by staring at him while he eats dinner, for example, Nnaife reminds her that she belongs to him—literally. She retorts that her brothers would have run him out of the compound if he had dared to approach her father himself. Then she reminds him that Amatokwu was her first and real love—at which point Nnaife threatens to beat her. Though neither Nnaife nor Nnu Ego is blameless in this exchange, our sympathies tend to lie with Nnu Ego. After all, how can we sympathize with a man who is affronted by a woman who watches him eat? How can we sympathize with a man who has just reminded his wife that she is nothing more than his possession? After their first baby has died, Nnu Ego has trouble recovering from the loss. In her grief she again romanticizes about her first husband. In contrast to Nnaife, who washes clothes "for a woman," her first husband was a man to respect, someone who represented the cultural standards of manliness (72). But what she has conveniently forgotten is that Amatokwu is the same man who refused to waste his "precious male seed" on her (32). When Nnaife suggests three months is a long enough time to mourn, therefore, Nnu Ego lashes out at him by retorting that she never would have come to Lagos in the first place if she could have had a baby in Ibuza. To this Nnaife asks if it makes her "happy to hurt other people." He continues by reminding her that it is not his fault the child died, that, in fact, he "gave [her] the child. He was mine too, remember?" (73). This is another rebuke that Nnu Ego seems to have earned. But it is easy for Western feminist readers to overlook because of other statements Nnaife has made. It is particularly irritating, for example, when Nnaife responds to news of Nnu Ego's first pregnancy with the self-centered remark that he is happy to learn that he is "a man" (50).

But Nnaife is not always as despicable as he seems. For example, unless we read the following passage carefully, we are tempted to implicate Nnaife in sexist statements he does not make. When Nnu Ego runs off, intending to kill herself, Nnaife is distraught and confides to his friend that his wife is unhappy: "Poor woman. She endures me only because of this child. . . . She thinks I'm ugly" (71). Though this passage gives us a very sympathetic view of a vulnerable and sensitive man, it is followed by remarks that are so offensive to women that it is easy to forget that Nnaife has taken his wife's side in the exchange. His friend Ubani assures Nnaife that Nnu Ego does not hate him, for how could she since, in contrast to women, "a man is never ugly and never old" (71).

What Western readers find hard to remember is the fact that there are reasons for Nnaife's unpleasant behavior. Many of the reasons are directly attributable to the white world. For example, when Nnu Ego complains about Nnaife to Ubani's wife, Cordelia, she gets no sympathy from the other woman, who reminds her that African men have been emasculated by their role as servants (51).[60] In other words, though Nnaife speaks in the Voice of the African Fathers throughout much of the novel, he has not been immune to the consequences of Western modernization. When he rejects Nnu Ego and their children, he speaks the language of modernization—in the Voice of the Western Individual who puts his own needs and desires before those of the community or family. Nnaife seems to have been caught up in what Mazrui calls "the rising trend of urbanization," a migration to the cities that has been accompanied by "a transition from the constraints of collective village life to the relative permissiveness of urban life" (Mazrui 1983, 66-67). Unlike his ancestors, as Nnaife ages he does not gain increasing respect in either the community or his family—respect is especially lacking in his rebellious sons. Though Nnaife's is not a particularly appealing voice, it is an important one that deserves our attention. For it is another anguished voice of post-independence Africa—one that wishes to retain all the benefits of African tradition without accepting its attendant responsibilities. Where Nnu Ego represents the old way of doing things (African master narratives), therefore, her husband represents the worst of the new ways (African master narratives corrupted by Western master narratives). In describing what he calls the "emotivist self," Alasdair MacIntyre seems to be describing Nnaife's transformation from a traditional member of a traditional society to a modern member of modern society. MacIntyre defines emotivism as "the doctrine that all evaluative judgments and more specifically all moral judgments are *nothing but* expressions of preference, expressions of attitude or feeling" (1984b, 11-12). The culture of the modern age he characterizes as "specifically emotivist" (22). The self, as conceived by emotivism, is one that has "suffered a deprivation, a stripping away of qualities" until it is seen as without "social identity" (33). Because Nnaife's cultural telos has lost both its integrity and its credibility under colonialism, he himself is adrift, without purpose. Unable to sort out his selfish motives from traditional values, he betrays his wife and his heritage.

SIGNIFYING AND THE QUESTION OF ENDINGS

Though the breakdown of Nigerian culture is attributed primarily to colonialism in *The Joys of Motherhood*, ironically enough the narrator reports that Nnu Ego is able to survive her travails because she has converted to Christianity (89). Because of this passage and similar ones in Emecheta's other novels, I think it is possible to argue that the imported patriarchal discourse (the master narrative) of Christianity has become an authoritative discourse nearly co-equal with the traditional discourse of the African fathers. But the ultimate goal of this alien discourse is to silence the African discourse it challenges. The ultimate goal is, after all, colonization of mind, body, and spirit. In *The Slave Girl*, for example, Ojebeta's devotion to Christianity occasions several arguments with Uteh. Concerned for her niece, Uteh asks Ojebeta why she has rejected her traditional religion, including its music and rituals (153). True convert that she is, Ojebeta responds that the old ways are the "work of the devil" (154). This passage expresses fears similar to those expressed by Nnaife when Nnu Ego gets pregnant before they have had their church ceremony. In *Marrying Well*, Kristin Mann argues that among the educated elite "Christian marriage stood as the perfect symbol of assimilation" (57). It is true that neither Nnaife nor Ojebeta is entirely assimilated; both adhere to Christian teachings and rituals pretty much when it pleases them to do so (see Gugler 1981, 175). Nnaife, it will be remembered, does not limit himself to the one wife Christianity allows, and Ojebeta marries in church primarily to keep her husband from taking other wives. But at one time or another both characters express genuine fear of the authority of Christian discourse. As is especially clear with Nnaife's worries that Mrs. Meers will fire him, this fear can be extrapolated to a more generalized dread of Western discourse itself.

The power of Western discourse to intimidate Nnaife and Ojebeta leads me to another question. Is it possible that the authoritative discourse of both British colonialism and Western literature (not to mention Western criticism) is somehow always present as a kind of background noise in African texts? Bakhtin argues that heteroglossia in low genres like songs and folk sayings is "parodic, and aimed sharply and polemically against the official languages of its given time" (1987, 273). I do not want to suggest that all African literature is parodic of Western literature. Nor do I mean at all to imply that it is another "low genre." But I do want to suggest that post-independence African literature questions the "official" literary language of its time. In this respect, as I have suggested, African fiction can be seen as signifying upon the West's cultural tradition and Western fiction—its *grands récits*. That is, the meaning toward which an African plot intends seems often to be dialogically opposed to the meaning of Western narrative. Rather than an affirmation of modernization, the African plot is a challenge (an often bitter challenge) to it—which brings us back to the question of endings.

Kate Ellis argues that "political theories are embedded in narratives of victory, tracing a path along which power, once lost, is regained" (1989, 43). Peter Brooks suggests that it may be "a defining characteristic of the modern novel (as of bourgeois society) that it takes aspiration, getting ahead, seriously"; the modern novel thus uses "ambition" to represent love, "that which totalizes the world as possession and progress" (1984, 39). For much modern African fiction, however, the desire to get ahead seems to lead more likely to disaster. One does not have to search far for examples: Achebe's *No Longer at Ease* (1960), Armah's *Fragments* (1970), Awoonor's *This Earth, My Brother . . .* (1971), and Soyinka's *The Interpreters* (1965), to name only four. One or more of the main characters in all of these powerful novels is a "been-to," a young man who has studied abroad and finally come home to make a success of his life. Achebe's hero, Obi Okonkwo, has spent nearly four years in England. When he returns to Nigeria, he gets a job in the civil service with a modest paycheck that does not begin to cover his expenses. As is the custom in Lagos, people offer him money so he will do them favors, but he scornfully refuses to be bribed. Eventually, when he is really pressed for money, however, he accepts—and is arrested for his crime (Achebe 1975a). Armah's hero, Baako, is so traumatized by his return to Ghana that he literally goes insane. Thinking about cargo cults, he notes bitterly that, in a world that exports people, it "is clearly understood that the been-to has chosen, been awarded, a certain kind of death. A beneficial death, since cargo follows his return. Not just cargo, but also importance, power, a radiating influence" (Armah 1970, 223-24). Awoonor's hero, Amamu, also goes insane, but not before he remarks that "the best of nature's freaks, African intellectuals, are returning from Oxford, where there is still a watering place by the name of a pub and we drowned our exile tears in gallons of good English beer" (Awoonor 1986, 135). These are brilliant, bitter, heartbreaking books that savage the Western world's effects on Africans. In the isolation and despair of their heroes, all three convey the terrible cost of modernization. Though getting ahead does not lead unequivocally to disaster for the heroes of Soyinka's novel, still he mercilessly mocks those African been-tos who most seriously pursue Western-style achievement.

Emecheta seems less angry than her male counterparts, but she manages nonetheless to fundamentally challenge both Western thought and Western plot—the West's master narratives. As we have seen, however, her fiction is most notable for the many voices it contains. This dialogic heteroglossia results in a plurality of meaning that directly affects how we understand the direction of her plots and their projected endings. Ellis is skeptical of hermeneutics because she thinks that it "takes place within the context of that projected end . . . [which] can become a totalizing strategy, one that admits to only one meaning" (1989, 43). I agree that hermeneutics occurs in the context of a projected end. As I have tried to show in the preceding pages, serious difficulties arise in our reading when we impose our own Western intentions on African plots. But I think Ellis overstates her case. Though novels surely come to an end, understanding never does—as reading an African novel should make perfectly clear to any Western reader. Emecheta's novels, in particular, seem to resist the kind of interpretive closure that worries Ellis, since it is virtually impossible for us to understand what their endings mean. Because we cannot determine if these endings are comic, tragic, or of another genre altogether, I think we can argue that hermeneutics does not have to become a totalizing strategy. Rather than assuming that we can ever reach closure with Emecheta's texts, we should accept the fact that reading them will give rise to both understanding and misunderstanding. We should, therefore, approach her alien texts in hopes of more fully understanding another culture—and more fully understanding our own Gadamerian prejudices and cultural expectations, expectations that become especially evident when we are faced with the problem of trying to make sense of her enigmatic endings and the plurality of meaning that precedes them.

I want to argue, then, that *The Joys of Motherhood,* if not strictly feminist, is feminine—in the French sense of *l'écriture féminine*.

INSCRIBING THE FEMININE

By refusing closure and overcoming the binary oppositions characteristic of phallologocentrism, does not this novel inscribe the feminine? In Emecheta's first two novels, the focus is primarily on a single character, the protagonist, whose point of view is almost indistinguishable from that of the narrator—though both are certainly double-voiced. In *The Bride Price,* the focus is still primarily on one double-voiced main character, though the Voice of the Fathers is always present. In *The Slave Girl* the focus continues to be directed on a single main character, but the heteroglossia in the novel seems to be reflected more in the narrator than in any of the characters themselves. In *The Joys of Motherhood,* however, the heteroglossia is spread among many characters, and the voice of the narrator is much less noticeable. Though some may dispute this point, I think *The Joys of Motherhood* is much less judgmental than any of the previous books Emecheta has written. In all of them she expresses both sympathy for, and reservations about, her own African culture. One function of the narrators in her earlier novels, as I have argued, has been to explain and defend her cultural traditions much as an ethnographer might. But in this novel she seems to be more convinced that her culture can speak for itself. Whether she is right in this estimation is an entirely different matter, for there is much that feminists take exception to in this novel. Perversely enough, we are permitted some of this outrage by the absence of a strong, single narrative voice. Much as we might despair over Nnu Ego's life and death, however, I think it is incumbent on feminist readers in particular to acknowledge the dialogic heteroglossia in this novel. If we listen to the other voices, we might not be so quick to judge Nnu Ego's life a failure. Instead of mourning her fate, we might find ourselves mourning the destruction of those humanistic values she tried to live by. When the traditions she followed were still intact, they protected her rights. But because things have changed with the advent of the modernist values imported by colonialism, Nnu Ego is left unprotected. In Bakhtin's terms, Nnu Ego's traditional discourse has been tested and found wanting. It is inadequate because the indigenous ways of her people have largely been supplanted by the alien ways of Western modernization.

As I mentioned earlier, both Amadi and Mazrui have identified several negative legacies in the aftermath of African colonialism. Though I do not want to contradict their negative views of colonialism, I want to take my cue from Ellis and suggest an alternative response—one that is not unrelated to her poststructuralist "interpretive strategy," in which she insists that even pornography has multiple and even conflicting meanings, arguing "that a *Playboy* centerfold . . . can be said to inscribe female submission to an invisible male viewer, or alternatively, an aggressive invitation to that same viewer" (1989, 46). My strategy is to suggest not that colonialism was positive but that, once contained and formally eradicated, its legacy on the African continent opens the possibility for a multiplicity of local narratives to co-exist. Since it seems unlikely at this time that the West will allow African narratives to speak in co-equal voices with the master narratives of the West (on Western soil), the *only* place we can see these narratives together is in Africa today. This cognitive model, is, of course, a poststructuralist one and, like the deconstructive "model of the world" proposed by Ellis, precarious and provisional, readily (pun intended) admitting to change (1989, 50).

It remains to be seen whether this model is too idealistic. But Mazrui has proposed one that is strikingly similar. In *The Africans: A Triple Heritage*, he argues that "there may be hope in the very instability which Africa is experiencing in the wake of [its] unnatural dis-Africanisation." Even though the instability gives him some hope, Mazrui describes the situation as combative, "a war of cultures. It is a war between indigenous Africa and the forces of Western civilisation. It takes the form of inefficiency, mismanagement, corruption and decay of the infrastructure" (1986, 12). He also suggests that the impact of colonization on Africa has not been as extensive or lasting as we might think. It was not so much "African *culture*" that the Europeans destroyed as "the indigenous African *structures*" (20). In *The Africans*, therefore, he is able to argue that the current bleak conditions in Africa should be seen "as a valuable opportunity for fundamental social, economic and political change—an opportunity for a reconciliation with the ancestors and a new relationship with the wider world of the twentieth century" (21). Ever hopeful for the future of Africa, Mazrui describes the three influences that give his project its name—"indigenous, Islamic and Western forces"—as in splendid, productive turmoil, "fusing and recoiling, at once competitive and complementary" (21).

The poststructuralist cognitive model that Mazrui's approach seems to echo, I would further suggest, describes Buchi Emecheta's fiction, as it, too, is created out of competing and complementary narratives. If we listen, for example, to all the voices in *The Joys of Motherhood* and not just Nnu Ego's, we will recognize the plurality of narratives in Emecheta's text. In so doing, we are helping her to overcome the either/or metaphor that Cixous describes (1981a). For Emecheta is not posing women against men in this novel. Rather, she is posing women with men in order to recover the traditional humane values of her Igbo people and overthrow the pernicious effects of colonization. Moreover, using this poststructuralist interpretive model, it is now possible to argue not that Emecheta poses the West *against* Africa but that she is trying to explore what might happen when the master narratives of both worlds are read (and rewritten) together. Seen in this light, what is *said* (spoken) during these novels seems to be just as important as what happens. In poststructuralist terms, what is said is co-equal to what events occur. The liberal division between speech and action has been overcome. Though the endings contain crucial information about Emecheta's African heritage, they should be read as clues to the heteroglossia that has preceded them. Instead of providing narrative closure, the endings, like the novels themselves, leave us wondering—about their meaning surely but also about ourselves and our Western way of life.

NOTES

1. Peter Brooks sees plots as "intentional structures, goal-oriented and forward-moving" (1984, 12). Brooks further argues that how well we understand a particular telos largely depends on the competency we have achieved as readers "of narrative" (19). According to Alasdair MacIntyre, any given present is "informed by some image of some future and an image of the future which always presents itself in the form of a *telos*—or of a variety of ends or goals" (1984b, 215).

2. This is based on MacIntyre's claim that "when we approach . . . an alien culture with a well-established classification of genres in our mind and ask of a given rite or other practice 'Is it a piece of applied science? . . . Or a piece of theology?' we may in fact be asking a set of questions to which any answer may be misleading" (1978, 252). Compare this with Mukherjee's assertion that "the universalist categories of criticism have no means of dealing with the specificity of a text except in terms of setting or backdrop. The universalist methodology, in its exaggerated focus on form and character, neglects referentiality and context, thereby failing to assign inventiveness to writers who structure their works on these principles" (1986, 346).

3. See, for example, Hollis and Lukes 1982 and Taylor 1985.

4. Lloyd Brown finds her work closely aligned with "the militant . . . rhetoric" of Western feminism; but he reminds us that she should also "be read . . . as an African or Third World writer whose quest for improvements in the situation of women is shaped by considerations that are of more immediate consequence to the non-Western, non-middle-class woman" (1981, 38, 39).

5. M. J. Daymond reads them this way, claiming that "each protagonist's story ends in defeat" (1988, 64).

6. In contrast, Petersen argues that in this novel Emecheta "describes the slow and seemingly inevitable destruction of a young girl by the forces of tradition" (1984, 43). I think the narrative telos is less certain than this. For commentary on Frye's Eurocentric criticism, see Asante 1987, 160.

7. For commentary on the ending, see Emenyonu 1987, 135.

8. Of the rewriting, Emecheta says that what weighed on her mind most was the

failure of her own marriage, her inability to live the kind of life scripted for her as a Nigerian woman; she thus "decided that people like [her] who go against tradition must die" (1986, 165).

9. Compare this with Anthony Barthelemy's argument that the "bitterly ironic conclusion . . . condemns that culture even as the narrator feigns neutrality. . . . Although tradition claims another victim, it is not triumphant. The victor disgraces itself as it claims its victim" (1989, 563).

10. Bazin claims, for example, that in this novel "Emecheta shows how numerous indigenous African customs and superstitions oppress and degrade the female" (1985a, 184; see also 1989, 8).

11. In contrast to my reading, Slomski argues that "the narrator seems to take particular delight in parodying Aku-nna and Chike's assimilation of the Western myth of romantic love; this delight, however, does not detract from the narrator's sympathy for the lovers and their plight" (1986, 70). She also argues that "it is the force of meaning or signification, and not any particular event, which blocks revolt and kills off the female protagonist at the end of her story" (62).

12. According to Afam Ebeogu, a fellow Nigerian, "Aku-Nna is an Igbo name which is borne by most Igbo males who have taken titles, and the title name suggests that it is their father who has initiated them into the cult." (It is worth noting at this point that Emecheta's own given name, Buchi, is also a man's name.) In those instances when a woman has this name, "it would mean, not that the females would fetch a large brideprice for their fathers, *but that they were born at that point in time when their fathers had become materially successful*" (1985, 86). I would add that if Aku-nna is indeed traditionally a man's name, it makes more complex the question of whose voice she speaks in: her own or that of the Fathers.

13. In defense of these customs it should be explained that during this ritualistic courting, the young women learn a great deal about how their suitors would treat them were they to marry.

14. This is a theme that also appears in Tess Onwueme's *The Broken Calabash* (1984; rpt. 1988) and Achebe's *No Longer at Ease* (1960; rpt. 1975a).

15. Or, at least the endings of the nineteenth-century, middle-class novel.

16. Echewa makes the same point in *The Land's Lord* (1976).

17. In contrast to the interpretive dilemma I see here, Dan Sperber (1982) argues: "If people of different cultures did hold apparently irrational *factual* beliefs, then it might be acceptable to try and reformulate the content of these beliefs so as to establish their rationality, even at the cost of having to imagine different cognizable worlds. But there is no reason," he insists, "either theoretical or empirical, to assume that the apparently irrational beliefs reported by anthropologists and historians are factual beliefs" (175).

18. Awoonor notes a similar "combination of Christianity and Igbo idiom" in *No Longer at Ease* (1975, 270).

19. As far as Ogunyemi is concerned, the presence of these explanations, which are "obviously meant for a foreign audience," is a serious flaw in Emecheta's writing (1983, 70).

20. Daymond argues that, ultimately, because "Aku-nna's incomprehension and silence [are] not part of her consciousness," there remains "an unbridged gap between reader and character" (1988, 65).

21. "Without men, no culture, certainly," Geertz concurs; "but equally, and more significantly, without culture, no men" (1973, 49).

22. Ogunyemi and Ebeogu would probably take strong exception to this assertion; Ogunyemi, for example, claims that Emecheta has "an outdated view of her country" (1983, 65).

23. Ward suggests that because Emecheta is both "an Igbo mother *and* storyteller, [she] is freer from the influence of the 'fathers'—the language of authority—than are many other women writers" (1990, 92). We might add that Emecheta is freer than her own female characters.

24. Geertz, who has himself taken these two terms from the psychoanalyst Heinz Kohut, defines an experience-near concept as that which a group of individuals would ordinarily use to describe themselves; conversely, an "experience-distant concept is one which various types of specialists . . . employ to forward their scientific, philosophical, or practical aims" (1979, 227).

25. For a similar approach see Slomski (1986) where she says that "in *The Bride Price* and *The Slave Girl* the narrator, simultaneously in the role of Ibuza ethnographer or 'insider,' and anti-traditionalist or 'outsider,' creates and maintains a narrative dialogue or tension between her revolutionary voice and the female hero's conservative perspective" (98).

26. Bernstein challenges us (Westerners) to "*exorcize* the Cartesian Anxiety and liberate ourselves from its seductive appeal" (1989, 19). Mae Gwendolyn Henderson defines plurality as the essence of black women's writing, "reflecting not only a relationship with the 'other(s),' but an internal dialogue with the plural aspects of self that constitute the matrix of black female subjectivity" (1990, 118).

27. Ebeogu claims that, technically, Ojebeta is not really a slave because one cannot be "sold" to a relative (1985, 88).

28. Katherine Frank claims, for example, that in this novel "Emecheta most fully explores her central vision of female bondage, her underlying metaphor of African womanhood as a condition of victimization and servitude" (1982, 479). Frank also argues, incorrectly, that the "slave masters, the tyrannical oppressors, in *The Slave Girl* are all men" (482)—apparently overlooking the powerful Ma Palagada. She might not technically own the slaves, but she certainly controls them.

29. Even though Emecheta's mother was named Alice, which seems reason enough to choose this name for a heroine based on her mother's life, Ogunyemi finds in this name "a connection with Alice in Wonderland" (1983, 71).

30. See also Frank 1982 and Awoonor 1975.

31. Later in the text the narrator informs us that at the turn of the century, Ojebeta's people made little distinction "between myth and reality" (20).

32. For a discussion of the oral tradition in Emecheta's fiction, see Ward 1990.

33. For a discussion of prefaces and their relationship to texts, see Spivak 1976.

34. This theme underlies the plot of *The Broken Calabash*—except the heroine refuses to stay home and marry a "wife" for her father's sake (Onwueme 1988).

35. Adewale Maja-Pearce argues that "any attempt to elicit concrete, material reasons for the behaviour of the characters in the novel is to approach it in terms of an alien, European system of beliefs, where individual psychology is paramount and where the gods have no place in the universe except as objects of 'sociology' and as quaint, wrong-headed remnants of a backward, pre-colonial Africa" (1985, 13-14).

36. For further discussion of the importance of motherhood in African culture, see Steady 1981 and Davies 1986b.

37. Bazin, for example, argues that "through her experiences with her father, husbands, and sons, [Nnu Ego] has come to understand the patriarchal nature of her culture and her own role in perpetuating it" (1985a, 33; see also 1985b, 186).

38. Aspects of the novel that Bazin focuses on (1985a).

39. See Bazin's response: "Although Nnu Ego's anger and her feminist consciousness come too late in her life to do much for her, the impulse towards freedom from indigenous patriarchal customs is reassuring" (1985a, 186).

40. For additional commentary, see also Umeh 1982.

41. More skeptical of his motives than I, Christian argues that Agbadi is primarily motivated to "make her dependent, to conquer her sexually and to make her a mother" (1985b, 229).

42. For DuPlessis, "the reproduction of [the sex-gender] relations . . . turns especially on the organization of family, kinship, and marriage, of sexuality, and of the division of all sorts of labor by gender. The *point at which these basic formations cross . . . is the heterosexual couple*" (1985, 1; emphasis added).

43. This term, too, presents interpretive problems for Western readers, which I have not gone into here; for discussion of its meaning, see "*Chi* in Igbo Cosmology" (Achebe 1975d).

44. According to Christian's reading of the novel, "Agbadi's effect on his cherished daughter," ironically enough, "is to render her a suitable wife, submissive and delightful" (1985b, 233). Though Nnu Ego may be submissive, she is hardly a delightful wife. The text also suggests that since Nnu Ego has known such loving attention from her father, she learns to expect it from a husband. I cannot think that this is all to the bad, especially in a culture that expects its women to marry.

45. See Davies 1986b.

46. As I understand it, the dibia is a kind of combination seer and root-worker or medicine-man.

47. On this subject, see Okonjo 1976 and Van Allen 1976.

48. From her studies of the women's associations composed of the "daughters of a lineage," Van Allen concludes that their "most important ritual function was at funerals of lineage members, since no one could have a proper funeral without their voluntary . . . participation" (1976, 68).

49. See Van Allen 1976 and Katrak 1988.

50. For a discussion of the deleterious changes wrought by colonialism on West African women, see Okonjo 1981.

51. See also Wipper 1972 and Nwapa 1987b.

52. See also Okonjo 1981, 91-95.

53. Barthelemy suggests that Nnaife has been "robbed of his manhood by the clock" (1989, 566).

54. In *Efuru* the villagers blame an increase in stealing on the Christians, who "tell us our gods have no power, so our people continue to steal" (Nwapa 1966, 223).

55. In *The Bride Price*, romance does occur in Ibuza when Okonkwo lingers in his hut, lovingly tracing the elaborate bridal tattoos on his youngest wife's breasts and back (49). Because no playful scenes like this occur between Nnaife and Nnu Ego, it makes it hard for Western women to understand why she stays with him.

56. Emecheta's public statement on polygamy has the effect of undermining Palmer's assertion that Nnu Ego's complaints to her first husband are an example of "the author making her propagandist point about the fate of mothers and the evils of the polygamous situation" (1983, 45).

57. For another view of polygamy, see Aidoo 1992.

58. She leaves with her daughters to make a life for herself as a prostitute; for commentary on her independence, see Andrade 1990.

59. Ward suggests that the irony here "is the kind that arises from a competition of two irreconcilable kinds of voices—the multivocal voices of oral subjectivity, represented by Emecheta's [sic] *chi*, and the univocal, literate voice of authority. All the voices are necessary and true" (1990, 96).

60. Barthelemy reads this to mean that "industrial time conspires with racism, capitalism, and imperialism to rob [African] men of [the time to be human and humane]" (1989, 567).

5

The Difference of View

Difference is redefined, not as male *versus* female . . . but as a multiplicity, ambiguity and heterogeneity which is that of textuality itself.

Mary Jacobus
Reading Woman: Essays in Feminist Criticism (1986, 30)

. . . writing is precisely *the very possibility of change*, the space that can serve as a springboard for subversive thought . . .

Hélène Cixous
"The Laugh of the Medusa" (1976, 879)

TRAVERSING (TRADITIONAL) BOUNDARIES

The novels discussed in this chapter present interpretive problems similar to those I have already discussed. But I want to suggest that in these three novels it becomes even more evident that Emecheta herself has *all along* been *writing* in the language of perspicuous contrast. By signifying on Western forms of literature and Western forms of thought, she has been, as it were, extending an open invitation to her readers to compare the limiting notions of her two cultures. The invitation to compare cultures, though present in all her fiction, seems all the stronger here because the main characters in these particular novels have been so clearly influenced by Western ideas. In *Destination Biafra*, for example, Emecheta uses as her heroine a Nigerian woman who, like herself, has studied in England. In *Double Yoke*, as the title itself implies, the heroine also carries the burden of two cultural traditions. In *The Rape of Shavi*, the worldviews of the modern West and traditional Africa collide, fuse, and separate—neither completely unaffected by their momentary conjunction. By the very nature of their composition, therefore, these novels seem to provide a model for cross-cultural conversation. In postmodern terms, we might say these texts spell out for us exactly how they should be read. As my epigraphs are meant to suggest, the theories of the French feminists and their Anglo-American adaptations can help us see how Emecheta invites her readers to join her in traversing traditional cultural and narrative boundaries. Mary Jacobus, for example, tackles the difficult question of what it means to write as a woman, suggesting not that women try to get behind or beyond language but that we find strategies for working "within" it and breaking down its conventional boundaries (1986, 29). Conceiving difference in writing as "multiplicity, ambiguity and heterogeneity," Jacobus argues that such a view of language makes it possible for writers to achieve a "traversal" of sexual boundaries that reveals them to be nothing more than "the product of phallocentric discourse"—and thus subject to change (30). Similarly, on Sally Robinson's view, novels that challenge "the (masculine) realist tradition are taking an important step toward reconstituting the female subject." "For both Cixous and Irigaray"—and Robinson herself—"a specifically female discourse would be open-ended, not controlled by the structures (or strictures) of narrative closure" (1988, 115). Multiplicity. Ambiguity. Heterogeneity. Open-endedness. Surely all of these terms also describe Buchi Emecheta's fiction. Could we not say, then, that the difference in her writing violates sexual, textual, *and cultural* boundaries—that she, too, is engaged in reconstituting the subject? In the preceding chapter we see how Emecheta's fiction signifies on the Western narrative telos, calling into question the desirability of always promoting the rights of individuals over those of society. In this chapter we see (again) how she uses the English language to deconstruct its own hegemonic status and how she uses the so-called English novel to deconstruct British colonialism. We also see how she interrogates the heterosexual couple even as she invokes it in all three novels as a model of social organization. From Emecheta's point of view, even the meaning of the Nigerian civil war comes down to the relationship between the sexes, as is apparent in *Destination Biafra*, a shocking novel that brilliantly conflates the bitter legacy of British colonialism with sexual politics.

Destination Biafra (1982)

FROM A WOMAN'S PERSPECTIVE

In this novel Emecheta re-creates the major events of the Biafran War (1967-70) through several fictional characters intended to represent the differing political positions of the time. She describes her novel as "historical fiction," though the history in question occurs less than a decade and a half before the novel was written (Emecheta 1982, ix). The brief temporal gap between event and fiction makes it relatively easy to maintain the sense of continuity between past and present that Lukács calls for in a historical novel (1986), but Emecheta still manages to give her readers the sense that they are, indeed, reading about a completely different era. She does so by suggesting throughout the novel that Nigeria was still under British domination in the decade that fell between its formal independence and the end of its civil war (1960-70). She thus implies that the war finally was able to shatter the long-standing relationship between the colonized and the colonizer—even as it worked to dismantle certain troubling sexual divisions and differences. In fact, she envisions the possibility of so much social change occurring as a result of this conflict that she challenges Soyinka's argument that the war was not worth the cost in lives and suffering because, on his view, it *failed* to "shatter the foundations of thought and re-create [society anew]" (1988, 183).

According to Emecheta's fictionalized account of events, after the first post-independence election, the British governor appoints the Mallam Nguru Kano, a Hausa, to be prime minister, leaving the Igbos especially bitter that their own great leader has not been chosen. Their bitterness soon leads to civil unrest, inspiring the Western-educated heroine Debbie Ogedemgbe to enlist in the army. After a military coup, the rebels name an Igbo head of state. By calling for a new nationalism and abolishing tribal meetings, Brigadier Onyemere manages to satisfy the embittered Hausas. But seeing this as a betrayal of their common heritage, the Igbos have him assassinated. In their turn, the Hausas escalate the civil unrest, and Saka Momoh takes power. Though Momoh tries to keep the federation intact, Chijioke Abosi demands that the predominantly Igbo eastern sector be given political autonomy. Instead, Momoh divides the country into twelve states, forcing Abosi to declare independence for Biafra on 30 May 1967. As the two countries gear up for war, Debbie is sent on a peace mission to Biafra; on the way she is illegally detained by Nigerian troops, who rape her. When she finally arrives, Abosi curtly informs her that he has no intention of surrendering. Outraged by the atrocities she has witnessed, Debbie returns to England, where she collects food for Biafrans. By the time she comes back to Nigeria, the war is nearly over.

Even though Emecheta herself was in England during the war, she felt compelled to bring to light the events that devastated her own Igbo village of Ibuza. But having been convinced from reading Soyinka's 1972 prison notes, *The Man Died* (rpt. 1988), that people other than Igbos suffered during this bitter war, she writes in her foreword that it became important to her to make her heroine a representative Nigerian figure who rises above rancorous tribal divisions (viii).[1] She thus portrays Debbie Ogedemgbe as attempting a mission of reconciliation between Nigeria and Biafra. Educated at Oxford University and daughter of a rich and powerful man, Debbie represents both the Nigerian intellectuals and a new type of modern Nigerian woman. She is also the girlhood friend of the two political leaders, Chijioke Abosi and Saka Momoh. She is, moreover, sexually involved with Alan Grey, the British military officer on unofficial assignment in Nigeria, who is responsible for protecting his country's political and financial interests. In her relationships with the novel's most important male characters, Debbie manages to become the focus of much of the debate about sexual politics. Though she comes from an elite family, while she is in the army, she spends considerable time among ordinary folk who are simply trying to escape the terrors of war. By crossing tribal, sex, class, and educational boundaries, she thus achieves the kind of representativeness that Emecheta envisioned for her heroine.

On the surface, however, though her main character is a woman, this novel, as Emecheta herself remarks, is more male-oriented than her earlier ones because its plot revolves around political intrigue and internecine warfare (viii). Nor is there a shortage of sexist attitudes among the male characters. As much as Debbie tries to overcome sexual stereotyping by enlisting as a soldier, for example, she simply cannot avoid the fact that she is seen first and foremost as female. Even though she comes from a distinguished family and is named an emissary of Momoh himself, she is still just a woman to the soldiers. No matter her family connections or that she herself is highly educated, she is just as sexually vulnerable as the group of refugee women and children she travels with, and she vows that once the war is over, she will testify to the horrors she has experienced as a woman in time of war. She will call her book *Destination Biafra* (246). Even though the civil war is the subject of Emecheta's novel, the events she has chosen to highlight are almost incidental side effects of the fighting. In fact, virtually all the politics of war have been transformed here into the politics of women and children. Because of this transformation and the emphasis on Debbie's (representative) femaleness, I argue that Emecheta has subverted the so-called masculine subject of war from within by the very act of writing about it herself from a woman's perspective.[2] In fact, she might be said to be signifying on those novels that glorify the heroics of soldiers and ignore the pain of civilians.[3]

It may be through Debbie's interaction with several key male figures that Emecheta most obviously raises the issue of sexual politics, but, in one form or another, sexual politics permeates the novel, affecting the lives of even those who lead their countries to war. Right before Abosi decides to declare Biafra's independence, for example, his wife has a miscarriage. Though the impending war is certainly not responsible for this domestic tragedy, the fact that Emecheta pauses to describe it in extensive, painful detail suggests a woman's perspective at work. Unlike his wife, the military commander cannot stop to mourn his loss because the affairs "of his people" were of paramount importance (98). The death of his baby is also clearly a metaphor for Biafra's abortive independence and early death—a death Abosi cannot bear to witness. Coincidentally and tellingly, the wife of his political foe is also in labor and in need of a cesarean section. Before giving the doctors permission to proceed with the operation—and save Elizabeth's life—Momah first asks how large the scar would be and if it would "disfigure her much" (202). Elizabeth survives the operation, but the baby does not. It is, in fact, a "monstrosity" whose disfigurement Momoh blames on his wife (203). As I have noted in other instances, attitudes like these make it very difficult for Western women to feel kindly toward the African men in Emecheta's novels. Because she continues to describe these sexist attitudes, it would appear that Emecheta herself hopes to see them end someday. But these passages are not simply reflective of a Western feminism in her work. Momoh's domestic tragedy, like Abosi's, must be symbolic; his monster baby, for which he claims no responsibility, is surely a metaphor of the inhuman state he now rules—a state that tries to destroy an entire tribe of its own people. But because the men rule the country and seem to rule the women, too, it is hard for us to see beyond their sexist behavior. The problem Western readers face in this novel, as elsewhere in Emecheta's fiction, therefore, is maintaining a distinction between the people of Nigeria itself and the heinous acts and attitudes of a few individual male characters—a problem compounded (fairly or not) by the fact that many readers of Emecheta know little of Nigeria outside her fictional representations of it.[4] Maintaining this distinction is also difficult because the novel seems to insist that the politics of war and sexual politics are intertwined—a view apparently endorsed by Ali Mazrui, who asks in *The African Condition* how we human beings can "change our values and perceptions fundamentally enough to drastically reduce the danger of war." The answer, he believes, could lie "in a world of transformed sex roles" (1983, 135).

I would not argue that Emecheta actually manages to transform the sex roles in her novel, but she certainly manages to question them successfully. For who would lead the soldiers to war if men like Abosi and Momoh were attending their wives in childbirth? Who would do the fighting if everyone felt about war as Debbie does? As evidence of the blurring of sex roles in the novel, at least one critic points to the fact that Debbie has enlisted as a soldier, indefinitely postponing becoming a wife and mother—and in so doing revealed her androgynous nature (Frank 1984, 40-41). While it is true that Debbie chooses the active life of soldiering, I argue that she never fully accepts its responsibilities. After she unwittingly participates in the torture and suffocation of several Igbo officers, for example, she recoils in horror from what she has done, and from this moment on, instead of fighting in the war, she spends her time fighting against it. Convinced that disparate (even warring) peoples can be brought together by common values, she maintains steadfastly that Biafra symbolizes an idealized good that everyone should strive for (236, 128). Rather than calling Debbie androgynous, therefore, I prefer to say that she transcends traditional sex roles—and she does so in the sovereign act of naming herself and naming her enemy.[5]

We witness Debbie's achievement near the end of the war, when Biafra is on the verge of collapse. Alan Grey is trying to convince Debbie she must use her feminine wiles to stop Chijioke Abosi from deploying biological weapons. If she does not succeed, Grey warns her that Momoh and his allies will take their superior armaments into Biafra and crush the uprising. Knowing that Abosi finds Debbie attractive, Alan advises her to get the rebel leader to surrender by flirting with him. In angry response, Debbie slaps him for the way he and his "country have fallen" in the estimation of African countries (255). She thus begins to assert her independence from her white lover. But because Debbie is portrayed as a representative Nigerian, this is also a reply that functions symbolically to break the colonial stranglehold on her country. Alan thinks he has spoken personally to her, but she recognizes the political significance of his command and has responded accordingly, reaffirming the connection in this novel between sexual politics and colonization.[6] A few days later, as a defeated Abosi flees the country, Alan, worried for Debbie's safety, asks if she wants to marry him and go to England. She responds by proudly declaring independence for herself and her country, rejoining angrily that she, for one, will never align herself with a former colonizer (258). When Alan pleads further, she retorts that it had not bothered her to have him as her lover, "but Africa will never again stoop to being your wife" (259). In this spirited exchange between the former oppressor and oppressed, Debbie Ogedemgbe is clearly intended to represent a unified and finally free Nigeria. That Debbie declares independence by refusing to become Alan's wife is significant, especially when she uses the same metaphor to declare Africa's independence. But she also describes herself as different from Abosi and other men who, in her eyes, remain "colonized"[7]—and establishes the thoroughness of her own decolonization by naming Alan Grey her "male concubine," thus reversing the balance of power between them (259). Fanon has argued that the colonized individual "is an oppressed person whose permanent dream is to become the persecutor" (1968, 53). Though Debbie may not want to become Alan's persecutor, their exchange at the end suggests that the (Western-educated) African (woman) has thrown off what Fanon calls the thinking "of the colonialist bourgeoisie"—just as Emecheta herself has thrown off the traditional narratives of the West (1968, 49).

Or, perhaps a better way to express what I see happening here is to say that Debbie Ogedemgbe has found a way to *contain* and *control* the "forms of thought" that would colonize her, whether these forms are Western or African in their origins (Fanon, 49). To borrow from Nina Auerbach, we might say that Debbie has found a way to "engorge" the patriarchy (1987). That is, she has taken from her African heritage and her Western education only what suits her. Taking these teachings as her own, she has found a way to make them work for her—by writing herself an identity as an independent, decolonized woman (much the way Adah Obi does in *Second-Class Citizen*). By extension, we can also argue that Emecheta has used her fiction in a Foucauldian effort to create a new subjectivity for herself. In "claiming power" over what would embrace and erase her identity (Auerbach 1987, 158), Emecheta helps establish an African corollary to the African American women's literary tradition. Elizabeth Fox-Genovese describes Zora Neale Hurston, for example, as a writer who "refused the limitations of gender and cultivated what she took to be the language of her readers only to subvert—or manipulate—their values" (1987, 176). Unlike Hurston, who was forced to negotiate an identity for herself as a black woman in a white culture, Debbie does not have to fight this battle. Hers is the (different but analogous) battle to negotiate an identity as a decolonized woman in a colonized culture. That Emecheta herself has successfully fought this battle on the playing fields of England is evidence of her own strength of character. But it also testifies to the strength and resilience of her African heritage—and the adaptability of the novelistic form. Although some of her heroines have been influenced by their Western education, they do not become Western heroines. Instead, in their attitudes and in the roles they play in Emecheta's narratives, these women remain very much African heroines.[8] But in portraying Debbie as a representative Nigerian, Emecheta once again invites us to compare certain Western feminist and African literary traditions—in this case, the tradition of collective protagonists.

SEXUAL/TEXTUAL POLITICS

This notion of a collective protagonist is introduced in its African context by Lewis Nkosi in *Tasks and Masks*. Here he discusses a group of novels—*A Grain of Wheat* (1967), *God's Bits of Wood* (1960), *Things Fall Apart* (1958), and *Arrow of God* (1967)—that have a common "vision of history as a collective working out of a people's destiny." In these four novels, individual characters still retain importance, but "it is the collective fate shared out among members of the community that provides the novels with their single most important source of energy" (1981, 31; see also Izevbaye 1986). Though the concept of a collective protagonist is uncommon in Western literature, it can readily be found in much feminist science fiction, as we see in DuPlessis's discussion of group protagonists in Charlotte Perkins Gilman, Joanna Russ, Marge Piercy, and Doris Lessing.[9] Seeming to echo Nkosi, DuPlessis argues that these speculative novels "replace individual heroes or sealed couples with groups, which have a sense of purpose and identity" (1985, 179). In short, these novels—whether written by Africans or Western feminists—help to subvert the public/private dichotomy that Myra Jehlen finds at the core of Western (middle-class) fiction.

A similar emphasis on a collective protagonist or history as hero is certainly at work in *Destination Biafra*, as Debbie Ogedemgbe experiences the same divisions and healing process as experienced by Nigeria itself. In the same way that the war ravages the country and its people, Debbie herself is brutally raped by soldiers until she is senseless. In the same way that the war divides the country, Debbie is also torn between her admiration for Biafra's socialistic ideals and her desire that it remain part of the Nigerian federation—though the federation itself, as the novel makes clear, remains enthralled to Great Britain. In the same way that Nigeria must learn to free itself from British meddling, therefore, Debbie must learn to free herself from Alan Grey. By describing Debbie as "simply a Nigerian" (viii), Emecheta herself suggests that she wants us to read her heroine as a collective protagonist, someone whose fate is tied ineluctably to that of her country and its people—a reading that returns to the concept of "individual" the meaning of "inseparable" that Williams reminds us it originally had in medieval England. But, more fundamentally, it also entails an African understanding of the text, as it is premised on the interconnection between an individual and her society. In other words, it allows us to see not only that Emecheta writes beyond Cixous's male/female metaphor but that she also writes beyond traditional Western romantic endings by giving voice to Fanon's contention that, in the process of true decolonization, "[i]ndividualism is the first [of the Mediterranean values] to disappear." During the colonial period, Fanon continues, the "colonialist bourgeoisie had hammered into the native's mind the idea of a society of individuals where each person shuts himself up in his own subjectivity." But when the revolution comes, "the interests of one will be the interests of all" (1968, 47). To reach this point of wholeness, however, Debbie and her people must first suffer almost intolerable pain—pain they primarily inflict on themselves with a little help from their British friends. Though their de jure independence is gained without violence, to achieve de facto independence, the country must endure a bloody and bitter war. According to Fanon, "decolonization is always a violent phenomenon"—whether the aspirations of the colonized are those of "[n]ational liberation, national renaissance, the restoration of nationhood to the people, [or] commonwealth" (35). In Emecheta's novel, much of this violence is committed by men upon the women.

Though Alan tries to use Debbie for his own political purposes, he does not abuse her sexually. Instead, the rape is left to her own people—just as other atrocities are committed by Nigerians on their own people. Weeks after the Nigerian soldiers have gang-raped Debbie, one of their officers, Lawal Salihu, pulls her out of the crowd of refugees and forces her to go into his quarters, threatening her with the promise that he will show her that she is "nothing but a woman"—surely a most graphic demonstration of the power men can wield over women (175). Debbie tells him that Allah will never forgive him for compounding the violence done her already by other soldiers (176). He offers a halfhearted apology but then asserts that because she has been raped, no man will ever want to marry her. Angered by the hypocrisy in Salihu's pious disgust, Debbie snaps back that "men have so many problems to solve," all of which they have brought on themselves (177). It is significant that instead of seeing Salihu's affront in strictly personal terms, she responds to the larger social situation by implying that the men have treated Nigeria as poorly as they treat women—once more establishing her role as a collective protagonist in the novel. Sexual politics also infiltrates the relationship between Debbie and her lifelong friends who are now powerful military officers. Seeing her as little more than a sexual pawn, these men do not hesitate to involve her in their scheming. After the coup, Abosi suggests that Debbie join them since she could use Alan (sexually) to get more weapons. Onyemere concurs, arguing that she could be a "useful tool" to them (69). Furthermore, when she is named Momoh's official emissary to Biafra, none of the men recognizes her new status. Chief Odumosu warns her, for example, not to interfere with things that do not concern her and never to forget that she is "a woman" (129). Though Abosi says she has been brave in undertaking her mission, he asks her scornfully what good she thinks she might have accomplished, "just you, little you?" To this taunt, Debbie responds angrily: "I am me. Debbie, daughter of Ogedemgbe." She then asks Abosi if he would have treated her so contemptuously had she been a man with the same credentials (239). Lest Western readers become too emotionally overwrought by how the African men mistreat Debbie, however, we should recall that in an earlier passage of free indirect discourse the narrator has informed us that women used to enjoy more sexual equality before their people had been colonized (118).[10]

If Alan and Debbie (literally) represent the love/hate relationship between England and Nigeria at this time, other couples represent conflicting attitudes toward the Biafran conflict. As the war comes to an end, Mrs. Elina Eze tells her husband that they have been defeated and should flee. Her husband, however, has faith in Abosi's plans to use biological weapons and so intends to stay. When she hears this, Mrs. Eze looks at her husband as though he were hallucinating (252). The best she can do is pity him for sharing the blindness of other men. As she departs in dismay, Dr. Eze is lost in dreams of a new Biafra where he will be rich and powerful beyond belief (253). This fantasy comes very close to the ambitions expressed by two real-life Nigerian leaders, Dr. Nnamdi Azikiwe and Chief Obafemi Awolowo. According to Achebe's account, in 1937 Azikiwe promised that he would "utilize [his] earned income to secure [his] enjoyment of a high standard of living and also to give a helping hand to the needy." For his part, Awolowo set out to make himself "formidable intellectually, morally invulnerable, to make all the money that is possible for a man with [his] brains and brawn to make in Nigeria." As Achebe remarks, these attitudes "are more likely to produce aggressive millionaires than selfless leaders of their people" (1984, 11). In this particular instance, it would appear that Africa has nothing to teach us, that its leaders are as corrupt as our own.

Like the men, many older women are also uncomfortable with the changes they see in the culture. Babs Teteku's mother and Debbie's mother, for example, openly dislike the new identities their daughters have assumed. Mrs. Teteku feels that Babs has been corrupted by her stay in England, where she has learned she can act like a man (122). After she learns that her daughter has been raped, Stella Ogedemgbe, speaking in the traditional Voice of the Fathers, fatalistically comforts Debbie by observing that women are destined to be violated (157). When she realizes that Debbie wants to continue her mission, her mother pleads with her to get married to protect her reputation, reminding her that she will gain no respect if she remains single (159). The attitudes taken by Debbie's mother seem to echo those of Nnu Ego and Ojebeta before her, both of whom cling to the notion that they have to be married to be respectable. But even in portraying such conventional attitudes in her women, as we have already seen, Emecheta questions them—and in the process questions what Cixous identifies as the patriarchal concept of the heterosexual *couple*, the concept around which culture itself has been organized (1981b, 44).[11] Though the worldview Emecheta learned growing up in Nigeria does not elevate women to the co-equal status demanded by Western (liberal) feminists, it does, as I have been suggesting throughout this study, express the feminist ideals of cooperation, community, and oneness with nature. When Emecheta focuses on the *couple* in these novels, therefore, though she may not critique the male as much as Western feminists might like (or think), I believe she is invoking a binary system (male/female) primarily to dismantle it. Other evidence of how Emecheta undermines Western discourse from within can be found in the many examples of double-voiced discourse in the novel.

DOUBLE-VOICED DISCOURSE AND INTERPRETIVE DILEMMAS

One such scene occurs when the soldiers crash Abosi's wedding party with a message for Onyemere. The newly appointed prime minister, Nguru Kano, is offended, but the narrator tells us that "Alan, somehow always at the right place at the right time," acted immediately to correct the officers' oversight by addressing Kano himself (47). Though it would appear that this statement is intended to be an ironic commentary on Alan's continual interference in Nigerian affairs, the narrator describes the officers' oversight as one of "neglect," implying that Alan has done the right thing by interfering. Indeed, it is possible to see that Alan has had to deliver the message himself because "[1] *in the eyes of those present*, it was presumably because [2] *[Kano] was too important to be approached by an ordinary black soldier*. After all, should he not as head of state be informed if anything had gone wrong [3] *in his democratic society?* [4] *Yet the poor man was living in cloud-cuckooland to be thinking of the kind of democratic society the British had been practising to perfection in their own country for hundreds of years* [5] *and which they now thought should work instantly in the colonies they had ruled for so long*" (48; emphases added). Whose point of view is expressed in this complex passage? Though the first italicized phrase [1] seems to suggest that the second one [2] is the view of the wedding guests, the other views cannot be so easily ascribed to them. Is there no irony in phrase three [3], for example? The wedding guests would probably not invoke any irony here, which means that the phrase is double-voiced, expressing two different points of view. The alien point of view is repeated in the next sentence [4] with the use of the phrase "cloud-cuckooland"; but whose voice is it? Is it the narrator's? If so, does the narrator really think the English have been practicing democracy "to perfection"? Somehow I doubt it. So this phrase must also be double-voiced, expressing the British view of themselves. But then the sentence continues with a criticism of the British [5] who (naively? arrogantly?) think they can impose their brand of democracy "instantly" on a former colony. I suspect, therefore, that the entire scene is yet another example of Emecheta's signifying on white colonial fiction—as she invokes the British phrases and points of view only to mock and delegitimate them.

Though she does give the British their own voice in this novel, Emecheta seems determined to warn all African peoples about the potential for political interference from Western powers (see Emecheta's foreword to this novel, viii). How the Nigerians are used by the British constitutes much of the story. But much of the criticism must be unlocked from a carefully modulated narrative voice that gives the appearance of impartiality. Alan Grey, for example, is a complicated figure. He may be self-serving, but he is no stereotypical monster. For all his double-dealing and treachery, he does seem to care for Debbie, though his feelings are clearly ambivalent. As arrogant as he is, however, he is not without knowledge of Nigerian customs and is astute enough to recognize the inherent weakness of tribalism, noting that the word "tribe" is able to bring people together and split them apart (8).[12] His huge collection of African artifacts provides further evidence of his complexity, increasing the ambivalence we ourselves feel toward him. Someday the collection will make him rich, but many of the things he ships back to England are religious artifacts that newly converted Nigerians have discarded. As the narrator indicates, "[b]y the time Nigerians came to appreciate the worth of their own products, irreplaceable valuables would have been sold to adorn the home of English aristocrats or rich Americans" (4). Who is being criticized here? The British for looting a national treasure? Or the Nigerians for letting them? What is the alternative? Is it better that the artifacts be thrown in the bush to rot? To answer this, we need to look beyond the situation and recognize that the artifacts would not have been thrown out in the first place if Western missionaries had not converted the Africans. So Grey and his ilk, while preserving priceless relics, are still benefiting from the ravages of colonialism.[13]

Western readers find these passages uneasy going, especially when the white men begin to characterize the Africans. For example, Sir Fergus, Alan Grey's father, proposes a toast to the British Empire, and Macdonald chastises him for living in the past. Fergus retorts that he "cannot imagine people like them" running a country (5). Because this is said in the context of a novel that is about to describe the horrors of the Biafran War, we, too, are tempted to agree with Sir Fergus's position. It is a position that even some Nigerians have taken; in *Sunset in Biafra*, for example, Elechi Amadi asserts, "[n]o African nation has truly emerged from colonialism. No African nation has shown that it is truly capable of running its own affairs" (1978, 89). Emecheta's novel suggests the same attitude with a twist: the *men* are incapable of ruling Nigeria, but perhaps the women could do it. During a heated discussion, Debbie tells Babs that anybody at all can see that Biafra is not strong enough to battle the whole country, and Babs retorts: "Any fool of a woman, perhaps, but not men"—especially the military leaders (109).

Though Western readers would probably have few qualms about aligning themselves with Babs and Debbie, we are nonetheless uneasy about claiming kinship to the Westerners in the novel—even if their attitudes often tempt us. Though we may be tempted to agree with Sir Fergus that Nigerians cannot rule themselves, our doubts about his judgment return when he and his friends make jokes about the African leaders. Macdonald goes so far as to be "amused by the Sardauna's great headdress" (5). As the spiritual leader of the Muslim Hausas, the Sardauna is a man to be respected, if not revered. Is this ignorant mockery what we want to align ourselves with? The question becomes more complicated when Alan addresses his compatriots: those who inhabit the northern part of the country, are "'comparatively ignorant and happy in their ignorance,' *Alan pointed out with regret*" (6; emphasis added). What a tempting position he takes: he criticizes the Hausas for being happy in their ignorance, but he does so "with regret." In other words, the text itself invites us to agree with him and share his sorrow that Africans have to be described in such negative terms. The temptation continues as Alan speaks about the problems inherent to returning the country's vast oil reserves to the control of Nigerians, who had sat on these resources for thousands of years without knowing "what to do with them." If we have been able to resist the impression that the Hausas are ignorant and the whole country backward for not utilizing its mineral and oil reserves, Alan then invites us to consider the corruption among even the "best" Nigerians, who can be bribed by anyone "with a few thousand pounds' 'dash' and some yards of shiny cloth" (6). After Alan calls the Igbos "ambition personified," his father agrees that they are "extremely intelligent. But they are greedy as well, and their arrogance could lead them into trouble" (7). Intelligent, yes. But also ambitious, greedy, and arrogant. Not much here to admire. If Western readers are looking for corroboration of this bigoted view of Igbos, they apparently need look no further than the other Nigerian tribes, who, according to Achebe, can "achieve consensus on no other matter than their common resentment of the Igbo. They would all describe them as *aggressive, arrogant* and *clannish*. Most would add *grasping* and *greedy*" (1984, 45). Achebe attributes this resentment to the Igbos' remarkable success in adapting themselves to the requirements of colonial society (46). In his words, their rise to power "was due to the self-confidence engendered by their open society and their belief that one man is as good as another, that no condition is permanent" (47). The same Igbo adaptability that is resented by other Nigerians is apparently seen as a kind of threat by the British, who want nothing more than to keep the country under their control. When Alan describes them as ambitious and intelligent, therefore, he reveals his concern that once the Igbos are free, they will want nothing to do with England.

The kind of corruption Alan mentions is also hard for many Western readers to fully understand.[14] Should we see Alan's statement as evidence of his own prejudice and dismiss the charge as inaccurate? Or should we accept the criticism as just? If so, what then? There is no simple solution. Though it has nothing to do with the question of magic or rationality, it is the same kind of cross-cultural interpretive dilemma addressed by Winch and Taylor. That is, we can try to see it in the context of Nigerian history and tradition and find the culture blameless (thus illustrating the error Taylor identifies as his incorrigibility thesis). Or, conversely, we can invoke our own (admittedly falsely idealized) value system as a standard and condemn the society for its rampant corruption (thus illustrating the error Taylor calls ethnocentric positivism). Or we can try to discover a human constant at work within the tradition and use the language of perspicuous contrast to try to understand both the Nigerians and ourselves. It is a complex problem that is capable of complicating our response to more than one African novel. In *No Longer at Ease*, for example, the main character, Obi Okonkwo, has studied in England and thus learned Western values, but he, too, is corrupted by the system. Hoping at first to initiate reform in his country, he refuses all bribes. But habitually spending more than he earns, he soon becomes hopelessly in debt. Facing financial ruin, he compromises his principles and accepts money. Unfortunately for Obi, he has been set up and is immediately arrested. Mr. Green, a British co-worker, claims that Obi succumbed because the "African is corrupt through and through" (Achebe 1975a, 3). Because I am offended by the corrupt system that has ruined Obi, I am tempted to agree with Mr. Green's interpretation. But this means I have agreed with someone who thinks all Africans are inferior. Lest readers are too tempted by his theory, however, the novel ends with the statement that no one could understand why Obi took the bribe: "The British Council man, even the men of Umuofia, did not know. And we must presume that, *in spite of his certitude*, Mr. Green did not know either" (154; emphasis added). The question we are left with, therefore, is, why did Obi violate his own moral code to accept an illegal bribe? Gerald Moore attributes Obi's fall from grace to character flaws, arguing that the novel portrays not "a situation in which an idealistic young man is bound to fail, but a situation in which a weak and indecisive one will" (1980, 130). Kofi Awoonor argues similarly that Obi is "vacillating, weak, and lacking any moral center whatever" (1975, 269). Achebe himself suggests that other forces are at work when he claims that corruption in his country "has passed the alarming and entered the fatal stage; and Nigeria will die if we keep pretending that she is only slightly indisposed." He explains that Nigerians are corrupt not because they are "fundamentally" different from other people but because "the system under which they live today makes corruption easy and profitable" (1984, 38). He concludes that "we are all living witnesses to the failure of helpless integrity to solve the problem of rampant corruption which threatens now to paralyse this country" (43).

A lesser form of corruption is seen in the behavior of the main character of Kole Omotoso's *The Edifice* (1971). Like Obi Okonkwo, Dele also goes to study in England. While there he cheerfully admits to paying too little for his biscuits in the common room: "Usually I paid according to the number of pennies I could find in my pocket. Invariably I underpaid. Or maybe I should say that since I'd been going there I'd not overpaid" (15). He also refuses to wash his dirty coffee cup, even though a sign posted in the room requests that he do so. But he does not feel guilty. To the contrary, he seems almost flippant, making a joke of cheating on his payment. Because Dele is dishonest in this scene, it is difficult for me to feel sympathy for him at other times. In short, I find it almost impossible to overcome the different cultural values that separate us—a situation that parallels the story itself, as Dele and his Western wife are torn apart by their conflicting values.

The same problem occurs in Emecheta's novel. Because of my own Western point of view, as war begins to break out in Nigeria, I confess to being tempted by Alan Grey's estimation of the country and its people. I doubt very much, however, that this is what Emecheta had in mind. In fact, the heteroglossia in this novel convinces me that Emecheta is, indeed, attempting to present an impartial account of this bitter war, where no side is more guilty than another—and where no one is innocent, except perhaps for the children. When I read about the genocide that Nigerians committed on their own people, however, I find myself, as a Western reader, withdrawing in horror from Emecheta's account of her native country. But, to the novel's credit, as the narrative progresses, I find it just as hard to justify my allegiance to Alan's Western perspective. What I am left with is sympathy for the women of Nigeria, a sympathy the novel is able to generate, in part, because it is narrated from a woman's point of view. Feeling such sympathy toward the women, however, I find myself deeply resenting the sexist behavior of the men—and must work to remember the distinction I made earlier: these novels are not reflections *of* Nigeria but Emecheta's personal reflections *on* it. Even so, this distinction does little to comfort me.

Because I am convinced that Emecheta herself would not entirely welcome the thoroughgoing resentment I feel toward the men in her novel, I think the depth of my own response cannot help but call into question the success of Emecheta's enterprise—the success, that is, of the cross-cultural conversation in which she engages me. Intellectually, I can appreciate how her text violates traditional boundaries by signifying on the master narratives of the West and documenting the violent decolonization of Nigeria. But to the end I remain emotionally incapable of understanding the African men she has portrayed. Incapable of understanding them, I find myself incapable of understanding the culture—at least as it has been portrayed here. This dilemma seems to be at the heart of a politicized postmodernism, as my feminist demands do battle with my postmodern desires. I want to be open to the newness of the text, but I refuse to extend that openness infinitely. In this respect, I think, Emecheta and her texts are more postmodern than their readers (at least this reader). She seems far more tolerant of Nigerian customs than I am—thus making it difficult for me to achieve a fusion of horizons with her texts. Perhaps this is yet another example of how cross-cultural readings necessarily involve misunderstandings. But, regardless of my failure, she has managed in this novel, as she manages elsewhere, to get me to read—and think—in the language of perspicuous contrast.

Double Yoke (1983)

DIDACTICISM AND HETEROGLOSSIA

Double Yoke marks the first time that Emecheta filters her story through the eyes of a male protagonist, and in so doing she manages to generate some sympathy for a character who clings all too tenaciously to his traditional upbringing. But even as her hero explains himself, his self-serving account is undermined by the novel's double-voiced discourse and by several passages where the authorial voice interjects itself to make an openly propagandistic feminist point. Although the authorial Voice of the Daughters seems genuinely to reflect a feminist perspective here, this novel presents me with as many moments of misunderstanding as any of Emecheta's previous ones—moments where the text itself seems to be ruptured, or I simply fail to understand the meaning. The story takes place at the University of Calabar and is dedicated to Emecheta's students in the Department of English and Literary Studies.[15] The major witness to the action, Miss Bulewao, has been hired to teach a course in creative writing largely because she is Nigeria's "most talked about" woman writer (Emecheta 1983b, 6). The narrative itself falls into four major sections: (1) the assignment Miss Bulewao gives the class; (2) the essay written by the hero, Ete Kamba; (3) Miss Bulewao's advice to Ete about his personal life; and

(4) her lecture to the rest of the class. Though hers is the dominant voice in the novel, the bulk of the narration is Ete's story, which is inexplicably infused with several scenes which are told from his girl friend's point of view. The plot of Ete's story is simple, however, inviting us to look elsewhere for the narrative complexity that always marks Emecheta's fiction.

Ete, as he tells it, falls in love with Nko, who allows him to have sexual intercourse with her before they are married. Convinced that Nko was not a virgin at the time, Ete, driven quite mad with anger and frustration, confides in Professor Ikot, who tells him to find someone more suited to his station in life —and then arranges to become her faculty adviser so he might force her to have sex. Nko gets her revenge, however, by blackmailing Ikot into promising her a first-class honors degree. When Ete discovers this illicit liaison, he and his friends attack Ikot in his office. But by now Nko is pregnant and will say only that she plans to raise the baby by herself. After Ete concludes his essay, Miss Bulewao meets privately with him (160). This scene is separated from the rest of the novel by a wide, black, horizontal bar, suggesting a different "author" is at work, though this author, too, has access to Ete's thoughts. Miss Bulewao's opening move is to ask Ete why he just does not marry Nko, who, like other up-to-date Nigerian women, is nearly "priceless" (161). When Ete expresses concern about the propriety of Nko raising the child on her own, Miss Bulewao lectures him again, reminding him that Nko will certainly be able to afford to do it since she is educated. Then she accuses him of worrying that people will think him weak if he forgives Nko. To convince him that a generosity of spirit is no sign of weakness, she (astonishingly) invokes the example of Adolf Hitler, whom she admires for having been able to love "cats and music"; in her eyes, having a "large heart" like Hitler makes a man "great" (162). How are we to understand these comments? Though this is surely a moment of rupture for Western readers, there is an explanation of sorts in *Head Above Water* (1986) where Emecheta recalls that her father named her brother "after the man [he] thought was the toughest on earth—Adolphus Hitler" (11). Even so, this memory does little to explain why a fascist monster is presented as a model of strength to a young African struggling with the burden of redefining his own manhood. Nor is Miss Bulewao through lecturing Ete, as she rebukes him for failing to keep up with his progressive girlfriend. Because Ete disagrees with Miss Bulewao, the scene seems on the surface to contain heteroglossia enough. But the ultimate effect of having this famous author do battle with the hero is to silence his point of view. It is just too easy to think that Emecheta herself is speaking here. Though Miss Bulewao says that writing the story has taught Ete to give up his quest for a virgin, the story itself has not shown us this transformation. Thus, what is supposed to be Ete's final rite of passage into maturity does little more than make us feel as though we ourselves are being instructed—even though many of Miss Bulewao's ideas are already our own.

This scene is separated from the next by another wide, horizontal bar. What follows and concludes the novel is Miss Bulewao's lecture to the class. During class she learns that Ete has left to help Nko, whose father has just died. She replies that she is glad to hear that her students are "bearing [their] double burdens or yokes or whatever heroically" (163). The outcome may constitute a happy ending for Ete and Nko (he goes to her aid, having recognized his communal responsibilities), but I find Miss Bulewao's lectures terribly contrived.[16] It would have been much more convincing if Emecheta had let the characters fight it out among themselves (it would also have been a good idea to subject this passage and others in the novel to some rigorous editing).

In some respects, the plot seems to reflect a modern version of Frye's comic mode. As if to make this connection herself, Emecheta calls chapter 3 "Boy Meets Girl." But it is the comic mode with a bitterly ironic twist. For when boy loses girl, he does not lose her because the old society disapproves of the match. He loses her because he has confided his secret to a depraved authority figure, a minister who decides that he wants Nko's sexual favors for himself—a man who habitually seduces young girls by playing the role of trusted elder. If Professor Ikot is functioning as a comic blocking agent who represents societal values, the society in question is hopelessly corrupt, as Achebe asseverates. But the hero is not particularly admirable either, as he stubbornly clings to the sexist attitudes of his upbringing. When Ete first meets Miss Bulewao, for example, he indulges in a little fantasy that someday he will be as famous as she is. But he is soon brought to his senses. Realizing that he has stooped to comparing himself with a woman, he asks, "How low could one sink?" (9).

Aside from its sexism, this passage presents readers with additional interpretive problems. Though we are privy to Ete's thoughts, we do not know who has given us access to them. Because Emecheta's novel is written from the premise that Ete is writing a story from life for his creative writing class, it is possible that he is the narrator here. If so, then he must assume his readers will agree with his assessment of women. But what does he gain by making himself look so foolish? Or is this passage evidence of another narrative voice at work in the novel, a female voice that more accurately represents Emecheta's own views? Is Ete's confession therefore double-voiced, expressing the depth of his own corruption that he feels no shame for having these sexist thoughts? If he is planning to get his revenge against Ikot, he gets off to a shaky start when he reveals his real feelings about women, for what he says is not calculated to win over any women readers—African or Western. Then there is his subsequent vow that he will get his revenge against Ikot by revealing "that masses in the university campus are oppressed. . . . He had nothing to lose but the chains which now bound his thoughts" (12). Surely this reference to Marx is a clear example of double-voiced discourse. Ete may be serious, but the context makes the connection sound parodic. What are the chains that bind his thoughts anyway? To him they may be one thing, but to the Western reader—and one presumes to the narrator—the chains are those of patriarchal thinking. His ideal woman, for example, is someone younger than he and not as far along in school, a woman like his mother but educated. "A very quiet and submissive woman, a good cook, a good listener, a good worker" (26). This sounds like the kind of idealized woman described in American popular fiction and magazines of the 1950s. In fact, Ete is a great fan of Western literature, and his friends even accuse him of being influenced by all the novels he has read (65). Nko, on the other hand, is a modern African woman who wants marriage, children, and a career—and not seriatim. Because she cares for Ete, she is willing to take the risk of having unprotected sex on the night they celebrate his winning a scholarship. But the more Ete thinks about it, the more he begins to suspect that it had not been the first time for Nko, and "[h]e wanted a virgin, an educated virgin" (54). An educated virgin. It would be hilarious if it were not so awful.

Completely demoralized, he tells Nko she is "a whore" who only pretends to be innocent (57). She suggests that if she is a whore, so is he for having sex with her. To this accusation Ete Kamba "reacted the way his father would have. . . . He resorted to . . . the brutal near animal method. He started to beat her" (59). If, indeed, the story is written from Ete's point of view, it would appear from this passage that the act of writing it has somehow helped him to overcome some of his patriarchal ways of thinking, for the passage seems to contain an implicit criticism of such brutal behavior. But the textual evidence is never very convincing one way or the other, leaving the question of authorship always in doubt. As the scene continues, for example, we are unexpectedly given access to Nko's private thoughts: she had decided to have sex again "because she said to herself, 'what is there to lose now?'" (60). It seems unlikely that Ete has written the account of their intercourse since it reveals his feelings of inadequacy, making him feel "like that little boy who had been holding his mother's lappa" for comfort (60). Would the manly Ete Kamba really put these feelings of sexual inadequacy on paper for the famous Miss Bulewao to read? The narration continues to reveal his innermost thoughts, but the writing seems more and more to be double-voiced, as we learn that if Nko had, indeed, been a virgin, Ete "would have happily hurt her, going through that masculine profound anguish. . . . Oh, how he would have loved her, how he would have held her" (61). Happily hurt her? Masculine profound anguish? Innocent, yet educated? Again, this passage would be hilarious if it did not so accurately express the crazy, harmful ideas Ete Kamba has about the woman he professes to love. But even if we cannot bring ourselves to laugh, surely we can appreciate (what I hope is) Emecheta's irony in this double-voiced passage. If I am wrong, and these passages are not double-voiced, they certainly provide additional moments of misunderstanding.

Because the novel often reflects Nko's point of view, the authorship of other passages is also in question. Nko and her friends are given so much to say, in fact, that it appears Ete's story has been embellished by another narrator. Even if the scenes are intended to show Ete's changing perspective, how could he know what these women say among themselves in their dormitory room? Whoever is responsible for including a female perspective, it does act as a corrective to Ete's. After he has accused her of being a whore, for example, Nko tells him that she wants him as he is, in contrast to him wanting her as he thinks she ought to be (62). When he observes that the prospects of remaining single do not seem to bother her, she retorts that he would like to see her kill herself if she has to remain single. Unable to see the irony in her assertion, he agrees that a single woman would be "better off dead" (63). Later, Nko reveals her own self doubts, confessing to her mother that she wants to be both a professional and an "obedient wife." Her mother responds sympathetically that Nko does, indeed, carry "a double yoke" (94).

Though the woman's perspective is very well represented in this narrative that has purportedly been written by a man, one of its more puzzling and disturbing aspects is the cruel way Sister Dr. Mrs. Edet is described. We are first introduced to this woman in chapter 8, where we learn that she is second only to Professor Ikot in the power she wields at the university. It is hard to tell whether it is her authority, her religion, or her appearance that the narrator finds most intolerable. When Sister Edet confesses her faith, she is said to lean toward her audience "with her long neck craned," as though her listener were expected to be overcome with "envy" or "gratitude." Such "power" makes her very nearly feel "like that Reverend John [sic] Jones," who had driven hundreds of people to suicide (79). Though we can reasonably assume this comparison reflects Ete Kamba's point of view, as he vowed to unveil the abuses of power in his creative writing essay, we cannot be sure. (And whose mistake is the "John" Jones?) We are then told that Sister Edet was a woman "who was desperately trying to be feminine, but whose height and flat chestedness" had made that goal impossible (81). I frankly find this judgment of Sister Edet offensive and would argue that the comment reflects only Ete's narrow point of view and not the narrator's (or Emecheta's), except for the fact that I am not sure Ete is really narrating these first few chapters, and the attack on Edet's appearance is repeated in chapter 11, "The Female Students." These students, one of whom is American, are Nko's roommates. When the subject of Sister Edet comes up, one of the young African students remarks that any woman who had "a neck like that, and a chest as flat as any man's" would want to convince everyone that she is, indeed, a female. Then Esther makes the shopworn accusation that Sister Edet is prouder of being married than of having a doctoral degree (102). Though these disparaging remarks are contained in dialogue and not narration, I cannot decide if they represent the values that the novel—or Emecheta herself—endorses.

Theoretically, of course, instead of trying to determine the origins of these remarks, I should be able to take refuge (if not comfort) in Bakhtin's notion of dialogized heteroglossia or that of textual plurality. Unfortunately, however, poststructuralist theory seems to fail us during emotional crises like these. Just as Ebeogu and Ogunyemi are provoked to anger by what they see as Emecheta's anti-African sentiments, I am provoked by what I see as evidence of a lingering misogyny in this novel. I want to know the source of this misogyny. I want to know if it is an accurate reflection of Emecheta's attitudes about professional women, especially since the rest of her writing seems absent such thinking. With the possible exception of Nnu Ego, who feels she must compete with Adaku for her husband's attention, there is also, for example, no fighting among women in Emecheta's novels. In fact, as I argued earlier, the loyal friendships that blossom between Adah Obi and the other women on the dole make for a rather extraordinary expression of female bonding. For these reasons, I am perplexed by the remarks in *Double Yoke*—especially because Nko and her mother seem so close and because the women in the dormitory are so supportive of one another. In a novel that otherwise seems sympathetic to ambitious, progressive women, why is there this need to attack the physical appearance of such a successful one? Is this a personal vendetta that has found its way into the narrative? Or have I missed the meaning of the novel altogether?

THAT WHICH DIVIDES US

If I cannot answer these questions nor determine the origins of the disparaging remarks about Sister Edet, I also cannot determine whether we are to accept Mrs. Nwaizu's remarks as representative of Emecheta's views. Mrs. Nwaizu, an older student who lives in the dormitory, is portrayed as someone whose background and knowledge of African culture "qualify her" to ask Nko certain questions (100). She certainly speaks with authority when she summarizes the difficulties involved with being a feminist in Nigeria, where feminism is associated with "everything the society says is bad in women. Independence, outspokenness, immorality, all the ills [imaginable]" (104). If, indeed, Mrs. Nwaizu speaks for Emecheta (and it sounds as if she could), she helps to exonerate the author by rebuking the girls for making unkind remarks about Sister Edet. But Mrs. Nwaizu also makes the astounding claim that cultures everywhere are "basically the same." She makes this remark after the American student compares African fattening rooms with the coming-out parties held for Victorian girls. Mrs. Nwaizu finds corresponding motives in the two practices, claiming that mothers nourish and watch over their daughters, and then, when the time is ripe, they show them off "either in high ceilinged ballrooms or get us to dance and show off our fat bodies in the open fields" (103). I think it fair to say that Emecheta's other fiction refutes this simplistic idea of cultural sameness—I think this novel refutes it. In some respects, however, the statement does reflect the feminist hunger for connections, for it would be so much easier to evaluate the status of women around the world if all cultures were the same—or if we all could agree on what equality entails.

But the problem I have with Mrs. Nwaizu's comments is nothing to the problem I have with what follows. Ironically enough, what follows specifically refutes Mrs. Nwaizu's assertion that all cultures are the same. In fact, it presents what I consider to be an archetypal moment in cross-cultural reading, a problem that none of our reading strategies adequately prepares us for or helps us resolve. In chapter 19, Nko tells her friends about Ete. They, in turn, confide in her and have a very frank discussion about sex. One girl wonders if she is still a virgin because once she fooled around with their houseboy (156). The girls advise her that she might as well have sex with the German boy she is dating because there is no virginity left for her to preserve. Then they warn her that lots of "white men are not circumcised," which makes their sex organs resemble "wet intestines." To this, Nko replies, "And their women are not clitorised . . . awful" (157; ellipses in original). At this moment the text loses me, all my efforts to remain open to its newness notwithstanding. This is the classic moment of refusal and rupture for me. Though it might be self-evident why I as a Western feminist resist this passage so vehemently, I think there is much to be learned from studying my reaction more closely.

First, some history of the practice. Exactly what Nko means by "clitorised" is unclear because there are varying degrees of female mutilation still being practiced in different parts of Nigeria and Africa itself.[17] Though it is more euphemistically referred to as "female circumcision," this term is quite misleading, as it suggests an operation analogous to that performed on the foreskin of a man's penis. It is true that the "mildest" form of mutilation (the Sunna type) is intended to remove "only the tip of the prepuce of the clitoris," which would theoretically make it comparable to male circumcision; but in actual practice it is not uncommon for more than the tip to be removed or destroyed because of primitive operating conditions (El Dareer 1982, 2). The most extreme version, the Pharaonic (or infibulation), can be subdivided into "the classical and the modernized" (1). What is removed from the young girl is virtually the same in both cases, the major difference being the more sanitized conditions of the modern version. During classical infibulation, the girl, who is usually between six and eight, has her clitoris, labia minora, and labia majora cut off—sometimes with a knife, sometimes with a razor, and sometimes with scissors. These tools are not sterilized and sometimes not even washed properly. Asma El Dareer reports, for example, that "all the knives [she] saw were rusty, dirty and old" (8). The girl receives no anesthetics but is sometimes doused with very cold water to numb the pain—or, if she is quite young, is thought to feel no pain at all. After the operation, various "adhesive substances" are used to seal the wound—"such as sugar, egg [or] cigarette papers" (1). The girl then has her legs tied together in three places to facilitate healing; this binding lasts from fifteen to forty days. In the modern version of infibulation, the clitoris and labia minora are excised but only part of the labia majora, anesthetics are used, and the wound is sealed with catgut or silk (2). In both cases only a very small hole is left for the urine and menstrual flow to dribble through—an opening so small that it not infrequently leads to serious health problems, such as urinary tract infections, pelvic inflammatory disease, and infertility. It also makes sexual intercourse painful and extremely difficult (if not impossible), which sometimes leads to lifelong psychological problems for the women involved. Various intermediate versions of the Sunna and Pharaonic are practiced, depending on the custom, the wishes of the family, or the skills of the midwives. A third type, excision, "is the removal of the prepuce, the clitoris itself and all or part of the labia minora, leaving the labia majora intact, and the rest of the vulva unsutured" (Koso-Thomas 1987, 17).

As this brief account might suggest, I find it virtually impossible to describe this so-called female circumcision with any degree of objectivity. Because of the pain and possible complications involved, one might think that it is an issue that women around the world would be able to agree on. But that has not been the case. What they call "female circumcision" is too ingrained in the cultures and traditions of those who practice it for most of them to see it the way Western women see it—as an atrocity beyond mention, a mutilation that should be outlawed everywhere. As Tobe Levin argues, such a view "simply does not occur to persons of both sexes embedded in a culture which has been circumcising for the extent of human memory, values pain in the building of character and has not (yet) been atomized into individuals claiming freedoms for themselves in defiance of tribal traditions" (Levin 1988, 6). And if the African women cannot understand the Western point of view, the reverse also holds true. Western women cannot begin to imagine what would convince African women to continue this tradition. Furthermore, because of its special nature as an exotic, painful sexual ritual, "female circumcision" has been a topic that easily lends itself to being sensationalized. Levin reports that during a recent United Nations Conference for Women in Copenhagen, for example, the African women in attendance seriously questioned whether white women should play any part in trying to eradicate circumcision, because Western media are so prone "to sensationalize mutilation, pandering to the prurient, often racist, views of those for whom not only the practice but also the practitioners [are] 'primitive' and brutal" (5).

Though the subject is fraught with controversy, Emecheta mentions it here without a single word of condemnation. To the contrary, the only comment made in response to Nko's statement is from one of the girls, who observes almost flippantly: "Well, different people, different customs" (157). How can this young woman respond so indifferently to the fact of genital mutilation, the very mention of which sends horrified chills through me?

Precisely because her culture is different from mine.
Different people. Different customs.

At this point in the text virtually all Western responses appear to break down. Liberals, convinced that, deep down, human beings are basically all alike—or, as in this case, hoping to avoid the appearance of racism—tend to accept or underplay the strange customs of different people. But what if this acceptance includes clitoridectomies? Does the famed tolerance of Western liberalism extend to female mutilation? If so, on what grounds? If the differences between peoples are so superficial, why do certain African women continue to insist on the need for clitorization, and Western women insist on its complete eradication? What about the feminists? How do we reach out to those African women who accept the custom of clitoridectomies? What common ground as females can we speak from? Mary Daly raises this same issue when she states bluntly, "I have chosen to name these practices for what they are: barbaric rituals/atrocities. Critics from Western countries are constantly being intimidated by accusations of 'racism,' to the point of misnaming, non-naming, and not seeing these sado-rituals" (1978, 154).

LIMITATIONS OF CULTURAL RELATIVISM

If liberal responses seem inadequate, is this not a moment when we are also faced with the limitations of relativism? Though I certainly share Geertz's dislike of anti-relativism (1984), I find I am equally persuaded by Sandra Harding's doubts about the merits of relativism. Harding notes, for example, that relativism "emerges historically only as an attempt to dissolve challenges to the legitimacy of purportedly universal beliefs and ways of life." For those of us who are not in power, relativism "accepts the dominant group's insistence that their right to hold distorted views . . . is intellectually legitimate" (1986a, 657).[18] If we take a relativistic position on the issue of clitorization, are we not helping to legitimate the mutilation of women? Kathleen Kilday thinks so, arguing as she does that "we must put aside cultural relativism and bring into the open this phenomenon which affects the health and lives of millions of African women" (1990, 38). But what would happen if we tried to understand this custom? Can we possibly invoke Winch's concept of limiting notions or Taylor's language of perspicuous contrast? What would invoking these concepts involve? Would we study cultures by focusing on the universal practice of female mutilations that include pierced ears (noses and so on), breast enlargements (or reductions), anorexia, bulimia, liposuction, fattening rooms, foot binding, and clitorization? Would we include in this list the cultural mandates that force (or otherwise induce)[19] women to wear hats, scarves, veils, robes? Would we include sequestration? Forced pregnancies? Forced abortions? Sterilization? Suttee? The list seems endless. Is it possible for us Westerners to imagine a world where clitoridectomies actually might be to a woman's benefit? Do we even want to imagine such a world? Though we may be willing to discuss and debate this issue, I think it unlikely that Western women will ever be able to accept the need for such mutilation—nor do I think we (necessarily) should. For Western women, this subject may be the one place where we find it impossible to make connections with an African text. The best we can probably hope to do is learn to reach out to the victims and practitioners of "female circumcision" without our customary sense of cultural superiority. But the differences run deep on this subject—as can be seen in my use of the word "victims" and my use of the quotation marks around *female circumcision*. Though I contemplated using a less emotional word (such as "subjects" or "participants") and omitting the quotation marks, I found myself unwilling to attempt an objectivity I do not feel. As a result, I would assume that I have not been able to achieve cultural humility at all but have, instead, invoked Winch's principle of hermeneutic charity.

Other African texts raise the same kind of problems for me. In *The Breast of the Earth*, for example, Kofi Awoonor discusses a whole series of events where Christian churches deservedly earned hostility by interfering with African customs. But then he continues with the observation that the "[c]hurches' position on female circumcision, which was one of unalterable opposition, equally drew a great deal of *legitimate resentment and popular hatred*" (29-30; emphasis added). In Ngugi's 1965 *The River Between*, the ritual of male and female circumcision separates traditional Africans from Christian converts. When the daughter of a prominent convert dies after having a forbidden circumcision, this tragedy "for ever confirmed the barbarity of Gikuyu customs" (Ngugi 1983, 55). "Circumcision was wholly evil. Thenceforth nobody would ever be a member of Christ's Church if he was so much as found connected in any way with circumcision rites" (59). The Christians are so horrified by the custom that they fail to recognize the important role it plays among the African people. "It kept people together, bound the tribe. . . . End the custom and the spiritual basis of the tribe's cohesion and integration would be no more" (68). In *Efuru*, Nwapa describes the rituals surrounding a woman's circumcision, which is euphemistically called a "bath" (because it "cleans" a woman) (1966, 8). "The women went to the back of the house and there it was done. Efuru screamed and screamed. It was so painful" (10). Afterward, she is pampered and feasted for a month. The day she emerges from the fattening room, her "body was exposed so that the people saw how well her mother or her mother-in-law had cared for her. A woman who was not beautiful on that day, would never be beautiful in her life" (15). Though Nwapa includes an account of Efuru's pain, she describes the event as though it were a necessary part of making a woman beautiful, desirable—and marriageable. Similarly, though Muthoni dies from her circumcision, Ngugi describes her motives as those of wanting to be fulfilled as a woman. Muthoni tells her sister: "I want to be a real girl, a real woman, knowing all the ways of the hills and ridges" (26). "I want to be a woman made beautiful in the tribe" (44). The language is compellingly seductive, for what woman would not want to be made "beautiful in the tribe"?

Though there is, indeed, much that binds African and Western women together, as both Ngugi's and Nwapa's novels suggest, there are still fundamental cultural differences that keep us apart.[20] But just how insurmountable are these differences?

ENLARGING OUR HORIZONS

Tobe Levin suggests Ngugi's novel treats the subject of clitorization "from a humanist and progressive standpoint, leading its readers gently and ironically to understand that male insistence on female 'rites' is . . . ultimately deconstructive" (1986, 211). She also argues that Muthoni's rebellion "serves better to expose Christian sexual hypocrisy than it does to support initiation. After all, [Muthoni] dies as a result of circumcision." Levin further modifies her own Western perspective when she is able to find some value in "female circumcision" because "the clitoris is at least acknowledged by the [Africans] (being too powerful, it is removed), while the organ has been treated by western [sic] ideology as though it didn't exist" (214).[21] One emendation to Levin's generalization is necessary, however: there was a period in the late nineteenth century and early twentieth century when a few Western doctors did perform clitoridectomies, primarily to reduce what was perceived as an increase in female masturbation.[22] Western women may be outraged by the female mutilation occurring today in Africa, but as this example suggests, our own culture is not without its own shameful historical incidents. In discussing current Western practices, moreover, Susan Bordo characterizes anorexia and bulimia as forms of "social control" and explains how "constraining, enslaving, and even murderous [conditions], come to be experienced as liberating, transforming, and life-giving" (1989, 14, 15). She concludes that the anorexics' attempts to gain control of their lives amount to "pathologies of female protest [which] function," ironically and paradoxically, to reproduce "that which is being protested"—leaving the anorexic with less, rather than more, power (22). For the woman who agrees to have her daughter clitorized or for the daughter who insists upon it, the situation seems to be significantly different but still analogous. These women, after all, are not trying to achieve power by rebelling; they are trying, on the contrary, to achieve power by fitting into their society. They do not, therefore, engage in the convoluted logic that Bordo calls pathologies of female protest, but these women *have* convinced themselves (because of social pressures to do so) that the "constraining, enslaving, and even murderous" conditions of genital mutilation are "liberating, transforming, and life-giving." Who is to say, then, which society is morally superior? That which openly requires women to mutilate themselves or that which surreptitiously does? In a recent interview Emecheta herself suggests the possibility that the practice of "female circumcision" could be eliminated if women no longer find value in it. "If women feel this is still meaningful, it should continue," she argues. "If it is no longer relevant, it has to be stopped—especially because these days, it is apparent that there is no advantage to it" (Topouzis 1990, 69).

If this has seemed like too much discussion about a relatively minor scene in *Double Yoke*, I would answer that my response to this scene distills the central question of bearing a double yoke that the entire novel is built upon: whose values are to prevail, those of the (traditional African) past or those of the (Westernized) present? In other words, the rupture with the text that I experience here is analogous to the ruptures within the culture that the text records. It has also been my intention throughout this study to seek out key moments of misunderstanding—an activity Emecheta's novel seems, on one level, to encourage. Also, to be fair to Nwapa's novel, it must be said that Efuru's slavish adherence to traditions (such as circumcision) is not its focus. Though Nwapa might be faulted for not challenging the need for such practices, her heroine is, at the very, least a proto-feminist. Similarly, although Nko is victimized by two men, she ultimately rejects the role of victim. She stands up to the man she loves and the one she despises. She has not set out to win a first-class honors degree by distributing sexual favors, but when the choice is made for her by Ikot, she decides to take full advantage of a bad situation. Fully aware of the conflicting demands made on her by the old and new ways of African life, she accepts her double burden with grace and dignity. The pull she experiences between being a mother and being a professional threatens to tear apart far too many African and Western women. But her courage and determination seem sufficient for the task of holding her together. Of all Emecheta's heroines she seems the most appealing to Western readers. In many respects, therefore, this is Emecheta's least traditional and most modern novel. At the same time that it is most openly feminist in much of its politics, it is also least feminist in its attitudes toward educated women. For the reasons I have already enumerated, it is also the least satisfying one, lacking the complexity and subtlety of the texts I feel less able to comprehend. But most important, perhaps, is its ability to remind me of the painful differences between cultures. In so much of its meaning, the novel echoes my own beliefs, yet that single passage about "female circumcision" calls into stark relief the reasons many feminists feel we are still in need of a standpoint theory—even if it is one we assume only provisionally for political purposes.

Emecheta may have transgressed traditional narrative (and cultural) boundaries here, and I would certainly argue for this interpretation, but once again I have to confess that her willingness to expand her horizon exceeds my own. The question might be asked, however, if this lengthy discussion on clitorization is not evidence that I have allowed Emecheta's text to expand my own horizon more than I admit.

The Rape of Shavi (1985)

THE AGONISTICS OF LANGUAGE GAMES

In *The Rape of Shavi* Emecheta takes her fiction for the first time into the speculative arena, imagining a fabulous African country that is visited by a group of whites who are fleeing what they think is imminent nuclear war. Though the novel is set in 1983, the world the whites discover in Shavi is that of a traditional, timeless culture, a world that has apparently escaped the influences of European civilization and modernization. Because of Shavi's isolation, the effect of the whites' sudden arrival is tantamount to colonization—even though the Europeans' only intent had been the guileless one of seeking refuge from a nuclear holocaust. The result is a study in cultural conflict, as the Shavians try to decide whether to adopt new ways of thinking the Europeans have introduced—and, to a lesser degree, the Europeans reconsider the putative superiority of their own culture. Since the Africans have their entire way of life destroyed, this exchange is a perfect illustration of what can go wrong in a so-called symmetrical discussion between peoples of different cultures, in which *we* try to understand them, and *they* try to understand us. It functions, in other words, as a warning to Western readers, reminding us of what can go wrong if we do not approach an alien text with the proper critical tools and the proper cultural humility.

Like Emecheta's other fiction, this novel also thematizes the heterosexual couple, using, in this case, the rape of an African woman by a white European man to symbolize the worst possible consequences of colonization. But the exchange between the West and Africa in this novel is not marked only by such obvious violence. It is also marked by the other Europeans' genuine attempt to engage in symmetrical conversation with their African hosts. Moreover, as Ali Mazrui might argue (1983), the African culture does seem perfectly capable, in the end, of throwing off the mantle of colonization. Before Shavi can reach this point, however, it suffers grievous harm as a direct consequence of the conversation it has had with the West. In contrast to the rebellious characters in Emecheta's earlier fiction, the person in Shavi most interested in engaging the West in conversation and thus challenging the voice of tradition is not a woman but a man—the crown prince himself who, one might think, had a vested interest in maintaining tradition rather than subverting it. Complicating his unexpected rebellion is the fact that the Voice of the Fathers is authenticated in the voice of a goddess who speaks through a corrupt priest.

Like the prince himself, none of the other characters does much more than serve the novel's ideas. This style is, of course, not without precedent in the West. In Western speculative fiction, according to DuPlessis, "the ideas, not the characters, are well rounded" (1985, 179). Because *The Rape of Shavi* has both flat characters and a simple plot, I think it likely the novel is intended to be a political parable or fable. But one major difference seems to distinguish Emecheta's speculative fiction from the feminist examples DuPlessis discusses. *The Rape of Shavi* does not speculate on what could occur in the future but on what has already happened: the subjugation of Africans by Western discourse. The fabulation that Emecheta has written, in other words, seems to be based on what Lyotard calls the agonistics of the language game, where the moves made by the West outmaneuver those made by the Africans. But even as Emecheta portrays the process of what is, after all, an inadvertent colonization, she also defends the value of what the Africans have lost. Implicit in her narrative, therefore, is a critique of Western discourse and a celebration of traditional African thought. Though her mythical kingdom has been inspired by the African past, Emecheta has thrust it into the future, where it functions as a model of society contrary to many Western principles of organization. The new African-inspired world Emecheta envisions here is based on an ethics of communal life where people really do care for and about one another.[23] But the alternative world she imagines is no utopia; it is marked by corruption, a falling away from traditional values, and an astonishing disregard for human beings who are born disabled. By focusing on the weaknesses in their own culture that make the Shavians vulnerable to colonization, Emecheta's fable folds back upon itself, reminding us that perfection in the body politic is a worthy but ultimately unattainable goal. Because the characters are not fully individualized, the dialogic heteroglossia in this novel is not as densely complex as it is in her earlier fiction. But as minimal as the heteroglossia may be, Emecheta does raise some interesting issues to contemplate as the competing voices of tradition and modernism jockey for supremacy in the novel.

When the story opens, King Patayon of Shavi is about to take his ninth wife, but he has failed to consult with his senior wife, who complains to the elders that he has not respected her status. While the elders are hearing her case, a mysterious "bird" (an airplane) crashes near the palace. Though they are never quite convinced that the survivors, who are white, are truly human, the Shavians welcome them into their village, and what appears to be a beneficent cultural exchange commences. Then one of the Europeans rapes the young woman who is betrothed to the king's son, Asogba. To protect Shavi's future, the older women keep Ayoko's secret and drag the rapist out to the desert where he would surely have died had Ayoko herself not let him go. Having successfully repaired their airplane, the Europeans leave, and Asogba goes with them to study in England. After he returns to Shavi, he violates sacred tradition by waging a series of military campaigns on the neighboring kingdoms. But his is an empty victory, since his people have been killed by a severe drought, and the country's wise men have died of shame because of the warfare. As a final humiliation, because Ayoko has been infected with syphilis, she and Asogba's other wives are unable to provide him with any heirs. At the end of the novel, having learned the white man's ways only too well, Asogba asks his brother Viyon why their goddess had created people like them who have "nothing to contribute to the rest of humanity" (a question that suggests the lack of symmetry in the conversation Asogba has had with the West) (Emecheta 1985, 178). Viyon responds thoughtfully that they have a lot to teach others, that they had, in fact, taught the whites "how to be responsible for one another" (a statement that appears intended to correct some of the imbalance and thus reestablish the symmetry of learning, though whether the trade-off has been equal is still doubtful). He thinks, moreover, that perhaps their goddess had been trying to teach them something about their own "way of life" by introducing them to the alien ideas of the European visitors (178).

Emecheta sets up a situation in Shavi similar to the one in Achebe's *Arrow of God*, where the weaknesses in the African culture make it vulnerable to the language games of British colonialism. In *The Rape of Shavi* the people and their gods also exist in a delicate equilibrium that has already been disturbed when the strangers arrive—a disturbance evident in the fact that the king and queen have begun to publicly humiliate each other. In failing to inform the queen of his intentions, the king, for example, has broken a crucial link with the past, which leaves his country vulnerable to Western influence. At the same time, Anoku, who serves as the chief priest of Ogene, has secretly begun to put his own self-interest before that of his people by attributing to the goddess a prophecy he himself has concocted in order to betroth his daughter to the crown prince. Just as Anoku ensures his power by claiming Ogene's authority for something he himself has spoken, the whites colonize Shavi through the language they speak, the worldview they represent. The whites make virtually no effort to learn their hosts' language though the crown prince quickly learns English—and he introduces European technology and warfare into his peace-loving country. I want to argue, therefore, that the social upheaval in Shavi is mainly caused by the fact that the language (worldview) of the white interlopers is able to supplant the language of African tradition. It does so, in Lyotard's terms, because the agonistics of the language game favor the West (1984, 16). The agonistics that Lyotard describes involve a pattern of conversational "moves" and "countermoves."[24] In such a game, "reactional" countermoves are not as strategically effective as "unexpected" moves. That is, the advantage lies in the ability to make "a new statement"—an ability neither the priest nor the king enjoys, as their power and influence lie primarily in tradition, the old ways of doing things (16).[25]

Unacquainted with Enlightenment thought, the Shavians have not divided the life-world into discrete spheres and thus fail to distinguish between what we in the West would call rationality and irrationality. In MacIntyre's terms, "their utterances [are] poised in ambiguity" (1978, 252). When the Europeans begin to interrogate the Shavians, therefore, the very act of answering the foreigners' questions forces the Shavians to think differently about themselves. Because the Europeans construct their questions based on their own intellectual divisions, for the Shavians to reply, they, too, must begin to think in these genres—even though they may not be at all suitable to their way of life. In short, the Europeans introduce them to unprecedented "alternatives to [their] established body of beliefs" (McCarthy 1988, 87). While some of these alternatives are surely harmless or their effects fleeting, McCarthy does think it possible, as I indicate in chapter 3, that "the very posing of such questions as: Is this science or theology, symbolic expression or applied technique, or all at once? can permanently upset the balance—as it did in our own past" (88). These may not be exactly the questions the Shavians are asked. But the balance in Shavian society, already precarious before the Europeans arrive with their Western technology and rationality, is certainly upset by the time they depart.

Another way to describe the events that ruin Shavi, therefore, is to say that Emecheta illustrates what happens when the pragmatics of narrative knowledge do battle with the pragmatics of (Western) scientific knowledge. Before the arrival of the Europeans, the Shavians affirmed their identity and organized themselves into a cohesive group through myths and the prophecies of their goddess—the kinds of narratives that Lyotard calls "the quintessential form of customary knowledge" (1984, 19). When authority lies in this kind of narrative, legitimation is not an issue. Moreover, as Lyotard hypothesizes, "a collectivity that takes narrative as its key form of competence has no need to remember its past" (22). One thus finds "an incommensurability between popular narrative pragmatics, which provides immediate legitimation, and the language game known in the West as the question of legitimacy" (23). Because narrative knowledge is not "subject to argumentation or proof," it is scorned by scientific knowledge, which characterizes it as "belonging to a different mentality: savage, primitive, underdeveloped, backward, alienated."[26] In short, practitioners of narrative knowledge are seen by the West to be uneducated and uncivilized—an appraisal of other peoples that, for Lyotard, lies behind "the entire history of cultural imperialism from the dawn of Western civilization" (27; see also Gilroy 1993). Given this distinction between two kinds of knowledge, it does not seem irrelevant in Emecheta's novel that the priest and priestess battle over whose prophecy has the greater legitimacy. Nor does it seem unimportant that the prince, having been introduced to the pragmatics of scientific knowledge, loses faith in his own people's narratives and accepts those of the West.

Since the strangers' unexpected arrival has occurred during Queen Shoshovi's complaints, some of the elders think she has asked the goddess Ogene to intervene on her behalf. Though King Patayon thinks Ogene might, indeed, have sent these visitors, he is frightened enough to pray for guidance. But the land remains silent. "For how could Ogene . . . who for centuries had been worshipped and consulted by the people of Shavi in their sheltered desert homeland, dream of a bird that flew with a noise like thunder"? Though Ogene has apparently served her people well for generations, this time she is unable to "answer Patayon" (10). In a novel that focuses on the question of which language will predominate, the language of tradition or that of change, it seems significant that Ogene does not answer. But it is not entirely clear whether this passage is intended to question Ogene's status as a goddess. Nor can we determine the origin of these remarks. On one hand, their objectivity suggests the narrator at work, for if the people have, indeed, worshipped Ogene for centuries, why would their king not expect her to have an answer even under these extraordinary circumstances? How likely is it, moreover, that he would use the phrase "sheltered desert homeland" to describe his own kingdom? But, on the other hand, if the narrator is speaking, why would she describe a plane as though it were a bird? Puzzling as the origins of this entire passage might be, Patayon himself is credited with saying aloud: "Things will never be the same again" (11). Even though the Shavians themselves have not yet been introduced to the language of scientific instrumentality, their exposure to the products of Western technology seems in itself sufficient to unbalance their delicate poise in ambiguity.

TEXTUAL AMBIGUITY: MOMENTS OF MISUNDERSTANDING

If the Shavians have trouble deciding what to do about the arrival of the Europeans, we Westerners have trouble deciding whether we are supposed to believe in the prophecies of Ogene. Egbongbele argues that if the Shavians kill the visitors, they will lose access to the strangers' culture (44). Iyalode, the priestess of Ogene, also defends them, arguing that the Shavians should take care of the strangers until they have a chance to learn the new language (37). But Anoku the priest, wanting a more "mystical interpretation," is annoyed by these secular suggestions and puts himself into a prophetic trance. Like Achebe's difficult novel, Emecheta's text does not make clear whether the priest subsequently speaks for himself or the goddess. Though hurt pride seems to motivate Anoku, during the trance "the spirit of Ogene took hold of him," the narrator reports, enabling him to see their beloved "river bubbling with blood" and predict that the strangers "will bring us destruction" (38). In some respects this is a very accurate foretelling of what is to come, but this prediction enrages Iyalode, who shouts that he is starting "to rave like a madman" (38). In its heteroglossia, the text refuses to satisfy our curiosity about Anoku's true motives as priest. Because we cannot be sure Anoku is a true priest, we do not know whether to accept Ogene as a true goddess (even within the parameters of Emecheta's fabulation). Of equal significance is what this acrimonious encounter between priest and priestess suggests about the Shavian world itself, as it seems to be disintegrating before our very eyes—losing out to the language game of scientific knowledge.

In yet another passage the ambiguity surrounding Anoku's priestly status is reinforced. The king, upset by his wife's demands for a cow, urges the elders to give her one so she will not call on the goddess for additional "bird-shaped monsters" (43). By using this language, the king seems to be agreeing with Anoku's perspective—even though he had previously given the impression that the priest was foretelling disaster "just for the joy of it" (43). Egbongbele addresses Anoku as one who "speaks for our great goddess Ogene," but then he challenges him by defending the visitors' right to live (44). Though the text shifts to Anoku's thoughts, the ambiguity is not resolved. If anything, it is intensified as he debates within himself what he ought to do to give his words authority. He knows that "ranting" would not be effective, because "[i]f he lost his dignity, he would lose his credibility" (45). Since we associate the concept of dignity with the concept of individualism, this passage seems all the more significant. It would seem less significant were Anoku to worry about his *honor*. For the concept of honor, according to Peter Berger, "lies in a world of relatively intact, stable institutions, a world in which individuals can with subjective certainty attach their identities to the institutional roles that society assigns to them" (1984, 156). When this world is weakened by the "forces of modernity," as seems to have occurred (or to be occurring) in Shavi, the concept of honor loses much of its meaning. "The reciprocity between individual and society, between subjective identity and objective identification through roles, now comes to be experienced as a sort of struggle" (156). This struggle certainly seems to describe Anoku's situation, as he cannot decide whether to "honor" his priestly role or act on his own (personal) behalf and thus retain his dignity. Significantly, the text then describes how Anoku had once abused his role as priest. Pretending to speak for Ogene, he has foretold (on her behalf) that his own daughter (Ayoko) will be queen one day—a false prophecy that everyone believes. Returning to the story present, the narrative reveals once more how calculating the priest can be. Realizing that Asogba is more powerful than himself, Anoku gives the prince permission to speak. To everyone's surprise, the prince, in violation of tradition, speaks of extending the borders of Shavi to encompass their "troublesome neighbours" (47). Thus the language of the priest, which apparently is and is not the language of Ogene, is being superseded by the language of Asogba, which is already infected by the language of the white world.

As the debate about the whites' humanity draws to a close, the narrator remarks that whatever Anoku had tried to say was lost in his overly emotional presentation, which sounded like the "raving of a lunatic" (39). Yet this raving is the most accurate foretelling we are privy to. So whose viewpoint is being expressed in this observation? The priestess concludes that the people are albinos, a remark that ends the discussion. But Anoku is furious. "And when the chief priest . . . is displeased, he can foretell many unpleasant happenings" (39). So once more the text casts doubt on his prophesying. Since what Anoku foretells comes true, however, we must question the origin of these statements. Are they the narrator's or those of the king? The physical description of Anoku is also puzzling, since we are told at least four times that he has a "skull-like head" (38, 76, and twice on 36). Why is he associated with death? Does foretelling death make him responsible for it? Though his lie about his daughter sets up much of the tragic decline in the kingdom, he does not cause the whites' arrival. Out of his own self-interest, however, he silences his well-founded fears about the foreigners because the future king has taken their side. He also reminds himself not to "encourage Ogene to predict anything against [Asogba]" (46). This statement, of course, suggests that somehow he can affect Ogene's prophesies. Does this make him a true or a false prophet? We cannot tell.

At other moments Western readers have trouble understanding the meaning of this speculative fiction. Although the peace-loving, tolerant Shavi is described as an idealized mythical country, superior in many ways to the industrial, militarized, colonizing West, the Shavian people continue to practice several customs that Westerners would find repugnant. For example, though the Shavians pride themselves on being a kingdom where a child can address the king, when the queen speaks to the elders, she refers to them as her "owners" (4). Before the women can marry, moreover, they are clitorized. When John Mendoza observes that he has seen "no deformity," Flip thinks maybe the climate "produces everything in perfection" (76). But the narrator is quick to point out that many people die during the country's frequent droughts, and "perfection was bought at a price" (76). That is, Shavians have no handicapped people because they practice infant euthanasia (77).

The textual debate about Shavi's relative perfection extends to the attitudes of the Westerners themselves, as Flip and Ista tend to admire the Shavians, while Ronje despises them, and Andria and Mendoza have mixed feelings. But even Ista has her moments of doubt. One key scene occurs when Ista sees that one of the Shavian women is about to undergo a breech birth. Convinced the woman needs the medical science that only she, Ista, can provide, she tries to interfere with the midwives' procedures. But they do not need her help, since the woman gives birth quite easily to a healthy baby, striking a serious blow to Ista's Western "arrogance" (132). Abashed, she explains to Andria that even though she admires the Shavians' way of life, she still feels that African ideas cannot hold a candle to Western ideas (133). Even so, the birth scene does seem to be an attempt on Emecheta's part to cast some doubt on the superiority of Western science, as the skills of the Western-trained doctor are simply not needed. But Ista's ambivalence increases after she has returned to England and undergone an abortion. In a moment of confused reasoning, she thinks maybe she should return to Shavi, where she could help raise the country's standard of living. Finally, she realizes that the Shavians have everything to teach her—and not the other way around (169). In another key scene Flip raves about the superiority of Shavian life, telling Ronje that he intends to return to Shavi and study its culture and remarking that maybe the West should destroy itself and let Africa repopulate the world, since "[a]ll we've so far produced are instruments of physical and moral destruction" (102). Because Flip is one of the scientists responsible for developing the nuclear bomb (31), at best this seems to be a disingenuous remark. Fond as he is of the Shavians, he does not return to study their life, though he does decide to marry Andria, having recognized the Shavian principle that "humans are communal at heart" (168). But being part of a European nuclear family is hardly parallel to the kind of complex communal living he has experienced in Shavi.

Ronje, of course, is obdurate. For him, it is all a question of power and whose narrative will reign supreme—that of the gentle Shavians or that of their European colonizers. Perversely enough, after he rapes Ayoko, he seems to have some remorse that she had been a virgin. As she runs away, he calls after her that he will marry her and take her to England, where he will make her "a lady"—not accepting the fact that she is already the most gracious person he has ever met (95). But to her he has lost his humanity, "for what human would rape?" (94). Echoing Lyotard's comments about Western arrogance, Ronje justifies his behavior by arguing that Europeans had always had the obligation "to impose their culture" on other peoples (106). Throughout his stay in Shavi, Ronje maintains his view that whites are "always superior" (87). Thinking only in terms of power, he determines he will not be deprived of Ayoko and thus begins to make plans as to how he will "talk to her" and subsequently begin to "civilise her" (106). That these people do not need Ronje's version of civilization is perhaps self-evident, but it is given some textual voice in the scene when the women capture him and sigh with regret, in the knowledge "that they were going to destroy such a specimen of health, strength and manliness" (107). It is also significant that Ronje's plan summarizes my argument: he would "talk" to her and thus silence her inferior narrative with his own superior one. Given the distinction Lyotard makes between narrative knowledge and scientific knowledge, it seems significant that Emecheta portrays the ravages of imperialism as a man raping a woman and then thinking he can civilize her. As Lyotard reminds us, in the view of scientific knowledge, the kind of narratives valued by the Shavians are mere "fables, myths, legends, fit only for women and children" (1984, 27). For the West, until quite recently, Africans were little more than women and children in need of Western guidance.

A NEW COMMUNITY OF INTERPRETERS

As we have already seen, Emecheta is not alone among her African contemporaries in using the heterosexual couple as a political metaphor. Sometimes, as in Head's 1971 *Maru* (rpt. 1986), the couple is African but of different tribes. Sometimes, as in Nkosi's 1986 *Mating Birds* (rpt. 1987), the couple is interracial but of the same nationality. Or, sometimes, as in Armah's 1972 *Why Are We So Blest?* and Bâ's 1981 *Scarlet Song* (rpt. 1985b), the couple is interracial and of different nationalities. Unlike the healing relationship between the two Africans in *Maru*, the relationships of interracial couples in these other novels seem especially unnatural and grotesque, as though to reconfirm the abominations of colonialism and justify the need for transformative violence. Nkosi's and Armah's novels almost seem to imply that no social intercourse should connect the white and black worlds, since such contact can lead only to destruction and colonization. Thus, it is possible to argue that, as revolutionary as these texts are intended to be, they nonetheless reinscribe, rather than overcome, dualisms (white/black, Western/African, male/female). At most I think it could be claimed that they invert the first two of these dualisms. They do little to challenge the thought that lies behind them. But in her 1974 novel, *A Question of Power* (rpt. 1979), Head provides us with an exception to this pattern and offers us some hope of overcoming dualism by showing how it is possible to form bonds with those who are different from ourselves. Though her heroine, Elizabeth, is tormented by demons who have taken the form of two African men, she is able to find respite in a platonic friendship with Tom, a sweet, thoughtful white American who has chosen to work in agriculture in order to help the African people become self-sufficient. Weakened and vulnerable from her bouts of madness, Elizabeth decides to focus on Tom as a "symbol of male nobility and compare his every word against [her own] inner chaos." In return, when she asks him if he will take care of her, he responds: "*Willingly*" (1979, 136). Indeed, he does help her regain her sanity and formulate a new view of the world that emphasizes the importance of ordinary people.

Interracial couples, however often they appear in other contemporary African novels, are quite rare in Emecheta's fiction—the most fully drawn example being Debbie Ogedemgbe and Alan Grey.[27] Though many of Emecheta's African characters have obviously been deeply affected by European colonization, most of the points she makes about cultural conflict occur within troubled African relationships or within a single unhappy or rebellious individual. But I think it is evident in the novels we have considered in this chapter that Emecheta uses couples and their strained relationships to question the foundations of (black) African and (white-dominated) Western society. She certainly uses the dynamics of the heterosexual couple to question the complex effects of colonization on Africans—if only symbolically, as in the case of Ayoko and Ronje. At the same time, as her characters try to make their way through a changing world, to one degree or another, they speak in the language of perspicuous contrast, weighing the value of their familiar African traditions against the glamour of Western discourse. Most of them are more than willing to listen to the conversation of the West, and many are harmed by their willingness, thus illustrating, as I have argued, the asymmetry in learning that can occur when cultures collide. But if her *characters* illustrate the asymmetry in learning, perhaps the conversation her readers have with her texts can be a more symmetrical exchange. If we are not to dominate the conversation and colonize her texts, we will, of course, have to work from the position of cultural humility that I have been advocating throughout this study. We must also be willing to question our own traditions and remain receptive to alien or new traditions we encounter in these texts. In short, we must help create a new and ever-changing community of interpreters.

Catharine Stimpson has raised some issues about gender and texts that are germane to my argument here. Discussing the work of Gertrude Stein, Stimpson argues that "[c]ultural laws of gender demand that feminine and masculine must play off against each other in the great drama of binary opposition" (1986, 1). In hierarchically structured patriarchal cultures such as our own, the masculine has traditionally been victorious. But the victory is not to the phallus in writing like Stein's. For according to Stimpson, even "as she polarizes kinds of literature and kinds of experience, Stein entangles them in thickets of contradictions—about both literature and gender" (9). I think we can make the same claim about Emecheta's writing. Though Emecheta does not begin to play the complex language games that Stein plays, her novels (replete as they are with signifying and heteroglossia) do serve finally to challenge traditional modes of thought—even while they sometimes appear to reinscribe them. Stimpson suggests that the elusive meaning of Stein's poetry "intensifies our sense of destabilization and subversively warns us against accepting the certainty of any text." The ultimate effect of her writing, therefore, is to dispel "our trust in the smoothness, regularity, and uniformity of our dominant discourses—including our discourse about gender" (10). Is this not exactly what Emecheta's fiction accomplishes for us, as it, too, destabilizes Western discourse and narrative? Just as Stein deconstructs the male in order to honor the female (5), Emecheta deconstructs Western discourse to honor the discourse of her African Fathers. But the challenge to the West's hegemony is also manifest in the African values her texts reinscribe and in the plurality they reflect. Sandra Harding argues that "feminine and African world views" can be seen as "categories of challenge" because they "name what is absent in the thinking and social activities of men and Europeans" (1986b, 186). By naming both what is present (the fathers' authoritative discourse) and what is absent (the daughters' internal discourse), Emecheta's novels achieve a level of plurality that goes beyond the old metaphors. Very simply, the old dualisms no longer obtain. Though Emecheta's novels, as we have seen in the previous pages, often *reflect* binary oppositions, it seems to me that her texts' plurality actually functions to *subvert* certain oppositions. For here, the authoritative discourse is no longer white Western male but black African male (reinscribed by the black African female narrator/author).[28] The internal discourse is not simply white female or black female but is instead a mélange of black African and Western female. Here "Man" is no longer "Western" but "African." "African" itself is not only "Man" but also "Woman."

Craig Owens's advice to those who wish to avoid binary thinking by embracing the playful plurality generated by postmodern texts revolves around learning to "conceive difference without opposition" (1983, 62). On this view, what is foreign may be strange (from another place and thus unfamiliar), but it does not have to be opposed to us. On my view, however, it is the very opposition of alien texts to our own tradition(s) that makes reading them such a valuable learning experience. It has thus been a central feature of my project to rehabilitate the concept of negative experience—to return dialectics to cross-cultural understanding. As difficult as Emecheta's fiction (all African fiction) can be for us Westerners to understand, therefore, I do not want to end on a negative note—or, I should say, the negative note I end on is, in fact, a positive or productive one. For, underlying all my examples and admonitions has lain the conviction that, while we cannot read Emecheta's texts as Africans would, we can ourselves learn to read them differently—even as we can (and must) learn to read ourselves and our culture differently. Reading these texts self-consciously and interactively allows us to participate, moreover, in the creation of a new kind of cross-cultural understanding. I want, then, to propose that Emecheta destabilizes not only the discourse within the text but also the discourse between the text and reader. As a function of destabilizing Western discourse and narrative, Emecheta disrupts our interpretive community—so that she may refashion it to suit her African self. Instead of offering discursive reassurance, she offers uncertainty and change.

The model of a reading community that I think is being fashioned here borrows from, but also inverts, the ideas of Judith Fetterley (1978) and Patrocinio Schweickart (1986). Fetterley, it will be recalled, urges women to become resisting readers in order to avoid being "immasculated" by male texts (xx), while Schweickart argues that as women read (female texts), they find themselves always making connections with the woman behind the text (52). On the surface, both of these theories of reading seem more than applicable. As I have shown in the preceding pages, for example, there is much that Western women will want to resist in African literature—even in Emecheta's so-called feminist texts. But if we protect ourselves by resisting everything in these texts, of course, we deny ourselves the pleasures of making those connections that Schweickart describes. The urge to make connections carries its own penalties, however, if in seeking connections with women in alien cultures, we elide our differences, finding sameness where none exists. If we yield to the feminist temptation of positing transcultural constants, we end up reading Buchi Emecheta's texts, for example, as a sub-category of Western feminist literature, which means we side with her mistreated heroines against their culture. Under these circumstances, in Geertz's terms, we confine ourselves to the limitations of our own experience-distant concepts and fail to utilize the complementary perspective of experience-near concepts found in the texts themselves (1979, 226). Without a balanced deployment of both kinds of concepts, where each corrects the weaknesses of the other, we will not be able to achieve the exchange of ideas on which communication depends. In the absence of an equal exchange, the temptation is to find in Emecheta's narrative voice a widespread and often bitter criticism of her own culture. As I hope to have shown throughout this study, this bitterness all but disappears when we read her novels as a reflection of a society that values the family and defines individuals not as isolated, atomistic selves but as *bound to* their social unit, whether it be family, village, or tribe.[29] Not only does the bitterness disappear, but understanding itself increases as we learn to employ more experience-near concepts. Just as beneficially, we begin to understand ourselves and our own culture differently—which returns us again to my theory of reading interactively.

By reading interactively, in the language of perspicuous contrast, we can, I believe, paradoxically enough, increase our chances of making connections or experiencing what Williams calls the "sharing of common meanings"—that sharing of commonality we sought to find in the first place (1961, 38). If we are to experience a fusion of horizons with Emecheta's African culture and its traditions, it may very well be that we must deny ourselves the more comforting but less challenging temptation of claiming we have (already) understood her heroines. In other words, by hoping to find our feminism reflected in her fictional heroines, we miss the "feminism" that is inherent in her cultural traditions. In ignoring or discounting the differences between her heroines and ourselves, moreover, we inadvertently but inevitably protect ourselves from the negative experiences in the texts that would introduce us to new knowledge. But in all of our encounters with these alien texts the hermeneutical problems, as we have seen, can be formidable. Rupture, refusal, and misunderstanding will all necessarily accompany our interactive reading project, for I am not envisioning a community of readers who all think alike or who think like the text. I imagine instead a shape-shifting, self-critical, postmodern community capable of recognizing without rejecting the authentic strangeness of the Other—an interpretive community also willing to go the distance and anthropologize itself. As we pursue a cross-cultural conversation with Emecheta's novels or those of other writers, therefore, we must be willing to experience the foreign with the familiar, the perils with the pleasures—else we may find that we have not left home at all.

NOTES

1. See McLuckie 1987. Debbie is, however, a member of the Itsekiri tribe (Emecheta 1982, 107).

2. Something similar might be said of her efforts in *The Bride Price*: that she is subverting a traditional Western comedic genre by writing about it from an African's perspective.

3. In Ekwensi's account of the war, the narrator also attends to the effects on families, observing at one point that "hundreds were dying every day—men, women, children—especially children" (1983, 3). Later, one of the characters bitterly explains the war as having been "fought to scatter our families" (54).

4. If Emecheta envisions a Western audience for her novels, perhaps she might be advised to consider more carefully the responsibility she has assumed in representing her culture to outsiders since we seem so prone to misunderstanding (see Alcoff 1991-92).

5. I take this phrasing from Daly 1978 (1–34). What Debbie achieves in naming herself and her enemy may have even more significance in an African setting. Jahn, for example, argues that "every human thought, once expressed, becomes reality. . . . Every word has consequences" (1990, 133).

6. In *Mating Birds*, Nkosi also uses the forbidden relationship of an interracial couple to highlight the socio-political problems concurrent with the presence of apartheid in South Africa. Perhaps even more than Emecheta's and Head's characters, Nkosi's are symbolic of cultural malaise (1987).

7. Onoge defines an "anti-colonial consciousness," for example, as one that acknowledges the fact that there are both "*true* and *false* decolonizations" (1986a, 27).

8. Debbie's efforts to reinscribe herself also place her in the tradition of African American women who, according to Michele Wallace, have had to assert their identity in opposition to "the unrelenting logic of dualism," a logic that has the effect of "automatically eras[ing] black female subjectivity" (1989, 60). More generally, see also Hodge 1990.

9. DuPlessis is discussing *Herland, The Female Man, Woman on the Edge of Time*, and *Children of Violence*.

10. Whether the narrator concurs with this claim is not entirely clear, since the novel portrays Nigerian women as enjoying precious little respect during the war. The narrator reports, for example, that it is *because* the women want a place in "the new nation" that they are brutalized by soldiers (119).

11. See also Cixous 1981a.

12. Amadi suggests that poverty "lends strength to this herd instinct. People see the tribe as an island of survival in a seething, unstable socio-economic sea" (1978, 10).

13. There is another way of looking at this. Jahn discusses the importance of what he calls "*the designation of the image*." The woodcarver, in other words, designates or *names* what the statue will represent. "Whether an orisha, a king, an ancestor, a peasant or one's neighbour was being represented, one figure could look like another and yet, thanks to its designation, be for the woodcarver in one case the image of an orisha, in another the image of king, ancestor, peasant, neighbour and so on" (1990, 157). In short, the image has no intrinsic meaning; a statue can therefore lose its significance by simply being unnamed. Moreover, once "it loses its functional efficacy it becomes valueless" (172). This belief would help explain why the people are so willing to throw out their statues once they have converted to Christianity. They had been in the habit of throwing them out anyway. Soyinka describes a similar process. "When gods die—that is, fall to pieces—the carver is summoned and a new god comes to life. The old is dis-

carded, left to rot in the bush and be eaten by termites. The new is invested with the powers of the old and may acquire new powers" (1990, 86).

14. But since all nations seem to be plagued by one form of corruption or another, this, too, might serve as one of Winch's limiting notions.

15. Cobham-Sander reports that "Emecheta's novel is said to be based on an actual incident at Calabar University, and her forthright treatment of sexually corrupt practices among academics created a furor" (1986, 18-19).

16. Cobham-Sander regards the ending as one of many "compulsive happy endings" being written today by Nigerian women, a pattern that suggests to her "a reformist, rather than revolutionary zeal on the part of the authors" (1986, 19).

17. See Koso-Thomas 1987, 17, and Sanderson 1981, 32-33.

18. Mary Hawkesworth expresses similar reservations about what she sees as the inevitable "slide into relativism that results from too facile a conflation of world and text" (1989, 555). Deeply skeptical of poststructuralist thought, she argues that "theories of life must deal with more than the free play of signifiers" (556). While I (clearly) do not share her distrust of poststructuralism and do not believe that seeing the world as a text in any way trivializes our material existence, I am aware that many feminists would agree with her that "the shift to intertextuality" is a politically irresponsible gesture in that it fails to disrupt the white-male-dominated status quo (557). I would hope, however, that my own study has shown how politically responsible a contextualized poststructuralist theory can be.

19. See Mohanty 1984.

20. In *Possessing the Secret of Joy* (1992), Alice Walker graphically describes these cultural differences in her account of the genital mutilation undergone by Tashi. See also Naylor 1992.

21. This is an observation borne out during the 1984-85 Museum of Modern Art exhibit "'Primitivism' in Twentieth-Century Art," where the clitoris was notably present on those statues created by African artists and absent on those by Western artists.

22. See Sanderson 1981, 28-31, and Daly 1978, 227.

23. See Young 1990a and 1990b.

24. During ordinary conversation, according to Lyotard, "the interlocutors use any available ammunition, changing games from one utterance to the next: questions, requests, assertions, and narratives are launched pell-mell into battle." In contrast, "an institution differs from a conversation in that it always requires supplementary constraints for statements to be declared admissible within its bounds" (1984, 17). What we have in Emecheta's novel seems to be discourse that falls between the two extremes of conversation and institution, as the Shavians and Westerners talk informally but also represent their own particular institutionalized way of life.

25. See Todorov 1992. *See also* Ryan 1982

26. Fanon describes a similar hierarchical division, wherein the native is said to be "the enemy of values, and in this sense he is the absolute evil. . . . The customs of the colonized people, their traditions, their myths—above all, their myths—are the very sign of that poverty of spirit and of their constitutional depravity" (1968, 41-42).

27. Others are Whoopey and her African lover, from *In the Ditch*, and Pa Noble and Sue, from *Second-Class Citizen*—Sue being also one of the white women with whom Francis Obi has an affair.

28. Bakhtin reminds us that "novelistic double-voicedness cannot be unfolded into logical contradictions or into purely dramatic contrasts." For this reason, he characterizes novelistic dialogues as capable of pushing "to the limit the *mutual nonunderstanding* represented by people who speak in different languages" (1987, 356; emphasis added). In other words, there is more double-voicedness at work in Emecheta's fiction than that of the fathers and daughters—so much, in fact, that we should ask if these novels have not already crossed into the realm of nonunderstanding for Western readers.

29. See also Geertz 1979, 229.

Bibliography

Achebe, Chinua. 1959. *Things Fall Apart*. Greenwich, CT: Fawcett.
———. 1969. *Arrow of God*. Garden City, NY: Anchor.
———. 1975a. *No Longer at Ease*. London: Heinemann.
———. 1975b. *Morning Yet on Creation Day*. London: Heinemann.
———. 1975c. "Africa and Her Writers." In *Morning Yet on Creation Day*. London: Heinemann. 19-29.
———. 1975d. "*Chi* in Igbo Cosmology." In *Morning Yet on Creation Day*. London: Heinemann. 93-103.
———. 1984. *The Trouble with Nigeria*. London: Heinemann.
Adorno, Theodor. 1986. "Reconciliation under Duress." *Aesthetics and Politics: The Key Texts of the Classic Debate Within German Marxism*. Trans. Rodney Livingstone. Ernst Bloch et al. Afterword. Fredric Jameson. London: Verso. 151-76.
Aidoo, Ama Ata. 1992. *Changes: A Love Story*. London: Women's Press.
Alcoff, Linda. 1988. "Cultural Feminism Versus Post-Structuralism: The Identity Crisis in Feminist Theory." *Signs* 13.3: 405-36.
———. 1991-92. "The Problem of Speaking for Others." *Cultural Critique* 20: 5-32.
Althusser, Louis. 1970. *For Marx*. Trans. Ben Brewster. New York: Vintage.
Althusser, Louis, and Etienne Balibar. 1987. *Reading Capital*. Trans. Ben Brewster. New York: Verso.
Amadi, Elechi. 1978. *Sunset in Biafra: A Civil War Diary*. London: Heinemann.
———. 1982. *Ethics in Nigerian Culture*. Ibadan: Heinemann.
———. 1986. *Estrangement*. London: Heinemann.
Andrade, Susan Z. 1990. "Rewriting History, Motherhood, and Rebellion: Naming an African Women's Literary Tradition." *Research in African Literatures* 21.1: 91-110.
Armah, Ayi Kwei. 1970. *Fragments*. Boston: Houghton Mifflin.
———. 1972. *Why Are We So Blest?* Garden City, NY: Doubleday.

Asante, Molefi Kete. 1987. *The Afrocentric Idea*. Philadelphia: Temple University Press.
———. 1988. *Afrocentricity*. Rev. ed. Trenton, NJ: Africa World Press.
Auerbach, Nina. 1987. "Engorging the Patriarchy." In *Feminist Issues in Literary Scholarship*. Ed. Shari Benstock. Bloomington: Indiana University Press, 1987. 150-60.
Awoonor, Kofi. 1975. *The Breast of the Earth: A Survey of the History, Culture and Literature of Africa South of the Sahara*. New York: Nok.
———. 1986. *This Earth, My Brother . . .* London: Heinemann.
Bâ, Mariama. 1985a. *So Long a Letter*. Trans. Modupé Bodé-Thomas. London: Heinemann.
———. 1985b. *Scarlet Song*. Trans. Dorothy S. Blair. Harlow, Essex, U.K.: Longman.
Babatope, Biola. 1987. "Women of Our Society with Emphasis on Economic and Political Problems Facing Women of Southern Nigeria." *Présence Africaine* 141.1: 15-27.
Bakhtin, M. M. 1987. *The Dialogic Imagination: Four Essays*. Trans. Caryl Emerson and Michael Holquist. Ed. Michael Holquist. Austin: University of Texas Press.
Barthelemy, Anthony. 1989. "Western Time, African Lives: Time in the Novels of Buchi Emecheta." *Callaloo* 12.3: 559-74.
Barthes, Roland. 1972. "Literature Today." In *Roland Barthes: Critical Essays*. Trans. Richard Howard. Evanston, IL: Northwestern University Press. 151-61.
———. 1974. *S/Z: An Essay*. Trans. Richard Miller. New York: Hill and Wang.
———. 1979. "From Work to Text." In *Textual Strategies: Perspectives in Post-Structuralist Criticism*. Ed. Josué V. Harari. Ithaca, NY: Cornell University Press, 1979. 73-81.
———. 1986. "The Death of the Author." In *Image, Music, Text*. Trans. Stephen Heath. New York: Hill and Wang. 142-48.
Baym, Nina. 1985. "Melodramas of Beset Manhood: How Theories of American Fiction Exclude Women Authors." In *The New Feminist Criticism: Essays on Women, Literature and Theory*. Ed. Elaine Showalter. New York: Pantheon. 63-80.
Bazin, Nancy Topping. 1985a. "Venturing into Feminist Consciousness: Two Protagonists from the Fiction of Buchi Emecheta and Bessie Head." *Sage* 2.1: 32-36.
———. 1985b. "Weight of Custom, Signs of Change: Feminism in the Literature of African Women." *World Literature Written in English* 25.2: 183-97.
———. 1986. "Feminist Perspectives in African Fiction: Bessie Head and Buchi Emecheta." *The Black Scholar* 17.2: 34-40.
———. 1989. "Feminism in the Literature of African Women." *The Black Scholar* 20.3-4: 8-17.
Bellah, Robert N., Richard Madsen, William M. Sullivan, Ann Swidler, and Steven M. Tipton. 1985. *Habits of the Heart: Individualism and Commitment in American Life*. New York: Perennial.
Belsey, Catherine. 1980. *Critical Practice*. London: Methuen.
Berger, Peter. 1984. "On the Obsolescence of the Concept of Honour." In *Liberalism and Its Critics*. Ed. Michael Sandel. New York: New York University Press, 1984. 149-58.
Berger, Peter L., and Thomas Luckmann. 1967. *The Social Construction of Reality: A*

Treatise in the Sociology of Knowledge. Garden City, NY: Anchor.
Bernstein, Richard J. 1986. "The Rage Against Reason." *Philosophy and Literature* 10.2: 186-210.
———. 1987. "One Step Forward, Two Steps Backward: Richard Rorty on Liberal Democracy and Philosophy." Liberalism and Philosophy 1. *Political Theory* 15.4: 538-63.
———. 1989. *Beyond Objectivism and Relativism: Science, Hermeneutics, and Praxis*. Philadelphia: University of Pennsylvania Press.
Berrian, Brenda F. 1981. "Bibliographies of Nine Female African Writers." *Research in African Literatures* 12.2: 214-36.
———. 1988. "An Update: Bibliography of Twelve African Women Writers." *Research in African Literatures* 19.2: 206-31.
Bhabha, Homi K. 1990. "Interrogating Identity: The Postcolonial Prerogative." In *Anatomy of Racism*. Ed. David Theo Goldberg. Minneapolis: University of Minnesota Press. 183-209.
Bialostosky, Don H. 1986. "Dialogics as an Art of Discourse in Literary Criticism." *PMLA* 101.5: 788-97.
Bjornson, Richard, ed. 1990. "Special Issue: Critical Theory and African Literature." *Research in African Literatures* 21.1.
Bloch, Ernst, Georg Lukács, Bertolt Brecht, Walter Benjamin, and Theodor Adorno. 1986. *Aesthetics and Politics: The Key Texts of the Classic Debate Within German Marxism*. Afterword. Fredric Jameson. London: Verso.
Bordo, Susan R. 1989. "The Body and the Reproduction of Femininity: A Feminist Appropriation of Foucault." In *Gender/Body/Knowledge: Feminist Reconstructions of Being and Knowing*. Ed. Alison M. Jaggar and Susan R. Bordo. New Brunswick, NJ: Rutgers University Press. 13-33.
Bourdieu, Pierre. 1984. *Distinction: A Social Critique of the Judgement of Taste*. Trans. Richard Nice. Cambridge, MA: Harvard University Press.
Brecht, Bertolt. 1986. "Against Georg Lukács." *Aesthetics and Politics: The Key Texts of the Classic Debate Within German Marxism*. Trans. Stuart Hood. Ernst Bloch et al. Afterword. Fredric Jameson. London: Verso. 68-85.
Brooks, Peter. 1984. *Reading for the Plot: Design and Intention in Narrative*. New York: Knopf.
Brown, Lloyd W. 1975. "The African Woman as Writer." *Canadian Journal of African Studies* 9.3: 493-501.
———. 1981. *Women Writers in Black Africa*. Contributions in Women's Studies, No. 21. Westport, CT: Greenwood Press.
Butler, Marilyn. 1985. "Against Tradition: The Case for a Particularized Historical Method." In *Historical Studies and Literary Criticism*. Ed. Jerome J. McGann. Madison: University of Wisconsin Press. 25-47.
Caputo, John D. 1989. "Gadamer's Closet Essentialism: A Derridean Critique." In *Dialogue and Deconstruction: The Gadamer-Derrida Encounter*. Ed. Diane P. Michelfelder and Richard E. Palmer. Albany: State University of New York Press. 258-64.
Carby, Hazel V. 1987. *Reconstructing Womanhood: The Emergence of the Afro-American Woman Novelist*. New York: Oxford University Press.
Chinweizu, Onwuchekwa Jemie, and Ihechukwu Madubuike. 1983. *African Fiction and*

Poetry and Their Critics. Vol. 1 of *Toward the Decolonization of African Literature*. Washington, DC: Howard University Press.

Christian, Barbara. 1985a. "Alternate Versions of the Gendered Past: African Women Writers vs. Illich." In *Black Feminist Criticism: Perspectives on Black Women Writers*. New York: Pergamon. 143-48.

———. 1985b. "An Angle of Seeing: Motherhood in Buchi Emecheta's *The Joys of Motherhood* and Alice Walker's *Meridian*." In *Black Feminist Criticism: Perspectives on Black Women Writers*. New York: Pergamon. 211-52.

Cixous, Hélène. 1976. "The Laugh of the Medusa." Trans. Keith Cohen and Paula Cohen. *Signs* 1.4: 875-93.

———. 1981a. "Sorties: Out and Out: Attacks/Ways Out/Forays." In *New French Feminisms: An Anthology*. Ed. Elaine Marks and Isabelle de Courtivron. Trans. Ann Liddle. New York: Schocken. 90-98.

———. 1981b. "Castration or Decapitation?" Trans. Annette Kuhn. *Signs* 7.1: 41-55.

Cobham, Rhonda. 1988. Introduction. "Special Issue on Women's Writing." *Research in African Literatures* 19.2: 137-42.

Cobham-Sander, Rhonda. 1986. "Class vs. Sex: The Problem of Values in the Modern Nigerian Novel." *The Black Scholar* 17.4: 17-27.

Coward, Rosalind. 1985. "Are Women's Novels Feminist Novels?" In *The New Feminist Criticism: Essays on Women, Literature and Theory*. Ed. Elaine Showalter. New York: Pantheon. 225-39.

Dallmayr, Fred R. 1984. *Polis and Praxis: Exercises in Contemporary Political Theory*. Cambridge, MA: MIT Press.

d'Almeida, Irene Assiba. 1986. "The Concept of Choice in Mariama Bâ's Fiction." In *Ngambika: Studies of Women in African Literature*. Ed. Carole Boyce Davies and Anne Adams Graves. Trenton, NJ: Africa World Press. 161-71.

Daly, Mary. 1978. *Gyn/Ecology: The Metaethics of Radical Feminism*. Boston: Beacon Press.

Dareer, Asma El. 1982. *Woman, Why Do You Weep? Circumcision and Its Consequences*. London: Zed.

Dasenbrock, Reed Way. 1987. "Intelligibility and Meaningfulness in Multicultural Literature in English." *PMLA* 102.1: 10-19.

Davies, Carole Boyce. 1986a. "Introduction: Feminist Consciousness and African Literary Criticism." In *Ngambika: Studies of Women in African Literature*. Ed. Carole Boyce Davies and Anne Adams Graves. Trenton, NJ: Africa World Press. 1-23.

———. 1986b. "Motherhood in the Works of Male and Female Igbo Writers: Achebe, Emecheta, Nwapa and Nzekwu." In *Ngambika: Studies of Women in African Literature*. Ed. Carole Boyce Davies and Anne Adams Graves. Trenton, NJ: Africa World Press. 241-56.

Daymond, M. J. 1988. "Buchi Emecheta, Laughter and Silence: Changes in the Concepts 'Woman,' 'Wife,' and 'Mother.'" *Journal of Literary Studies/Tydskrif Vir Literatur Wetenskap* 4.1: 64-73.

Dixon, Vernon J. 1976. "World Views and Research Methodology." In *African Philosophy: Assumption and Paradigms for Research on Black Persons*. Ed. Lewis M. King, Vernon J. Dixon, and Wade W. Nobles. First Annual J. Alfred Cannon Research Conference Series. Los Angeles: Fanon Center. 51-102.

DuPlessis, Rachel Blau. 1985. *Writing Beyond the Ending: Narrative Strategies of Twentieth-Century Women Writers*. Bloomington: Indiana University Press.
Ebeogu, Afam. 1985. "Enter the Iconoclast: Buchi Emecheta and the Igbo Culture." *Commonwealth Essays and Studies* 7.2: 83-94.
Echewa, T. Obinkaram. 1976. *The Land's Lord*. Westport, CT: Lawrence Hill.
Egejuru, Phanuel Akubueze. 1980. *Toward African Literary Independence: A Dialogue with Contemporary African Writers*. Westport, CT: Greenwood Press.
Ekwensi, Cyprian. 1983. *Survive the Peace*. London: Heinemann.
Ellis, Kate. 1989. "Stories Without Endings: Deconstructive Theory and Political Practice." *Socialist Review* 19.2: 37-52.
Emecheta, Buchi. 1976. *The Bride Price*. New York: George Braziller.
———. 1977. *The Slave Girl*. New York: George Braziller.
———. 1979a. *In the Ditch*. Revised ed. London: Allison and Busby. First published in 1972.
———. 1979b. *The Joys of Motherhood*. New York: George Braziller.
———. 1982. *Destination Biafra*. London: Allison and Busby.
———. 1983a. *Second-Class Citizen*. New York: George Braziller. First published in 1974.
———. 1983b. *Double Yoke*. New York: George Braziller.
———. 1985. *The Rape of Shavi*. New York: George Braziller.
———. 1986. *Head Above Water*. London: Ogwugwu Afo.
Emenyonu, Ernest N. 1975. "Who Does Flora Nwapa Write For?" *African Literature Today* 7: 28-33.
———. 1987. "Technique and Language in Buchi Emecheta's *The Bride Price*, *The Slave Girl* and *The Joys of Motherhood*." *Journal of Commonwealth Literature*: 22.1: 130-41.
Esonwanne, Uzo. 1990-91. "The Madness of Africa(ns): Or, Anthropology's Reason." *Cultural Critique* 17: 107-26.
———. 1992. "'Race' and Hermeneutics: Paradigm Shift—From Scientific to Hermeneutic Understanding of Race." *African American Review* 26.4: 565-82.
Fanon, Frantz. 1968. *The Wretched of the Earth*. Trans. Constance Farrington. New York: Grove.
Fetterley, Judith. 1978. *The Resisting Reader: A Feminist Approach to American Fiction*. Bloomington: Indiana University Press.
Fido, Elaine Savory. 1986. "Okigbo's *Labyrinths* and the Context of Igbo Attitudes to the Female Principle." In *Ngambika: Studies of Women in African Literature*. Ed. Carole Boyce Davies and Anne Adams Graves. Trenton, NJ: Africa World Press. 223-39.
Fish, Stanley. 1980. *Is There a Text in This Class: The Authority of Interpretive Communities*. Cambridge: Harvard University Press.
———. 1987. "Change." *South Atlantic Quarterly* 86.4: 423-44.
Foucault, Michel. 1971. "The Discourse on Language." In *The Archaeology of Knowledge and the Discourse on Language*. Trans. A. M. Sheridan-Smith. New York: Pantheon. 215-37.
———. 1979. "What Is an Author?" In *Textual Strategies: Perspectives in Post-Structuralist Criticism*. Ed. Josué V. Harari. Ithaca, NY: Cornell University Press. 141-60.

———. 1984. "Truth and Power." (From *Power/Knowledge*) *The Foucault Reader*. By Foucault. Ed. Paul Rabinow. New York: Pantheon. 51-75.

Fox-Genovese, Elizabeth. 1987. "To Write My Self: The Autobiographies of Afro-American Women." In *Feminist Issues in Literary Scholarship*. Ed. Shari Benstock. Bloomington: Indiana University Press. 161-80.

Frank, Katherine. 1982. "The Death of the Slave Girl: African Womanhood in the Novels of Buchi Emecheta." *World Literature Written in English* 21.3: 476-97.

———. 1984. "Feminist Criticism and the African Novel." *African Literature Today* 14: 34-48.

Frye, Northrop. 1957. *Anatomy of Criticism: Four Essays*. Princeton, NJ: Princeton University Press.

Fuss, Diana. 1989. *Essentially Speaking: Feminism, Nature and Difference*. New York: Routledge.

Gadamer, Hans-Georg. 1976a. "On the Scope and Function of Hermeneutical Reflection." In *Philosophical Hermeneutics*. Trans. and ed. David E. Linge. Berkeley: University of California Press. 18-43.

———. 1976b. "On the Problem of Self-Understanding." In *Philosophical Hermeneutics*. Trans. and ed. David E. Linge. Berkeley: University of California Press. 44-58.

———. 1976c. "Man and Language." In *Philosophical Hermeneutics*. Trans. and ed. David E. Linge. Berkeley: University of California Press. 59-68.

———. 1987. "The Problem of Historical Consciousness." Trans. Jeff L. Close. In *Interpretive Social Science: A Second Look*. Ed. Paul Rabinow and William M. Sullivan. Berkeley: University of California Press. 82-140.

———. 1989. *Truth and Method*. Trans. and revised by Joel Weinsheimer and Donald G. Marshall. 2nd rev. ed. New York: Crossroad.

Gates, Henry Louis, Jr. 1984. "The Blackness of Blackness: A Critique of the Sign and the Signifying Monkey." In *Black Literature and Literary Theory*. New York: Methuen. 285-321.

Gearhart, Sally Miller. 1979. *The Wanderground*. Watertown, MA: Persephone.

Geertz, Clifford. 1973. *The Interpretation of Cultures*. New York: Basic Books.

———. 1979. "From the Native's Point of View: On the Nature of Anthropological Understanding." In *Interpretive Social Science: A Reader*. Ed. Paul Rabinow and William M. Sullivan. Berkeley: University of California Press. 225-41.

———. 1983. *Local Knowledge: Further Essays in Interpretive Anthropology*. New York: Basic Books.

———. 1984. "Distinguished Lecture: Anti Anti-Relativism." *American Anthropologist* 86.2: 263-78.

Gikandi, Simon. 1987. *Reading the African Novel*. London: James Currey.

Gilligan, Carol. 1982. *In a Different Voice: Psychological Theory and Women's Development*. Cambridge, MA: Harvard University Press.

Gilman, Charlotte Perkins. 1979. *Herland*. New York: Pantheon.

Gilroy, Paul. 1993. *The Black Atlantic: Modernity and Double Consciousness*. Cambridge, MA: Harvard University Press.

Goldberg, David Theo, ed. 1990. *Anatomy of Racism*. Minneapolis: University of Minnesota Press.

Golden, Marita. 1983. *Migrations of the Heart*. New York: Ballantine.

Gould, Stephen Jay. 1981. *The Mismeasure of Man*. New York: Norton.
Gourdine, Angeletta Kim Marie. 1994. "Bridging the Middle Passage: Reading and [R]eading Diasporic Politics in Alice Walker's *Possessing the Secret of Joy* and Ama Ata Aidoo's *Changes*." Diss. Michigan State University.
Gugelberger, Georg. 1986. Introduction. *Marxism and African Literature*. Trenton, NJ: Africa World Press. v-xiv.
Gugler, Josef. 1981, 1985. "The Second Sex in Town." In *The Black Woman Cross-Culturally*. Ed. Filomina Chioma Steady. Rochester, VT: Schenkman. 169-84.
Habermas, Jürgen. 1981. "Modernity Versus Postmodernity." *New German Critique* 22: 3-14.
Harding, Sandra. 1986a. "The Instability of the Analytical Categories of Feminist Theory." *Signs* 11.4: 645-64.
———. 1986b. *The Science Question in Feminism*. Ithaca, NY: Cornell University Press.
Harris, Eddy L. 1992. *Native Stranger: A Black American's Journey into the Heart of Africa*. New York: Vintage.
Hartsock, Nancy. 1983. "The Feminist Standpoint: Developing the Ground for a Specifically Feminist Historical Materialism." In *Discovering Reality: Feminist Perspectives on Epistemology, Metaphysics, Methodology, and Philosophy of Science*. Ed. Sandra Harding and Merrill B. Hintikka. Boston: Reidel. 283-310.
———. 1987. "Rethinking Modernism: Minority vs. Majority Theories." *Cultural Critique* 7: 187-206.
Hawkesworth, Mary E. 1989. "Knowers, Knowing, Known: Feminist Theory and Claims of Truth." *Signs* 14.3: 533-57.
Head, Bessie. 1979. *A Question of Power*. London: Heinemann.
———. 1986. *Maru*. London: Heinemann.
Heidegger, Martin. 1927. *Being and Time*. Trans. John Macquarrie and Edward Robinson. New York: Harper Collins, 1962.
Held, Virginia. 1985. "Feminism and Epistemology: Recent Work on the Connection Between Gender and Knowledge." *Philosophy and Public Affairs* 14.3: 296-307.
Henderson, Mae Gwendolyn. 1990. "Speaking in Tongues: Dialogics, Dialectics, and the Black Woman Writers' Literary Tradition." In *Reading Black, Reading Feminist: A Critical Anthology*. Ed. Henry Louis Gates, Jr. New York: Meridian. 116-42.
Herskovits, Melville J. 1990. *The Myth of the Negro Past*. Boston: Beacon Press.
Hodge, John L. 1990. "Equality: Beyond Dualism and Oppression." In *Anatomy of Racism*. Ed. David Theo Goldberg. Minneapolis: University of Minnesota Press. 89-107.
Hollis, Martin, and Steven Lukes, eds. 1982. *Rationality and Relativism*. Cambridge, MA: MIT Press.
Holloway, Joseph E., ed. 1990. *Africanisms in American Culture*. Bloomington: Indiana University Press.
Holloway, Karla F. C. 1992. *Moorings and Metaphors: Figures of Culture and Gender in Black Women's Literature*. New Brunswick, NJ: Rutgers University Press.
Hutcheon, Linda. 1988. *A Poetics of Postmodernism: History, Theory, Fiction*. New York: Routledge.

Huyssen, Andreas. 1986. "Mapping the Postmodern." In *After the Great Divide: Modernism, Mass Culture, Postmodernism*. Bloomington: Indiana University Press. 178-221.
Ifemesia, Chieka. (1979?). *Traditional Humane Living Among the Igbo: An Historical Perspective*. Enugu, Nigeria: Fourth Dimension.
Irele, Abiola. 1991. "The African Scholar: Is Black Africa Entering the Dark Ages of Scholarship?" *Transition*, 51: 56-69.
Izevbaye, Dan. 1986. "Reality in the African Novel: Its Theory and Practice." *Présence Africaine* 139.3: 115-35.
Izevbaye, D. S. 1975. "The State of Criticism in African Literature." *African Literature Today* 7: 1-19.
Jacobus, Mary. 1986. "The Difference of View." In *Reading Woman: Essays in Feminist Criticism*. New York: Columbia University Press. 27-40.
Jaggar, Alison M. 1988. *Feminist Politics and Human Nature*. Totowa, NJ: Rowman and Littlefield.
Jaggar, Alison M., and Susan R. Bordo, eds. 1989. *Gender/Body/Knowledge: Feminist Reconstructions of Being and Knowing*. New Brunswick, NJ: Rutgers University Press.
Jahn, Janheinz. 1990. *Muntu: African Culture and the Western World*. Trans. Marjorie Grene. Rev. ed. New York: Grove Weidenfeld Evergreen.
Jameson, Fredric. 1986. Afterword. "Reflections in Conclusion." In *Aesthetics and Politics: The Key Texts of the Classic Debate Within German Marxism*. By Ernst Bloch et al. London: Verso. 196-213.
Jardine, Alice, and Paul Smith, eds. 1987. *Men in Feminism*. New York: Methuen.
Jay, Martin. 1985. "Habermas and Modernism." In *Habermas and Modernity*. Ed. Richard J. Bernstein. Cambridge, MA: MIT Press. 125-39.
Jehlen, Myra. 1981. "Archimedes and the Paradox of Feminist Criticism." *Signs* 6.4: 575-601.
Kaplan, Caren. 1987. "Deterritorializations: The Rewriting of Home and Exile in Western Feminist Discourse." *Cultural Critique* 6: 187-98.
Katrak, Ketu H. 1988. "Womanhood/Motherhood: Variations on a Theme in Selected Novels of Buchi Emecheta." *The Journal of Commonwealth Literature* 23.1: 159-70.
Kilday, Kathleen. 1990. "Female Circumcision in Africa: Not Just a Medical Problem." *Iris* Spring/Summer: 38-43.
Kolodny, Annette. 1985. "Dancing Through the Minefield: Some Observations on the Theory, Practice, and Politics of a Feminist Literary Criticism." In *The New Feminist Criticism: Essays on Women, Literature and Theory*. Ed. Elaine Showalter. New York: Pantheon. 144-67.
Koso-Thomas, Olayinka. 1987. *The Circumcision of Women: A Strategy for Eradication*. London: Zed.
Levin, Tobe. 1986. "Women as Scapegoats of Culture and Cult: An Activist's View of Female Circumcision in Ngugi's *The River Between*." In *Ngambika: Studies of Women in African Literature*. Ed. Carole Boyce Davies and Anne Adams Graves. Trenton, NJ: Africa World Press. 205-21.
———. 1988. "Cutting Out Circumcision." *Women's Review of Books* 5.6: 5-6.
Levine, Lawrence W. 1977. *Black Culture and Black Consciousness: Afro-American*

Folk Thought from Slavery to Freedom. New York: Oxford University Press.
Lugones, María C., and Elizabeth V. Spelman. 1983. "Have We Got a Theory for You! Feminist Theory, Cultural Imperialism and the Demand for 'The Woman's Voice.'" *Women's Studies International Forum* 6.6: 573-81.
Lukács, Georg. 1971. *Realism in Our Time: Literature and the Class Struggle.* Trans. John Mander and Necke Mander. New York: Harper.
———. 1983. *The Historical Novel.* Trans. Hannah Mitchell and Stanley Mitchell. Lincoln: University of Nebraska Press.
———. 1986. "Realism in the Balance." In *Aesthetics and Politics: The Key Texts of the Classic Debate Within German Marxism.* Trans. Rodney Livingstone. Ernst Bloch et al. Afterword. Fredric Jameson. London: Verso. 28-59.
Lyotard, Jean-François. 1984. *The Postmodern Condition: A Report on Knowledge.* Trans. Geoff Bennington and Brian Massumi. Theory and History of Literature, vol. 10. Minneapolis: University of Minnesota Press.
Macherey, Pierre. 1978. *A Theory of Literary Production.* Trans. Geoffrey Wall. London: Routledge.
MacIntyre, Alasdair. 1978. "Rationality and the Explanation of Action." In *Against the Self-Images of the Age: Essays on Ideology and Philosophy.* Notre Dame, IN: University of Notre Dame Press. 244-59.
———. 1984a. "Is Understanding Religion Compatible with Believing?" In *Rationality.* Ed. Bryan A. Wilson. Worcester, England: Basil Blackwell. 62-77.
———. 1984b. *After Virtue: A Study in Moral Theory.* 2nd ed. Notre Dame, IN: University of Notre Dame Press.
MacKinnon, Catharine A. 1982. "Feminism, Marxism, Method, and the State: An Agenda for Theory." *Signs* 7.3: 515-44.
McCarthy, Thomas. 1988. "Scientific Rationality and the 'Strong Program' in the Sociology of Knowledge." In *Construction and Constraint: The Shaping of Scientific Rationality.* Ed. Ernan McMullin. Notre Dame, IN: University of Notre Dame Press. 75-95.
McDowell, Deborah E. 1989. "Boundaries: Or Distant Relations and Close Kin." In *Afro-American Literary Study in the 1990s.* Ed. Houston A. Baker and Patricia Redmond. Chicago: University of Chicago Press. 51-70.
McLuckie, Craig W. 1987. "A Preliminary Checklist of Primary and Secondary Sources on Nigerian Civil War/Biafran War Literature." *Research in African Literatures* 18.4: 510-27.
Maja-Pearce, Adewale. 1985. "Flora Nwapa's *Efuru*: A Study in Misplaced Hostility." *World Literature Written in English* 25.1: 10-27.
Mann, Kristin. 1985. *Marrying Well: Marriage, Status and Social Change Among the Educated Elite in Colonial Lagos.* Cambridge, England: Cambridge University Press.
Marcus, George E., and Michael M. J. Fischer. 1986. *Anthropology as Cultural Critique: An Experimental Moment in the Human Sciences.* Chicago: University of Chicago Press.
Marcuse, Herbert. 1964. *One-Dimensional Man: Studies in the Ideology of Advanced Industrial Society.* Boston: Beacon Press.
Martin, Emily. 1987. *The Woman in the Body: A Cultural Analysis of Reproduction.* Boston: Beacon Press.

Martini, Jürgen. 1986. "Linking Africa and the West: Buchi Emecheta." In *Festschrift zum 60. Geburtstag von Carl Hoffmann*. Ed. Franz Rottland. Hamburg: Buske. 223-33.

Mascia-Lees, Frances E., Patricia Sharpe, and Colleen Ballerino Cohen. 1989. "The Postmodernist Turn in Anthropology: Cautions from a Feminist Perspective." *Signs* 15.1: 7-33.

Matustik, Martin J. 1989. "Habermas on Communicative Reason and Performative Contradiction." *New German Critique* 47: 143-72.

Mazrui, Ali A. 1983. *The African Condition: A Political Diagnosis*. London: Cambridge University Press.

———. 1986. *The Africans: A Triple Heritage*. Boston: Little Brown.

Meese, Elizabeth A. 1990. *(Ex)Tensions: Re-Figuring Feminist Criticism*. Urbana: University of Illinois Press.

Memmi, Albert. 1991. *The Colonizer and the Colonized*. Exp. ed. Boston: Beacon Press.

Miller, Christopher L. 1986. "Theories of Africans: The Question of Literary Anthropology." In *"Race," Writing, and Difference*. Ed. Henry Louis Gates, Jr. Chicago: University of Chicago Press. 281-300.

———. 1988. "Ethnicity and Ethics in the Criticism of Black African Literature." *South Atlantic Quarterly* 87.1: 75-108.

———. 1990. *Theories of Africans: Francophone Literature and Anthropology in Africa*. Chicago: University of Chicago Press.

Miller, J. Hillis. 1981. "The Ethics of Reading: Vast Gaps and Parting Hours." In *American Criticism in the Poststructuralist Age*. Ann Arbor: Michigan Studies in the Humanities. 19-41.

Miller, Nancy K. 1986. "Changing the Subject: Authorship, Writing, and the Reader." In *Feminist Studies/Critical Studies*. Ed. Teresa de Lauretis. Bloomington: Indiana University Press. 102-20.

Mintz, Sidney W., and Richard Price. 1992. *The Birth of African-American Culture: An Anthropological Perspective*. Rpt. Boston: Beacon Press. Originally published in 1976 as *An Anthropological Approach to the Afro-American Past*.

Mitchell, W.J.T. 1992. "Postcolonial Culture, Postimperial Criticism." *Transition* 56: 11-19.

Mlama, Penina Muhando. 1990. "Creating in the Mother-Tongue: The Challenges to the African Writer Today." *Research in African Literatures* 21.4: 5-14.

Mohanty, Chandra Talpade. 1984. "Under Western Eyes: Feminist Scholarship and Colonial Discourses." *Boundary 2* 12.3/13.1 (Spring/Fall): 333-58.

Mohanty, S. P. 1989. "Us and Them: On the Philosophical Bases of Political Criticism." *Yale Journal of Criticism* 2.2: 1-31.

Moi, Toril. 1985. *Sexual/Textual Politics: Feminist Literary Theory*. London: Methuen.

Moore, Gerald. 1980. *Twelve African Writers*. Bloomington: Indiana University Press.

Mudimbe, V. Y. 1988. *The Invention of Africa: Gnosis, Philosophy, and the Order of Knowledge*. Bloomington: Indiana University Press.

———. 1990. "Which Idea of Africa? Herskovits's Cultural Relativism." *October* 55: 93-104.

Mukherjee, Arun P. 1986. "The Vocabulary of the 'Universal': Cultural Imperialism

and Western Literary Criticism." *World Literature Written in English* 26.2: 343-53.
Mullings, Leith. 1976. "Women and Economic Change in Africa." In *Women in Africa: Studies in Social and Economic Change*. Ed. Nancy J. Hafkin and Edna G. Bay. Stanford, CA: Stanford University Press. 239-64.
Naylor, Gloria. 1992. *Bailey's Cafe*. New York: Harcourt Brace Jovanovich.
Newton, Judith. 1988. "History as Usual?: Feminism and the 'New Historicism.'" *Cultural Critique* 8: 87-121.
Ngugi, James [Ngugi wa Thiong'o aka Ngugi]. 1964. *Weep Not, Child*. London: Heinemann.
Ngugi wa Thiong'o. 1981. "Literature and Society." In *Writers in Politics*. London: Heinemann. 3-33.
———. 1983. *The River Between*. London: Heinemann. First published in 1965.
———. 1989. *Decolonising the Mind: The Politics of Language in African Literature*. Portsmouth, NH: Heinemann.
Nikiforova, Irina D. 1987. "The Development and Distinctive Features of Forms of the Novel in African Literature." *Research in African Literatures* 18.4: 422-33.
Nkosi, Lewis. 1976. "Women in Literature." *Africa Woman* 6 September/October: 36-37.
———. 1981. *Tasks and Masks: Themes and Styles of African Literature*. Harlow, Essex, U.K.: Longman.
———. 1987. *Mating Birds*. New York: Harper.
Nwapa, Flora. 1966. *Efuru*. London: Heinemann.
———. 1987a. *Idu*. London: Heinemann.
———. 1987b. "Women in Politics." *Présence Africaine* 141.1: 115-21.
Ogunyemi, Chikwenye Okonjo. 1983. "Buchi Emecheta: The Shaping of a Self." *Komparatistische Hefte* 8: 65-77.
———. 1985. "Womanism: The Dynamics of the Contemporary Black Female Novel in English." *Signs* 11.1: 63-80.
Okhamafe, E. Imafedia. 1989. "African Feminism(s) and the Question of Marital and Non-Marital Loneliness and Intimacy." *Sage* 6.1: 33-39.
Okonjo, Kamene. 1976. "The Dual-Sex Political System in Operation: Igbo Women and Community Politics in Midwestern Nigeria." In *Women in Africa: Studies in Social and Economic Change*. Ed. Nancy J. Hafkin and Edna G. Bay. Stanford, CA: Stanford University Press. 45-58.
———. 1981, 1985. "Women's Political Participation in Nigeria." *The Black Woman Cross-Culturally*. Ed. Filomina Chioma Steady. Rochester, VT: Schenkman. 79-106.
Okpaku, Joseph. 1970a. "The Western Africanist versus the African Intellectual: An Examination of the Present State of African Humanities." In *New African Literature and the Arts*. New York: Crowell. 6-12.
———. 1970b. "Culture and Criticism: African Critical Standards for African Literature and the Arts." In *New African Literature and the Arts*. New York: Crowell. 13-23.
Omotoso, Kole. 1971. *The Edifice*. London: Heinemann.
O'Neill, John. 1985. "Decolonization and the Ideal Speech Community: Some Issues in

the Theory and Practice of Communicative Competence." In *Critical Theory and Public Life*. Ed. John Forester. Cambridge, MA: MIT Press. 57-76.

Onoge, Omafume F. 1986a. "The Crisis of Consciousness in Modern African Literature: A Survey (1974)." In *Marxism and African Literature*. Ed. Georg Gugelberger. Trenton, NJ: Africa World Press. 21-49.

———. 1986b. "Towards a Marxist Sociology of African Literature." In *Marxism and African Literature*. Ed. Georg Gugelberger. Trenton, NJ: Africa World Press. 50-63.

Onwueme, Tess. 1988. *The Broken Calabash*. Ibadan, Nigeria: Heinemann.

Ousmane, Sembène. 1983. *Xala*. Trans. Clive Wake. Westport, CT: Lawrence Hill.

Owens, Craig. 1983. "The Discourse of Others: Feminists and Postmodernists." In *The Anti-Aesthetic: Essays on Postmodern Culture*. Ed. Hal Foster. Port Townsend, WA: Bay Press. 57-82.

Palmer, Eustace. 1982. "A Powerful Female Voice in the African Novel: Introducing the Novels of Buchi Emecheta." *New Literature Review* 11: 21-33.

———. 1983. "The Feminine Point of View: Buchi Emecheta's *The Joys of Motherhood*." *African Literature Today* 13: 38-55.

Petersen, Kirsten Holst. 1984. "First Things First: Problems of a Feminist Approach to African Literature." *Kunapipi* 6.3: 35-47.

———. 1986. "Unpopular Opinions: Some African Women Writers." In *A Double Colonization: Colonial and Post-Colonial Women's Writing*. Ed. Kirsten Holst Petersen and Anna Rutherford. Mundelstrup, Denmark: Dangaroo Press. 107-20.

Piercy, Marge. 1976. *Woman on the Edge of Time*. New York: Fawcett.

Poster, Mark. 1989. *Critical Theory and Poststructuralism: In Search of a Context*. Ithaca, NY: Cornell University Press.

Povey, John F. 1970. "Changing Themes in the Nigerian Novel." In *New African Literature and the Arts*. New York: Crowell. 27-41.

Rabinow, Paul. 1986. "Representations Are Social Facts: Modernity and Post-Modernity in Anthropology." In *Writing Culture: The Poetics and Politics of Ethnography*. Ed. James Clifford and George E. Marcus. Berkeley: University of California Press. 234-61.

Rawls, John. 1971. *A Theory of Justice*. Cambridge, MA: Harvard University Press, Belknap.

Ricoeur, Paul. 1965. "Universal Civilization and National Cultures." In *History and Truth*. Trans. Charles A. Kelbley. Evanston, IL: Northwestern University Press. 271-84.

Robinson, Sally. 1988. "The 'Anti-Logos Weapon': Multiplicity in Women's Texts." *Contemporary Literature* 29.1: 105-24.

Rorty, Richard. 1982. *Consequences of Pragmatism (Essays: 1972-1980)*. Minneapolis: University of Minnesota Press.

———. 1985. "Habermas and Lyotard on Postmodernity." In *Habermas and Modernity*. Ed. Richard J. Bernstein. Cambridge, MA: MIT Press. 161-75.

Rosaldo, M. Z. 1980. "The Use and Abuse of Anthropology: Reflections on Feminism and Cross-Cultural Understanding." *Signs* 5.3: 389-417.

Rowell, Charles H. 1990. "An Interview with Chinua Achebe." *Callaloo* 13.1: 86-101.

Russ, Joanna. 1978. *The Female Man*. New York: Bantam.

Ryan, Michael. 1982. *Marxism and Deconstruction: A Critical Articulation*. Baltimore: Johns Hopkins University Press.
Said, Edward W. 1979. "The Text, the World, the Critic." In *Textual Strategies: Perspectives in Post-Structuralist Criticism*. Ed. Josué V. Harari. Ithaca, NY: Cornell University Press. 161-88.
———. 1979. *Orientalism*. New York: Vintage.
Sanderson, Lilian Passmore. 1981. *Against the Mutilation of Women: The Struggle to End Unnecessary Suffering*. London: Ithaca.
Schipper, Mineke. 1985. "Women and Literature in Africa." In *Unheard Words: Women and Literature in Africa, the Arab World, Asia, and Caribbean and Latin America*. Trans. Barbara Potter Fasting. London: Allison and Busby. 22-58.
Schweickart, Patrocinio P. 1986. "Reading Ourselves: Toward a Feminist Theory of Reading." In *Gender and Reading: Essays on Readers, Texts, and Contexts*. Ed. Elizabeth A. Flynn and Patrocinio P. Schweickart. Baltimore: Johns Hopkins University Press. 31-62.
Siebers, Tobin. 1988. *The Ethics of Criticism*. Ithaca: Cornell University Press.
Slomski, Genevieve T. 1986. "Dialogue in the Discourse: A Study of Revolt in Selected Fiction by African Women." Diss. Indiana University.
Smitherman, Geneva. 1988. *Talkin and Testifyin*. Detroit: Wayne State University Press.
Solberg, Rolf. 1983. "The Woman of Black Africa, Buchi Emecheta: The Woman's Voice in the New Nigerian Novel." *English Studies* 64.3: 247-62.
Songolo, Aliko. 1977. "The Writer, the Audience and the Critic's Responsibility: The Case of *Bound to Violence*." In *Artist and Audience: African Literature as a Shared Experience*. Selected Proceedings from the 1977 African Literature Association Meeting. Ed. Richard K. Priebe and Thomas A. Hale. Washington, DC: Three Continents Press. 126-40.
Soyinka, Wole. 1965. *The Interpreters*. London: Andre Deutsch.
———. 1988. *The Man Died: The Prison Notes of Wole Soyinka*. New York: Noonday.
———. 1990. *Myth, Literature and the African World*. New York: Cambridge University Press.
Spelman, Elizabeth V. 1988. *Inessential Woman: Problems of Exclusion in Feminist Thought*. Boston: Beacon Press.
Sperber, Dan. 1982. "Apparently Irrational Beliefs." In *Rationality and Relativism*. Ed. Martin Hollis and Steven Lukes. Cambridge, MA: MIT Press. 149-80.
Spivak, Gayatri Chakravorty. 1976. Translator's Preface. In *Of Grammatology*. By Jacques Derrida. Baltimore: Johns Hopkins University Press. ix-xc.
Steady, Filomina Chioma. 1981, 1985. "The Black Woman Cross-Culturally: An Overview." In *The Black Woman Cross-Culturally*. Ed. Filomina Chioma Steady. Rochester, VT: Schenkman. 7-41.
Stimpson, Catharine R. 1986. "Gertrude Stein and the Transposition of Gender." In *The Poetics of Gender*. Ed. Nancy K. Miller. New York: Columbia University Press. 1-18.
Stratton, Florence. 1988. "The Shallow Grave: Archetypes of Female Experience in African Fiction." *Research in African Literatures* 19.2: 143-69.
Sudarkasa, Niara. 1981, 1985. "Female Employment and Family Organization in West Africa." In *The Black Woman Cross-Culturally*. Ed. Filomina Chioma Steady.

Rochester, VT: Schenkman. 49-63.

Taylor, Charles. 1985. *Philosophy and the Human Sciences*. Philosophical Papers 2. Cambridge, England: Cambridge University Press.

Thompson, John. 1982. "Universal Pragmatics." In *Habermas: Critical Debates*. Ed. John B. Thompson and David Held. Cambridge, MA: MIT Press. 116-33.

Todorov, Tzvetan. 1992. *The Conquest of America: The Question of the Other*. Trans. Richard Howard. New York: Harper Perennial.

Topouzis, Daphne. 1990. "Buchi Emecheta: An African Story-Teller." *Africa Report* (May-June): 67-70.

Torgovnick, Marianna. 1990. *Gone Primitive: Savage Intellects, Modern Lives*. Chicago: University of Chicago Press.

Umeh, Marie. 1982. "*The Joys of Motherhood*: Myth or Reality?" *Colby Library Quarterly* 28.1: 39-46.

Van Allen, Judith. 1972. "'Sitting on a Man': Colonialism and the Lost Political Institutions of Igbo Women." *Canadian Journal of African Studies* 6.2: 165-81.

———. 1976. "'Aba Riots' or Igbo 'Women's War'? Ideology, Stratification, and the Invisibility of Women." In *Women in Africa: Studies in Social and Economic Change*. Ed. Nancy J. Hafkin and Edna G. Bay. Stanford, CA: Stanford University Press. 59-85.

Visel, Robin. 1988. "A Half-Colonization: The Problem of the White Colonial Woman Writer." *Kunapipi* 10.3: 39-45.

Walker, Alice. 1983a. *In Search of Our Mothers' Gardens: Womanist Prose*. New York: Harvest.

———. 1983b. "A Writer Because of, Not in Spite of, Her Children." In *In Search of Our Mothers' Gardens: Womanist Prose*. New York: Harvest. 66–70.

———. 1992. *Possessing the Secret of Joy*. New York: Harcourt Brace.

Wallace, Michele. 1990. "Variations on Negation and the Heresy of Black Feminist Creativity." In *Reading Black, Reading Feminist: A Critical Anthology*. Ed. Henry Louis Gates, Jr. New York: Meridian. 52-67.

Ward, Cynthia. 1990. "What They Told Buchi Emecheta: Oral Subjectivity and the Joys of 'Otherhood.'" *PMLA* 105.1: 83-97.

Weedon, Chris. 1987. *Feminist Practice and Poststructuralist Theory*. New York: Basil Blackwell.

Williams, Adebayo. 1991. "Toward a Theory of Cultural Production in Africa." *Research in African Literatures* 22.2: 5-20.

Williams, Raymond. 1961. *The Long Revolution*. New York: Columbia University Press.

———. 1977. *Marxism and Literature*. New York: Oxford University Press.

Winch, Peter. 1964. "Understanding a Primitive Society." *American Philosophical Quarterly* 1.4: 307-24.

———. 1990. *The Idea of a Social Science and Its Relation to Philosophy*. Second edition. Atlantic Highlands, NJ: Humanities Press International. First published in 1958.

Wipper, Audrey. 1972. "African Women, Fashion, and Scapegoating." *Canadian Journal of African Studies* 6.2: 329-49.

Yezierska, Anzia. 1975. *Bread Givers*. New York: Persea.

Young, Iris Marion. 1990a. "The Ideal of Community and the Politics of Difference." In

Feminism/Postmodernism. Ed. Linda J. Nicholson. New York: Routledge. 300-23.

———. 1990b. *Justice and the Politics of Difference.* Princeton, NJ: Princeton University Press.

Index

Achebe, Chinua, 6, 33, 38–40, 42, 45, 49 n.8, 52, 117–18, 122 n.14, 124 n.43, 138–40, 143, 155, 157
Adorno, Theodor, 46
aesthetics, communal, 40; relationship between, and worldviews, 33–50
The African Condition (Mazrui), 131
African discourse, 116–17
African men, criticism of, 67, 140; negative portraits of, 57, 113–15, 130–31, 143–44. *See also* criticism
African narratives, 120
African novel, themes in, 35–37
African novelists, differences between, and Western writers, 36; issues facing, 35–36
African scholarship, 8
African socialist writers, 63
African women: negative portraits of, in Emecheta's fiction, 145–46; problems faced by, 21–22; status in community, 71, 103, 107–112, 123 n.28, 135, 165 n.10
African worldview, 73
Afrocentrism, 14 nn.10, 16, 15 nn.25–27, 31, 16 n.32; 29 n.1, 31 n.27, 50 n.19
agonistics of language games. *See* language games, agonistics of
Alcoff, Linda, 8, 26, 28, 31 n.26, 165 n.4
alienation, cultural, 41; Western, 34
alien: beliefs, 124; cultures, 11, 18, 78, 91, 121 n.2, 163; customs, 5, 59, 63, 83, 119, 148–51; discourse, 17, 117; texts, 5, 9, 25, 119, 153, 163–64; worldviews, 45, 59, 124. *See also* customs; differences
Althusser, Louis, 48
Amadi, Elechi, 35, 60, 66, 109, 120, 138, 165
ambiguity, 127–28, 155, 157–60
ambivalence, of narrator, 64, 93, 96
American literature, characteristics of, 34
Andrade, Susan Z., 125 n.58
anorexia, 149, 151
anthropologizing the West (Rabinow), 25, 164. *See also* interactive reading; interrogating ourselves
anthropology, 11; debates in, 78; usefulness of, 19–20
anti-relativism, 16, 149. *See also* relativism
application, 14 n.11. *See also* understanding

archetypal patterns, 100
Armah, Ayi Kwei, 35, 52, 75 n.24, 117–18, 161
Arrow of God (Achebe), 133, 155, 157
art for art's sake, 33, 38–40
artist and society, relationship between, 33, 49 n.9
artistic commitment, 40–43
artist, relationship of African, to audience, 37, 41–42, 102
art, Western view of, 38–39
Asante, Molefi Kete, 10, 13 n. 2, 16 n.32, 30 n.5, 49 n.7, 121 n.6
assisting readers, questions of how much novelists should engage in, 41–42
atomistic selves, 34, 71, 164
Atwood, Margaret, 78
audience, Emecheta's reading, 101–102, 165 n.4
audience participation, 41
Auerbach, Nina, 132–33
author: as Other, 25–28; need for an, 25; situatedness of, 37; subjectivity of, 27. *See also* Other, reader as
authorial authority, 30
authorial voice, 141. *See also* narrative voice
authoritative discourse. *See* discourse, authoritative. *See also* voice of authority; Voice of the Fathers; voice of tradition; word of the fathers
authority, 2–3; voice of, 84
Awoonor, Kofi, 52, 117–18, 122 n.18, 123 n.30, 140, 150

Bâ, Mariama, 36–37, 42, 52, 65, 113, 161
Babatope, Biola, 21
Bakhtin, Mikhail, 6, 33, 44–45, 54, 73, 84–85, 90, 94, 114, 117, 119, 145–46, 167 n.28
Barthelemy, Anthony, 122 n.9, 124 n.53, 125 n.60
Barthes, Roland, 24–25, 28, 46, 50 n.26, 92
Baym, Nina, 31 n.17, 34
Bazin, Nancy Topping, 74 nn.12, 14, 75 n.18, 122 n.10, 124 nn.37–39
Bellah, Robert, 34, 49 n.5
Belsey, Catherine, 22, 31 n.19, 46–48, 73
Berger, Peter, 158; and Thomas Luckmann, 53, 89–90
Bernstein, Richard J., 1, 8, 10, 12–13, 13 n.4, 14 n.12, 78, 87–88, 92, 123 n.26
Bhabha, Homi, 31 n.21
Biafran War, 62, 128–29, 165 n.3. *See also Destination Biafra* (Emecheta); independence; *Sunset in Biafra* (Amadi)
Bialostosky, Don, 31 n.28
biblical authority, extent of, in African literature, 30 n.15. *See also* Christianity
binary oppositions, 119, 134, 136, 161–62. *See also* Cixous, Hélène; difference; plurality
Bloch, Ernst, 45
Bordo, Susan, 31 n.26, 151
Bourdieu, Pierre, 49 n.11
Bread Givers (Yezierska), 75 n.19
breast enlargements, 149
Breast of the Earth (Awoonor), 150
Brecht, Bertolt, 47, 50 n.23
bride price, custom of, 59, 64, 66, 68, 82, 88
The Bride Price (Emecheta), 42, 50 n.13, 51–52, 59, 70, 74 n.15, 79–94, 119, 123 n.25, 124 n.55, 165 n.2
The Broken Calabash (Onwueme), 122 n.14, 123 n.34
Brooks, Peter, 77, 82, 117, 121 n.1
Brown, Lloyd, 74 n.11, 100, 121 n.4
bulimia, 149, 151
Butler, Marilyn, 13 n.2

Cane (Toomer), 71
Caputo, John D., 4, 14 n.7

Carby, Hazel, 74 n.2
Cartesian anxiety, 92, 123 n.26
categories of thought (Winch), 18, 87–88
childlessness, 105. *See also* motherhood
child raising, 61
Children of Violence (Lessing), 165 n.9
Chinweizu, 23, 39–41, 43, 102
Christian, Barbara, 20–22, 106–107, 124 nn.41, 44
Christian dogma, 99
Christianity: as authoritative discourse, 116; as enslavement, 94, 100; believing in, 54–55; effects of, on African peoples, 60, 103, 108, 112, 116, 124 n.54, 150, 165 n.13; meaning of, to Emecheta's characters, 89, 99; understanding, 54–55. *See also* biblical authority; colonialism; colonization; missionaries
civil war, Nigerian. *See* Biafran War; *Destination Biafra* (Emecheta)
Cixous, Hélène, 120, 127–28, 134, 165 n.11. *See also* binary oppositions; difference; French feminists; plurality
classic realism. *See* realism, classic
classification, problems of, 88, 121. *See also* genres, question of literary
clitoridectomies, 5, 149, 151; performed in West, 151. *See also* clitorization
clitoris, 166 n.21
clitorization, 59, 147–52, 159, 166 n.20; Emecheta's comments on, 152. *See also* clitoridectomies
closure, 29; interpretive, 118; narrative, 121; refusing, 119, 121
Cobham, Rhonda, 20
Cobham-Sander, Rhonda, 166 nn.15–16
collective protagonists, 133–35. *See also* protagonist
colonialism, 10, 155; effects of, 50, 52, 108–112, 120, 124 nn.50, 53, 135, 137. *See also* Christianity; colonists; colonization; colonized and colonizer; decolonization; Fanon, Frantz
colonialists, values imported by Western, 71, 103, 111. *See also* colonialism; colonization
colonization, 4, 117, 121, 153, 161; ability of Africans to throw off effects of, 153. *See also* Christianity; colonialism; colonialists; decolonization; Fanon, Frantz
colonized and colonizer, relationship between, 129, 132. *See also* decolonization; Fanon, Frantz
comic mode, 102, 143. *See also* New Comedy
commonalities: between Igbo and feminist values, 59, 136. *See also* community
common language, finding a, 27; myth of a, 10, 28, 44–45. *See also* discourse; English language; language
communal ethics, 154
communal responsibility: among Igbo, 60. *See also* community; interdependence
community: Igbo attitude toward, 58–59; in Emecheta's fiction, 59, 62, 136; relationship of individual to, 84, 134, 164; values of, reaffirmed, 81. *See also* communal ethics; communal responsibility; interdependence
competing voices: in Emecheta's fiction, 85, 154. *See also* dialogic heteroglossia: in Emecheta's fiction; plurality
conflicting cultural traditions, 59. *See also* alien: cultures, customs
connections, feminism hunger for, 21, 30 n.9, 146–47, 163; impossibility of achieving, 150–51; literary, 50 n.22; making, 164. *See also* correspondence; standpoint theory; universalism, false

constructions of gender, 56
contextualized approach, 24–25. *See also* foregrounding; interactive reading; interrogating ourselves; readers
conventional endings. *See* endings; happy endings; narrative *telos*
conversation, reading as, 4, 13, 14 n.11, 26, 28, 162, 164; theories of, 13 n.1. *See also* cross-cultural: conversations; dialogics; interactive reading; language games
correspondence, 12; warning not to assume too much, 50 n.20. *See also* alien: texts; connections
corruption: of Africans by Western values, 60, 67, 108–109; societal, 135, 138–40, 143, 166
couple, significance of the heterosexual, 108, 124 n.42, 128, 136, 153, 160–63, 165 n.6, 166 n.27
Coward, Rosalind, 31
critical bias of Western readers, 63, 74 n.5. *See also* expectations; feminist readers; prejudices; Western criticism; Western responses
critical signification, 72. *See also* signifying
criticism: of African men, 67; of African tradition, 106; of Nigerian men in Emecheta's fiction, 53, 140. *See also* African men; defense; sympathy
cross-cultural: conversations, 62, 103, 128, 141; encounters, 56, 147. *See also* conversation; dialogics; interactive reading
cultural alienation, 41
cultural anthropology, 8
cultural differences, 61, 64, 68, 80, 96, 106, 146–51; Emecheta remarking on, 67. *See also* alien
cultural heritage, loss of, by Africans, 60; resilience of African, 133. *See also* Christianity; colonialism; colonization
cultural humility, 150; need for, 18, 153, 162
cultural imperialism, 156. *See also* ethnocentric responses; ethnocentricity; ethnocentrism
cultural prejudices. *See* prejudices. *See also* critical bias; expectations
cultural sameness. *See* universalism, false
culture, African, defense of, 68, 100. *See also* displaced African values
customs, mix of African and Western, 88–89, 97, 122. *See also* alien customs

Dallmayr, Fred, 13 n.1, 31 n.22
d'Almeida, Irene Assiba, 22
Daly, Mary, 149, 165 n.5, 166 n.22
Dareer, Asma E., 147–48
daughters, language of. *See* voice of the daughters. *See also* discourse; language; Voice of the Fathers; voice of tradition
Davies, Carole Boyce, 20, 22, 30 n.8, 105, 124 nn.36, 45
Daymond, M. J., 121 n.5, 122 n.20
death of the author (Barthes), 24–25
decolonization, 132, 141, 165 n.7; need for, 40. *See also* colonialism; colonization; Fanon, Frantz
defamiliarizing: Western customs, 61; Western language, 95–96
defense: of African culture, 68, 74 n.14, 100, 122 n.13. *See also* African men; criticism; displaced African values; sympathy
Derrida, Jacques, 4
Destination Biafra (Emecheta), 127–41, 161, 164 n.1, 165 n.5
dialectics. *See* negative experience
dialogic heteroglossia, 43, 45, 69, 73, 117, 146; in Emecheta's fiction, 87–92, 96–99, 101, 104, 107, 118–19, 142, 154, 157, 162. *See also* competing voices; dialogics; discourse; plurality
dialogic model of understanding, 2

dialogics, 89; Gadamerian, 2, 28; in novels, 84–85. *See also* conversation; cross-cultural: conversations; dialogic heteroglossia; interactive reading
dialogic voices, 84
Dib, Mohammed, 40
difference: as multiplicity, 127–28. *See also* binary oppositions; Cixous, Hélène; French Feminists; plurality
differences: between Africa and West, 10; cultural, 19–20, 61; in texts, 7, 12; in values, 56, 140. *See also* alien: beliefs, cultures, customs, worldviews
differing aesthetic values, 83. *See also* expectations; prejudices
differing meaning for readers, 87
dignity, 158
discourse, authoritative, 54, 85–87, 90, 114, 116; double-voiced, 97, 119, 136–37, 141, 143–44, 167 n.28; internally persuasive, 85, 93; potential, 86, 93. *See also* dialogic heteroglossia; master narratives; voice of the daughters; Voice of the Fathers; voice of tradition; word of the fathers
discursive familiarity, 25, 27, 31 n.19, 47, 73. *See also* familiarity
displaced African values, 59–61. *See also* defense; sympathy
disrupting old stories, 79
distinguishing Emecheta's novels from English novels, 73
divorce, meaning of, to Igbos, 63
Dixon, Vernon, 34–35
double-voiced discourse. *See* discourse, double-voiced
Double Yoke (Emecheta), 5, 127, 141–52
dualisms. *See* binary oppositions
DuBois, W. E. B., 71
DuPlessis, Rachel Blau, 52, 78–79, 103, 108, 124 n.42, 133, 153, 165 n.9

Ebeogu, Afam, 122 n.12, 123 nn.22, 27
Echewa, T. Obinkaram, 122 n.16
economic independence, loss of women's, 11–12. *See also* Christianity; colonialism; colonization
The Edifice (Omotoso), 140
Efuru (Nwapa), 42, 67, 105–106, 109, 124 n.54, 150–52
Egejuru, Phanuel Akubueze, 40
Ekwensi, Cyprian, 165
Ellis, Kate, 20, 117–18
Emecheta: as political writer, 52
Emenyonu, Ernest, 49 n.12, 50 n.13, 121 n.7
emotivism, 116
endings, conventional, 79, 134; dislike of Westerners for Emecheta's, 80, 82, 84–85, 102–103, 106, 121, 122 nn.9, 11; problem of interpreting, 81–82, 85, 94–95, 118–19, 121 nn.5–7; significance of Emecheta's, 77–79; writing beyond conventional, 134. *See also* DuPlessis, Rachel Blau; feminist readers; genres; happy endings; interpretive problems; misunderstanding; narrative *telos*; problems in interpretation; understanding; Western fiction
English language, Achebe's view of, 43; Chinweizu's view of, 43; Emecheta's use of, 33, 43; Ngugi's renouncing of, 43; used by Africans, 6. *See also* common language, myth of a; language
Enlightenment, the, 3, 14 n.12, 25–26, 38, 155–56. *See also* modernity
enslavement: of African women, 94, 100, 102–103, 123 nn.27–28
epic: and novel distinguished, 84–85; comparing Emecheta's novel to an, 90–91
epistemology, interrogation of Western, 24; relationship to narrative form, 33; Western, 18, 26
Esonwanne, Uzo, 15 n.22, 75 n.23

Estrangement (Amadi), 109
ethical criticism, 25–26
ethical responsibilities, 8
ethics of reading, 1, 12, 31 n.25, 59
ethnocentric compulsions, 95
ethnocentricity, 3; luxury of, 42
ethnocentric positivism, 21, 139
ethnocentric prejudice, 8
ethnocentric responses, 61
ethnocentrism, 6–7, 11, 29 n.2, 52
ethnographic documentation, Emecheta's novels as, 58
ethographer, narrator as, 98–99. *See also* meditation on culture
Eurocentric arrogance, 49 n.7
Eurocentrism, 16 n.32, 23, 121 n.6
European novel, changes in, 35
expectations, 65–66, 80, 102–103; comedic, 102; cultural, 81, 119; feminist, 102. *See also* critical bias; feminist readers; genres; happy endings; narrative *telos*; prejudices; Western criticism; Western responses
experience-distant concepts, 91, 99, 123 n.24, 164
experience-far concepts. *See* experience-distant concepts
experience-near concepts, 91, 123 n.24, 164
experience-near context, 99
explanations, textual, 41–42, 45, 122 n.19

fabulation, 154, 157. *See also* science fiction
false consciousness, 72
familiarity, 9–10, 31, 65, 78. *See also* discursive familiarity
Fanon, Frantz, 4, 132, 134, 166 n.26
Farr, Cecilia K., 74
fathers and daughters, relationship of, in Emecheta's fiction, 82
fathers, language of the. *See* discourse, authoritative; Voice of the Fathers; voice of tradition; word of the fathers
fattening rooms, 146, 149
female circumcision, 147–48, 150. *See also* clitoridectomies; clitorization
female hero, 70
The Female Man (Russ), 165 n.9
female mutilation. *See* clitoridectomies; clitorization; female circumcision
female self, changing definition of, 70
feminism, African, 30 n.8; apparent Western, in Emecheta's fiction, 50 n.14, 74 n.12, 75 n.18, 121 n.4, 122 n.10, 124 n.39, 141, 146; influence of Western, on Emecheta, 50; limitations of Western, 6, 8–9, 19–22, 58; rejection of, by African writers, 21; socialist, 58; Western, Emecheta's differences with, 79. *See also* standpoint theory; universalism, false; universalizing questions; womanism
feminist ideals, 136
feminist readers, difficulty faced by Western, 91; displeasure of Western, toward portraits of men, 63–64, 113–16, 131, 140–41. *See also* critical bias; expectations; interpretive problems; misunderstanding; prejudices; problems in interpretation; Western criticism; Western responses
feminist, temptation to treat Emecheta as Western-style, 69, 163
Fetterley, Judith, 31 n.17, 163
Fido, Elaine Savory, 50, 88, 108
Fischer, Michael M. J., and George Marcus, 19, 49
Fish, Stanley, 14 n.13, 22, 30 n.12
foot binding, 149
forced abortions, 149
forced pregnancies, 149
foregrounding: expectations, 78; prejudices, 59, 85. *See also* anthropologizing the West; contex-

tualized approach; interactive reading; interrogating ourselves fore-meanings, 5
Foucault, Michel, 14 n.13, 24, 70, 133
Fox-Genovese, Elizabeth, 133
Fragments (Armah), 117–18
Frank, Katherine, 7, 15 n.20, 123 nn.28, 30
French feminists, 86, 128. *See also* Cixous, Hélène; Irigaray, Luce; Jacobus, Mary
Frye, Northrop, 80, 102, 121 n.6, 143
Fuss, Diana, 30 n.9, 31 n.23

Gadamer, Hans-Georg, 1–13, 13 nn.1–2, 5–6, 14 nn.7, 11–12, 14, 15 nn.17–18, 26–29, 44, 47, 50 n.18, 53–54. *See also* hermeneutic circle; hermeneutics
Gates, Henry Louis, Jr., 71–72, 75 n.23
Gearhart, Sally Miller, 49 n.3
Geertz, Clifford, 16 nn.33–34, 49 n.5, 91, 123 nn.21, 24, 149, 163–64, 167 n.29
genital mutilation. *See* clitoridectomies; clitorization, female circumcision
genres, different, of understanding, 78, 121 n.2; question of literary, 83–87, 91, 102. *See also* endings; expectations; happy endings, questions of; interpretive problems; narrative forms; narrative *telos*; novel; prejudices; problems in interpretation
Gikandi, Simon, 48
Gilligan, Carol, 74 n.6
Gilman, Charlotte Perkins, 133, 165 n.9
Gilroy, Paul, 13 n.2, 49 n.10
God's Bits of Wood (Ousmane), 35, 133
Goldberg, David Theo, 15 n.23
Golden, Marita, 49 n.6

Gould, Stephen Jay, 15 n.22
Gourdine, Angeletta Kim Marie, 31 n.20
A Grain of Wheat (Ngugi), 133
Gugelberger, Georg, 7, 50 n.25
Gugler, Josef, 117

Habermas, Jürgen, 31 n.25, 38, 61
Haggard, Rider, 72
happy endings, questions of, 80–82, 94, 99, 102–103, 166 n.16. *See also* endings; expectations; genres, question of literary; interpretive problems; narrative *telos*; novel; problems in interpretation; Western fiction
Harding, Sandra, 49 n.4, 149, 162
Harris, Eddy L., 49
Hartsock, Nancy, 25–26, 31 n.16, 74 nn.1, 6
Hawkesworth, Mary E., 14 n.15, 166 n.18
Head Above Water (Emecheta), 59, 79, 81, 94, 101, 105, 121 n.8, 142
Head, Bessie, 21, 39–40, 49, 52, 65, 160–61, 165
Hegel, G. W. F., 14 n.7, 26
Heidegger, Martin, 2, 13 n.3
Held, Virginia, 74 n.8
Henderson, Mae Gwendolyn, 123 n.26
heritage, cultural. *See* cultural heritage
heritage, loss of African. *See* Christianity; colonialism; colonists; colonization
Herland, (Gilman), 165 n.9
hermeneutical conversation, 26
hermeneutic charity (Winch), 17, 103; principle of, 18, 29 n.2, 74 n.4, 150
hermeneutic circle, 2–3, 13 n.3. *See also* Gadamer, Hans-Georg; hermeneutics
hermeneutic dialogue, 29
hermeneutics, 4, 9, 14 n.11, 118, 164. *See also* Gadamer, Hans-Georg;

hermeneutic circle
heroine, African, 133; conventional, 93, 102, 114; Western fictional, role of, 71. *See also* protagonist
Herskovits, Melville, 13 n.6, 14 n.16, 15 n.26
heteroglossia, unintended, 75 n.25. *See also* dialogic heteroglossia
historical fiction, 128–29
historicism, 3
history: as hero, 134. *See also* collective protagonists
Hodge, John L., 165 n.8
Hollis, Martin, and Steven Lukes, 121 n.3
Holloway, Joseph, 14 n.16, 15 n.26
Holloway, Karla, 14 nn.10, 16, 15 nn.21, 25, 30 n.10, 31 nn.20, 27, 50 n.22
honor, 158
horizon, alien, 28; expansion of, 152; limitations of, 29; of the question, 27
horizons, 9, 11; fusion of, 10, 23, 141, 164
human constants (Taylor), 11, 77, 99, 104, 106–107, 139. *See also* limiting notions
humility, cultural. *See* cultural humility
Hurston, Zora Neale, 133
Hutcheon, Linda, 24, 26, 29
Huyssen, Andreas, 31 n.16
hybrid construction, 94, 96–97

ideals, feminist. *See* feminist ideals
ideology inscribed in form of novel, 48
Idu (Nwapa), 42, 67, 109
Ifemesia, Chieka, 35, 51, 60, 68
Igbo cosmology, 35, 51, 124 n.43
Igbo customs, traditional, 68
Igbo living, humane tenets of, 62, 113, 120–21. *See also* interdependence
Igbo philosophy, 56
Igbos characterized, 138–39
Igbo thought, 60
Igbo tradition: defended in Emecheta's fiction, 64; explained in Emecheta's fiction, 64. *See also* defense; displaced African values
Igbo values, 58, 67
Igbo vocabulary, 68
In the Ditch (Emecheta), 51–63, 73, 146, 166 n.27
incorrigibility thesis, 21, 139
independence, Nigerian, 129. *See also* Biafran War
indeterminacy, 103–105, 118, 145–47, 157. *See also* competing voices; dialogic heteroglossia; interpretive problems; plurality; problems in interpretation
individual, definitions of, 34–35, 134, 164; Western view of, 30 n.30, 48, 164. *See also* self; subject; subjectivity
individualism, 10, 17, 124 n.35, 158; as a Western prejudice, 59; inappropriateness of applying Western concepts of, 20; in Western novel, 34–35; Western 34–35, 37, 46, 58; Western, ill effects of, on African tradition, 60. *See also* self; subject; subjectivity
individuality, 24; definitions of, 33–35
individual rights, believed in by Western readers, 84; Western emphasis on, 66
infibulation, 147–48. *See also* clitoridectomies; clitorization; female circumcision
intellectual humility, need for, 18. *See also* cultural humility; hermeneutic charity
intelligibility, 52. *See also* misunderstanding; understanding
interactive reading, 1–2, 4–5, 11, 13, 26, 164. *See also* anthropologizing the West; contextualized approach; conversation; cross-cultural: conversations; foregrounding; interrogating ourselves
interdependence: in Igbo thought, 60;

of society and individual, 56, 158.
See also communal ethics; communal responsibility; community; Igbo living, humane tenets of
internal discourse, 54
internally persuasive discourse, 85, 93, 114. See also discourse
interpretation, problems in. See endings; feminist readers; genres; happy endings; indeterminacy; interpretive problems; misunderstanding; narrative *telos*; prejudices; problems in interpretation; understanding
The Interpreters (Soyinka), 72, 75 n.24, 118
interpretive approach (Taylor), 11
interpretive communities (Fish), 14 n.13, 30, 160–64. See also reader-response criticism
interpretive problems: for Western readers, 64, 66, 74 n.15, 122 n.17, 124 n.43, 127, 138–39, 143, 145–46, 150, 157–59. See also endings; expectations; feminist readers; genres; happy endings; indeterminacy; misunderstanding; narrative *telos*; prejudices; problems in interpretation; understanding
interrelatedness, 17
interrogating ourselves, 26, 30 n.4, 58. See also anthropologizing the West; contextualized approach; foregrounding; interactive reading
intertextuality, 10, 71. See also signifying
Irele, Abiola, 8, 30
Irigaray, Luce, 128
Islam, 60; effects of, 120
isolation, of Emecheta's heroines, 62
Izevbaye, Dan, 35–36, 133

Jacobus, Mary, 31 n.18, 127–28. See also French feminists
Jaggar, Alison, 19, 31 n.26, 48 n.2, 58, 72, 75 n.20

Jahn, Janheinz, 165 nn.5, 13
Jameson, Fredric, 47, 50 n.24, 63
Jardine, Alice, 30 n.11
Jay, Martin, 39
Jehlen, Myra, 34, 48 n.1, 58, 69–71, 133
The Joys of Motherhood (Emecheta), 67, 79, 103–121, 136
juju, 53–55, 62, 78. See also magic

Katrak, Ketu H., 124 n.49
Kilday, Kathleen, 149
knowledge, narrative. See narrative knowledge
knowledge, scientific. See scientific knowledge
Kohut, Heinz, 123 n.24
Kolodny, Annette, 31 n.17, 47
Koso-Thomas, Olayinka, 148, 166 n.17

l'écriture féminine, 119. See also Cixous, Hélène
The Land's Lord (Echewa), 122 n.16
language, as a worldview, 45, 155; as culture, 50 n.17; as instrument of socialization, 89–90; as patriarchal construct, 50 n.21; as reservoir of tradition, 53–54; of African fathers, 54; of scientific instrumentality, 157; of self-understanding, 11; of tradition, 155, 157; opacity of, 44; transparency of, 44; Western, defamiliarization of, 95–96. See also common language, myth of a; discourse; English language
language differences, 17
language games, 155–57, 166 n.24; agonistics of, 153–55. See also conversation
language of perspicuous contrast, 11–13, 21, 59, 72, 139, 141, 149, 161; Emecheta writing in, 43, 127, 161; need for, 43, 164
legitimation, 10, 156. See also scientific instrumentality; scientific

knowledge
Lessing, Doris, 52, 78, 133, 165 n.9
Levin, Tobe, 148, 151
Levine, Lawrence, 14 n.16, 15 n.26
liberal humanism, 19–20, 24. *See also* individual; individualism; Western liberalism
liberalism, limits of, xi, 149. *See also* expectations; prejudices; Western liberalism
limitations of learning, 62
limiting notions (Winch), 11, 15, 61, 64, 127, 149, 166 n.14. *See also* human constants
linguistics, post-Saussurean, 47
liposuction, 149
loss of African values, 60, 69, 124. *See also* Christianity; colonialism; colonization
love and marriage, differing concepts of, 64–65. *See also* alien: customs; romance
love stories, Western, 65
loyalty to community: shown by Emecheta's characters, 58. *See also* communal ethics; community
Luckmann, Thomas, and Peter Berger, 53, 89–90
Lugones, María, 30 n.9
Lukács, Georg, 45–46, 48, 50 n.23, 129
Lyotard, Jean-François, 15 n.22, 154–56, 160, 166 n.24

Macherey, Pierre, 103 n.5
MacIntyre, Alasdair, 49, 54–55, 70–71, 84, 116, 121 nn.1–2, 155
MacKinnon, Catharine A., 74 n.16
McCarthy, Thomas, 61–62, 156
McDowell, Deborah, 74 n.2
McLuckie, Craig W., 164 n.1
magic, 54, 78; Asande, 87–88. *See also* juju
Maja-Pearce, Adewale, 123 n.35
The Man Died (Soyinka), 129
Mann, Kristin, 112, 117

Marcus, George, and Michael M. J. Fischer, 19, 49 n.5, 91
Marcuse, Herbert, 52
marginality, 52, 74 n.1
Martin, Emily, 31 n.26
Martini, Jürgen, 74 nn.13–14
Maru (Head), 160–61
Marxism, 7, 9
Marxists, debates among German, 45–46
Mascia-Lees, Frances E., 31
master narratives, 50 n.21, 116, 118, 120–21, 141, 162. *See also* discourse
Mating Birds (Nkosi), 160–61, 165 n.6
Matustik, Martin, 29 n.2
Mazrui, Ali, 30 n.6, 60, 108–109, 116, 120, 131, 153
mbari, 38–40, 49 n.8
meditation on culture: by Emecheta, 65, 140. *See also* ethnographer
Meese, Elizabeth, 30 n.9, 31 n.18
Memmi, Albert, 25
menstruation, customs surrounding, 85–86
methodology, 14 n.8, 121 n.2
Miller, Christopher L., 7, 9, 15 nn.19, 22, 16 n.34, 50 n.25, 80
Miller, J. Hillis, 28, 31 n.25
Miller, Nancy K., 31 n.16
Mintz, Sidney, 14 n.16
misogyny, 145–46
missionaries, Christian, 92, 110, 137. *See also* Christianity
misunderstanding, 28, 58, 99, 165 n.4; inevitability of, 2, 6, 118–19, 141, 164; moments of, 5, 21, 141, 144, 152; origins of, 1. *See also* endings; expectations; feminist readers; genres; interpretive problems; narrative *telos*; prejudices; problems in interpretation; understanding
Mitchell, W. J. T., 14 n.9
Mlama, Penina Muhando, 50 n.16
modernity, effects of, 49 n.5, 61, 114, 116, 118–19, 158; project of cul-

Index 195

tural, 38–39. *See also* Enlightenment, the
modernization, language of, 116
Mohanty, Chandra Talpade, 19, 22, 166 n.19
Mohanty, S. P., 15 n.30
Moi, Toril, 25
moments of misunderstanding. *See* misunderstanding, moments of
Moore, Gerald, 139–40
motherhood, importance of, in Africa, 67–68, 124 n.36; views of, 105–106
Mphahlele, Ezekiel, 41
Mudimbe, V. Y., 13 n.6, 14 n.16
Mukherjee, Arun P., 74 n.5, 121 n.2
Mullings, Leith, 113

naming, act of, 132, 165 nn.5, 13
narrative ambivalence. *See* ambivalence of narrator
narrative audience, 11
narrative closure. *See* closure, narrative
narrative forms, 54. *See also* endings; genres; happy endings; narrative *telos*; novel; Western fiction
narrative knowledge, 156, 160
narrative mode of conceiving of self, 70–71
narrative poetics, 11, 77
narratives, determining our lives in, 77
narrative structures, 11
narrative struggles. *See* language games, agonistics of
narrative *telos*, 77–78, 94, 104, 117–18, 121 nn.1, 6, 128. *See also* endings; expectations; interpretive problems; misunderstanding; prejudices; problems in interpretation; understanding
narrative voice, 11, 137, 143, 164; heteroglossia in, 107; plurality in, 101. *See also* narrator
narrative, Western, Emecheta's rejection of, 132. *See also* master narratives; signifying
narrator, 11, 122 nn.9, 11; ambivalence of, 93, 96, 103; as ethnographer, 91, 98–99, 119, 123 n.25; as mediator, 91, 119; function of, 91, 119; open-mindedness of, 52, 95, 101; problem of understanding attitudes of, 81, 95, 99, 115; silence of, 102–103; Western perspective shared by, 89, 95, 98–99
native: characterized (Fanon), 166 n.26
Naylor, Gloria, 166 n.20
negative experience, 28–29, 163–64
New Comedy, 80, 102. *See also* comic mode
New Criticism, 11, 14 n.14, 23
new realism, 63. *See also* realism
Newton, Judith, 74 n.1
Ngugi, 15 nn.24, 28; 20, 23, 30 n.7, 33, 40, 43–44, 49 n.9, 50 n.17, 52, 74 n.10, 75 n.24, 150–51
Nikiforova, Irina D., 36, 65
Nkosi, Lewis, 1, 10, 44, 48, 61, 75 n.24, 133, 160–61, 165 n.6
No Longer at Ease (Achebe), 117–18, 122 n.14, 139
nonunderstanding, 167 n.28. *See also* misunderstanding, moments of
novel, adaptability of, 36; African adaptations of Western, 15; characteristics of African, 35–37; Western middle-class, characterized, 58, 122 n.15, 133. *See also* narrative forms; sentimental novel; signifying; Western art forms; Western fiction
nuclear family: as Western value, 111. *See also* polygamy
Nwapa, Flora, 21, 42, 52, 67, 105, 109, 124 nn.51, 54, 150–52

objectification of women, 66
Ogunyemi, Chikwenye Okonjo, 21, 74 n.2, 83, 103, 122 n.19, 123 nn.22, 29
Okhamafe, E. Imafedia, 14 n.14

Okonjo, Kamene, 110, 124 nn.47, 50, 52
Okpaku, Joseph, 17, 65, 113
Omotoso, Kole, 140
O'Neill, John, 40–41
Onoge, Omafume F., 49 n.11, 63, 165
Onwueme, Tess, 122 n.14, 123 n.34
openness, 13 n.5
oppositions: subverted in Emecheta's fiction, 162–63. *See also* binary oppositions; difference; heterosexual couple; plurality
oral tradition, 15 n.28, 50 n.22, 123
Other, authentic strangeness of, 164; author as, 25–28; constructing the subjectivity of the, 26; reader as, 26
Ousmane, Sembène, 35, 113
Owens, Craig, 163

Palmer, Eustace, 75 n.25, 106, 125 n.56
past and present, relationship of, 101, 114, 129
Petersen, Kirsten Holst, 121 n.6
philosophical hermeneutics, 1. *See also* Gadamer, Hans-Georg; hermeneutic circle; hermeneutics
philosophy, Emecheta's communitarian, 46; Igbo, 56. *See also* communal ethics; community; Igbo cosmology; Igbo thought; Igbo values; interdependence
philosophy of the social sciences. *See* social sciences, philosophy of the
pierced ears, 149
Piercy, Marge, 133, 165
The Pilgrim's Progress (Bunyan), 73
plots. *See* narrative *telos*
plurality: in texts, 92, 103, 123 n.26, 146, 162–63; of meaning, 57, 59, 93, 101, 103, 107, 118; of protest, 52. *See also* binary oppositions; competing voices; dialogic heteroglossia; difference
politics, sexual. *See* sexual politics

polygamy, 59, 94, 103, 111, 113, 125 nn.56–57. *See also* nuclear family
Possessing the Secret of Joy (Walker), 166 n.20
Poster, Mark, 8, 70
postmodern approach to African literature, 22–29
postmodernism, 11, 17, 128, 141; characterization of, 24–25; contextualized, 29; limitations of, 23; usefulness of, 23–24, 29. *See also* poststructuralism
postmodern texts, 163
poststructuralism, 15, 19; limitations of, 146; usefulness of, 23, 166 n.18. *See also* postmodernism
poststructuralist model of reading, 28, 121
potential discourse, 86, 93. *See also* discourse
Povey, John F., 42
power, 8, 12–13; balance of, 31 n.25, 132; imbalance of, 2, 9, 14 nn.11, 13; question of, 28, 160
prefaces, 123 n.33. *See also* prologues
prejudices, cultural, 19, 37; disenabling, 2, 28; enabling, 2, 28; Gadamerian, 2–6, 9–10, 14 n.12, 119; hidden, 7; limitations of Western, 47; Western, 13, 23, 26, 58. *See also* critical bias; expectations; feminist readers; *Vorurteil*; Western Criticism; Western response
pre-understanding, 2. *See also* expectations; prejudices
principle of hermeneutic charity. *See* hermeneutic charity, principle of
problems in interpretation, 88, 98–101, 103–106, 114, 140, 150. *See also* endings; expectations; feminist readers; indeterminacy; interpretive problems; misunderstanding; prejudices; narrative *telos*; understanding
prologues, 101–102, 104. *See also* prefaces

propaganda, feminist, in Emecheta, 141
protagonist, Emecheta's use of male, 141; Western concept of, changed in African novels, 35. *See also* collective protagonists; heroine; romantic hero
Proudhon, J. P., 39, 49 n.11
public/private division, 71, 75 n.20, 133. *See also* individualism

question, horizon of the, 27; logic of the, 27
question of authorship, 144–45. *See also* Other, author as
A Question of Power (Head), 39–40, 49 n.6, 161
questions: raised by Western readings, 100–101. *See also* endings; expectations; indeterminacy; interpretive problems; misunderstanding; prejudices; problems in interpretation; narrative *telos*; understanding
The Quest of the Silver Fleece (DuBois), 71
Quo Vadis (Sienkiewicz), 73

Rabinow, Paul, 5
racism: encountered in England, 52, 61–62; scientific, 15 n.22
rape: as subject in Emecheta's fiction, 134–35, 153
The Rape of Shavi (Emecheta), 15 n.22, 127, 153–61
rationality, 17, 29 n.2, 155; criteria of, 56; question of, 78; scientific, 6; social construction of, 52; varying standards of, 18; Western, 10, 48 n.2, 54, 56
Rawls, John, 28
reader-response criticism, 4, 22–23. *See also* interpretive communities
readers: as situated, 26, 29, 39. *See also* contextualized approach
readership, Emecheta's dependence on Western, 41–42
reading: as conversation, 26; from an Africanized perspective, 84; interactively, 4, 13, 59; ourselves, x, 15 n.29, 163. *See also* interactive reading; Other, reader as
realism, classic, 47, 73, 128; Emecheta's signifying on Anglo-American white, 72, 137, 141; European, 33–34; European, characteristics of, 45–48; formal characteristics of, 50 n.23; ideal of, 50 n.24; new, 48, 63; nineteenth-century European, 46; poetics of, 46. *See also* narrative forms; novel; Western fiction
reality, social construction of, 53, 89
regime of truth (Foucauldian), 8, 13, 24
relativism, debates over, 16 n.33, 78; limitations of, 149–50, 166 n.18
religion, understanding, 54–55
representation: of others, 28
resisting, feminist, 147. *See also* feminist readers; Fetterley, Judith
The River Between (Ngugi), 150–51
Robinson, Sally, 128
role of women: in Africa, 111–12. *See also* African women: status in community
romance, interpretive difficulties posed by, 74, 124 n.55. *See also* interpretive problems; love and marriage; misunderstanding; problems in interpretation; understanding
romantic: hero, 65; love, theme of, 77, 104, 122 n.11, 125; myths, 94
Rorty, Richard, 13 n.1
Rosaldo, M. Z., 30 n.9, 75 n.22
Rowell, Charles, H., 49 n.8
rupture, 12, 142, 147, 152; necessity of, 1, 28, 164
rupturing: narratives, 52; old stories, 80
Russ, Joanna, 133, 165 n.9
Ryan, Michael, 166

Said, Edward, 25, 30 nn.13, 15–16
sameness, cultural. *See* universalism, false
Sanderson, Lilian Passmore, 166 nn.17, 22
Scarlet Song (Bâ), 36–37, 161
Schipper, Mineke, 67, 75 n.17
Schreiner, Olive, 78
Schweickart, Patrocinio, 4–5, 30 n.11, 31 n.17, 74 n.6, 163
science fiction, 48 n.3, 133. *See also* speculative fiction
scientific instrumentality, 17, 56, 78, 157
scientific knowledge, 156–57, 160
scientific positivism, 30 n.14
Second-Class Citizen (Emecheta), 51, 57, 63–73, 74 n.15, 75, 80, 133, 166 n.27; ending of, 80
self-constitution, 70. *See also* subjects
self versus society, 34
self, Western view of, 19, 24–26, 30, 34–35, 49 n.5. *See also* individual; individualism; individuality; subject; subjectivity
sentimental novels, 94. *See also* endings; genres; happy endings; narrative forms; novel; narrative *telos*
separate spheres, importation of, to Africa, 111. *See also* colonialism; colonists; woman's sphere
sequestration, 149
sexism, apparent attacks on, in Emecheta's fiction, 57–58. *See also* African men; defense; feminism; sympathy
sex roles, questioning, 131, 136
sexual boundaries, traversal of, 127–28. *See also* binary oppositions; difference; heterosexual couple; plurality
sexual politics, 130–31, 135
sexual stereotyping, 130
She (Haggard), 72
Siebers, Tobin, 31 n.25
signifying, 69, 71–72, 75 n.24, 117, 130; Emecheta's, on Western culture, 72, 94, 127–28, 162. *See also* intertextuality; narrative, Western; novel
Signifying Monkey (Gates), 71
The Slave Girl (Emecheta), 79, 92–104, 106–107, 110, 117, 119, 123 n.25, 136
slave trade, 10
Slomski, Genevieve T., 91, 122 n.11, 123 n.25
Smith, Paul, 30 n.11
Smitherman, Geneva, 14 n.16
social construction: of race, 74 n.2; of rationality, 52; of reality (*see* Berger, Peter, and Thomas Luckmann)
socialist feminism, 58
social mythology, 78
social patterns, 78
social roles, 90
social sciences, philosophy of the, 54, 78. *See also* Bernstein, Richard; MacIntyre, Alasdair; Taylor, Charles; Winch, Peter
Solberg, Rolf, 64, 74, 79, 113
So Long a Letter (Bâ), 113
Songolo, Aliko, 39, 41
Soyinka, Wole, 42, 49 n.9, 52, 72, 75 n.24, 118, 129, 165–66
speculative fiction, 153–54. *See also* science fiction
Spelman, Elizabeth, 30 n.9, 31 n.18
Sperber, Dan, 122 n.17
Spivak, Gayatri Chakravorty, 123 n.33
standpoint theory, 19, 152. *See also* connections; universalism, false
Steady, Philomina Chioma, 20, 67, 86, 113, 124 n.36
Stein, Gertrude, 162
sterilization, 149
Stimpson, Catharine, 162
strangeness, 10, 163. *See also* alien
Stratton, Florence, 15 n.20, 100, 108, 112
subject: as positionality, 31 n.26; nature of the, 31 n.16. *See also* individual; individualism; self;

subjectivity
subjectivities, alien, 27
subjectivity, 19; as negativity, 26; black woman's, 123 n.26, 165 n.8; of author, 27; poststructuralist view of, 19; reconstruction of, 70, 128. *See also* individual, individualism; self; subject
subject matter, 26–27
subjects, need to constitute ourselves as, 26. *See also* self-constitution
Sudarkasa, Niara, 111
Sunset in Biafra (Amadi), 138
suttee, 149
symmetrical conversations, 61, 153
symmetry, failure to achieve, 62; in learning, 155, 161–62
sympathy: for male characters, 141; for women characters, 63, 66, 82, 106, 140, 146; toward African culture, 52, 63, 92. *See also* defense; displaced African values; tradition

Taylor, Charles, 7–8, 11–12, 21, 28, 42, 72, 99, 106, 121 n.3, 139, 149
teleology, 29
telos, narrative. *See* narrative *telos*
terminology, 29 n.3, 124 nn.43, 46
test, heroine's the, 91
text, detachment of, from author, 27
textual plurality. *See* plurality, textual
Their Eyes Were Watching God (Hurston), 71
Things Fall Apart (Achebe), 133
This Earth, My Brother . . . (Awoonor), 117–18
Thompson, John, 31 n.24
Todorov, Tzvetan, 166 n.25
Toomer, Jean, 71
Topouzis, Daphne, 41, 50 n.15, 152
Torgovnick, Maria, 10
tradition, 9, 13 n.2, 50 n.18; as source of truth, 14 n.11, 15 n.18; authority of, 3; benefits in violating, 100; challenge to, 99; changes in, 111–13; endurance of, 82; importance of, 84; metaphysics of, 14 n.7; possibility of failure of, 81, 122; possibility of female, 15 n.20; power of, 82, 84, 121 n.6, 122 nn.8–9; relationship to, 13; sacred, 90; unified, 2; Western, 12
traditionary texts, 3. *See also* Gadamer, Hans-Georg
traditions, alien, 4–5, 10; literary, comparing, 133; questioning Western, 162
tribalism, 137
truth and power, 24
truth claims, 2–3, 8, 27, 29
Two Thousand Seasons (Armah), 35

Umeh, Marie, 124 n.40
understanding, achieving, 9, 13 n.2; African, 134; cross-cultural, 147–48, 163–64; definition of, 17; difficulty of achieving, 53, 91, 118–19, 139, 141, 150–51; failure to achieve, 12–13; interdependence of, and misunderstanding, 28, 164; nature of, 14 nn.11, 14; need to extend Western, 18, 87; prejudices that interfere with, 19; reciprocity of, 4. *See also* expectations; interpretive problems; misunderstanding; prejudices; problems in interpretation
unintelligibility, 55
universalism, false, 22–23, 121 n.2, 146–47, 163. *See also* connections; standpoint theory
universalizing questions, dangers of starting with, 75 n.22. *See also* feminism

values, differences in, 56
Van Allen, Judith, 110–11, 124 nn.47–49
veil of ignorance (Rawls), 28
verstehen view (Taylor), 11
Visel, Robin, 10

voice of authority, 84, 125 n.59. *See also* discourse, authoritative; Voice of the Fathers; voice of tradition; word of the fathers
voice of the daughters, 91, 107, 141. *See also* discourse
Voice of the Fathers, 50 n.21, 89, 92–93, 99, 107, 109, 114, 116, 122 n.12, 123 n.23, 153. *See also* discourse, authoritative; voice of authority; voice of tradition; word of the fathers
voice of tradition, 82, 89, 153. *See also* discourse, authoritative; voice of authority; Voice of the Fathers; word of the fathers
Vorurteil, 14. *See also* prejudices

Walker, Alice, 21, 74 n.3, 78, 166 n.20
Wallace, Michele, 165 n.8
Ward, Cynthia, 20, 41, 50 n.22, 74 n.9, 80, 84, 123 nn.23, 32, 125 n.59
Weedon, Chris, 30 n.5, 75 n.21
Weep Not, Child (Ngugi), 74 n.10
Weiss, Peter, 38
welfare system, British, 52–53
Western art forms, adaptation of, by Africans, 101–102, 133. *See also* novel
Western criticism, applicability of, 15 n.20; weaknesses in, 20. *See also* expectations; prejudices
Western discourse, 116–17; 154, 161–63. *See also* master narratives
Western fiction, characteristics of, 69–70. *See also* endings; happy endings; narrative forms; narrative *telos*; novel; realism
Western hero, similarity to, 83. *See also* protagonist; romantic hero
Western ideas, ill effects of, on role of women, 110–11; influence of, in Emecheta's fiction, 127. *See also* Christianity; colonialism; colonization
Western individualism, ill effects of, on African tradition, 60. *See also* individual; individualism; individuality; self
Western liberalism, 30 n.7, 48 n.2, 59, 149. *See also* individualism; liberal humanism; liberalism
Western love, concept of, 66; displays of, 65. *See also* romance; romantic love
Western love stories, 65. *See also* romance
Western mythology, 78
Western prejudices, 61, 111. *See also* expectations; prejudices
Western responses, 149. *See also* feminist readers; indeterminacy; interpretive problems; misunderstanding; problems in interpretation; understanding
wholeness, 17. *See also* communal ethics; community; Igbo cosmology; Igbo philosophy
Why Are We So Blest? (Armah), 161
Williams, Raymond, 34–35, 46–47, 77, 134, 164
Winch, Peter, 11, 15 n.30, 17–18, 29 n.2, 56, 61, 64, 74 n.4, 87–88, 103, 139, 150, 166 n.14
Wipper, Audrey, 21, 124 n.51
womanism, 21. *See also* feminism
Woman on the Edge of Time (Piercy), 165 n.9
woman's sphere, 71. *See also* separate spheres
Women's War, the, 110
Woolf, Virginia, 52, 78
word of the fathers, 85, 87, 91. *See also* discourse, authoritative; Voice of the Fathers; voice of tradition
working-class women, 73; alliance with, 63
worldview, African, 35, 44, 162; endurance of Emecheta's 54; Emecheta's, 44, 136; Euro-American, 35, 155; feminine, 162; Igbo, 48 n.3
worldviews, alien, 45, 59, 124. *See*

also alien: beliefs, cultures, customs
Writing Beyond the Ending (DuPlessis). *See* DuPlessis, Rachel Blau

Xala (Ousmane), 113

Yezierska, Anzia, 75 n.19
Young, Iris Marion, 14 n.15, 19, 27, 30 n.9, 166 n.23

About the Author

KATHERINE FISHBURN is Professor of English at Michigan State University. She is the author of *The Unexpected Universe of Doris Lessing* (Greenwood, 1985) and *Women in Popular Culture: A Reference Guide* (1982).

ISBN 0-313-29589-1

HARDCOVER BAR CODE

DATE DUE			